India-Russia-China and the Emerging World Order in 21st Century

India-Russia-China and the Emerging World Order in 21st Century

Ashutosh Kumar

PRASHANT PUBLISHING HOUSE
DELHI-110094

Published by :
PRASHANT PUBLISHING HOUSE
C-34, 28 Foota Road, Gali-3,
West Karwal Nagar, Delhi-110094
Phone : 011-22963970, Mob. : 9810396373, 8826258746
e-mail.: prashantpublishinghouse@gmail.com

India-Russia-China and the Emerging World Order in 21st Century

First Published 2019

ISBN : 978-93-88526-17-3

PRINTED IN INDIA

Published by Mr. R.K. Jha M/s Prashant Publishing House and Published at H.S. Offset House Press, Delhi.

Contents

Preface

The 21st century is touted to be the Asian age, belonging to China and India. The end of the Cold War and the growing impacts of globalisation are also making India redefine its position and role both at the regional and at the global level. Since the economic liberalisation of the 1990s, which lead to growth rates of 6-7 percent p.a., India's global presence has been steadily visible. Two issues are shaping India's rise – the political dividend it has garnered as the world's largest democracy and its growing economic status, which, according to projections, will cause it to emerge, along with China, as a key economic driver of the future. India, the acknowledged leader of the South, is transcending that role to play a larger global role, a development that is endorsed by both the US and the European Union (EU) in their respective Strategic Partnerships with India. But this is an ongoing process, not a signpost, and so it is important to examine the political and economic values the new evolving India endorses in the context of global governance (multilateralism, political and economic values and international security).

Indian Prime Minister Narendra Modi and Russian President Vladimir Putin had an "informal" meeting in Sochi in late May, the two leaders discussed a number of bilateral issues such as military and defense cooperation and international issues relevant to both India and Russia. The meeting once again put the attention on the strategic partnership between New Delhi and Moscow, which continues to be significant, but also faces a number of challenges.

The end of the Cold War and the growing impacts of globalisation are also making India redefine its position and role both at the regional and at the global level. Since the economic liberalisation of the 1990s, which lead to growth rates of 6-7 percent p.a., India's global presence has been steadily visible. Two issues are shaping India's rise – the political dividend it has garnered as the world's largest democracy and its growing economic status, which, according to projections, will cause it to emerge, along with China, as a key economic driver of the future.

Russia's tilt towards Asia has been a gradual process and comes with limitations. Russia must avoid relying excessively on China in harnessing its Arctic energy. Currently, its relation with Japan is constrained due to Japan's strategic relations with the US. This US factor will continue to impede the growth and potential of Russia–Japan relations. Asia is not yet in a position to completely replace Europe in terms of the volume of energy imports from Russia, due to geographical and political constraints as well as competition from the Gulf countries and the US. However, while Russia's economic engagement with Europe will continue, political distrust may also be prevalent. This could influence Russia to further its engagement with Asia, leading to the establishment of new institutions and the redefining of the existing ones. The success or failure of Russia's tilt towards Asia thus depends on the extent to which it is able to align Asian institutions to its interests.

The mainstay of India-Russia strategic partnership and the Indo-Soviet Peace and Friendship Treaty of 1971 was to make India secure against threats from China and Pakistan. Russia in acceding to the 1971 Treaty had made a conscious strategic choice between India and China. Gorbachev set in motion the paradigm switch towards China. It is unclear whether the Indian authorities sensed it. His successor Yeltsin followed this switch more vigorously. Following Yeltsin, President Putin seems to be continuing the policies set by his two predecessors in giving China overriding priority in Russia's foreign policy relationship.

China's and Russia's strategies for international expansion, in each of their respective areas of policy specialization, are not necessarily mutually exclusive. Arguably, both countries' intensified involvement on the world stage is not only complementary but to a growing extent directly and indirectly supportive of each other's increasingly commonly-defined interests. The growing international significance of China and Russia's key political and economic partnership must be considered a major factor in global policymaking going forward.

This is a reference book. All the matter is just compiled and edited in nature, taken from the various sources which are in public domain.

This book provides a comprehensive analysis of the India-Chinese-Russian bilateral relationship, grounded in a historical perspective, and discusses the implications of the burgeoning 'strategic partnership' between these two major powers for world order and global geopolitics.

—*Editor*

1

Introduction

A RUSSIA-INDIA-CHINA TRIANGLE

Apart from the Indian and Pakistani nuclear tests, another major event made 1998 a watershed year: the Anglo-American bombing campaign on Iraq to punish Saddam Hussein for obstructing U.N. inspections of his alleged development of weapons of mass destruction elicited a much more dramatic response from Russia than international criticism of India's nuclear tests. Russian President Boris Yeltsin's Prime Minister Yevgeny Primakov called for the establishment of a *'strategic triangle'* among India, Russia and China to ensure peace and stability in the world. Primakov strongly criticized the air strikes by the United States and the United Kingdom on Iraq as being conducted without the mandate of the United Nations Security Council. Primakov's 'triangle' was variously described in US media as 'a coalition of the weak great powers pitted against its one superpower' or the *'Anti-NATO Axis'*.

China immediately rejected Primakov's call, saying that China pursues an independent and peaceful foreign policy, and furthermore kept a low profile. However, Russian diplomats said that China and Russia both feared that the US attacks against Iraq would become a model for unilateral action taken and carried out by Washington against the Democratic People's Republic of Korea and other countries. The Clinton administration had been close to attacking North Korea in 1993 and peace was saved only by the surprise self-styled mission of former US President Jimmy Carter.

Within one year of the bombing of Iraq, the Clinton presidency had set the trend for unilateral action in disregard of the United Nations with two large-scale aerial bombardment campaigns: first in Iraq; and then in Kosovo. Russia, and particularly Primakov himself, had strong links with Iraq, whereas

China, having just entered into a 'Strategic Partnership' with the United States during Clinton's July 1998 visit to China, had no specific interest to defend there. However, Kosovo was to Serbia/Yugoslavia what Taiwan was to China and thus China went all the way in criticizing US and NATO policy in further dismembering the Yugoslav Federation. Russia had multiple interests in Kosovo, foremost in Huntingtonian terms as the core nation of Slavic-Orthodox civilization and secondly as the erstwhile leader of the Communist bloc to which Yugoslavia had once belonged. The weakened Russian military wanted to show that it still had some muscle and guts, and had taken a short cut to the airport of Pristina, Kosovo's capital, which stirred NATO Supreme Commander General Wesley Clark into ordering the British local commander, Lieutenant-General Michael Jackson, to evict the Russians with American air support. Jackson refused and the showdown between the American four-star and British three-star generals is recorded on dozens of websites. Jackson asked Clark: "What is your authority, Sir?". Clark smugly said: "Me, I am a four-star general, Michael". "I am a three-star general", Jackson thundered, "but I am not going to start World War III for you". Although a direct US–Russian confrontation was avoided, bilateral ties never recovered. After appointing five different Russian prime ministers in 1998 and 1999, and in failing health, Yeltsin abruptly resigned at the turn of the millennium. His chosen successor, Vladimir Putin, decided to await the outcome of the 2000 American presidential election before re-engaging with the United States.

The Chinese suffered even more dramatically from American transgressions in Serbia/Kosovo, when US B-2 bombers under NATO's command 'erroneously' dropped five guided bombs on the Chinese Embassy in Belgrade, killing three Chinese and injuring twenty. US President Clinton telephoned China's President Jiang Zemin to make an instant apology, but Jiang refused to take the call. A spate of presidential, ministerial and ambassadorial apologies followed during the next few days, but no Chinese could believe that the bombing had been accidental.

The whole episode is described in detail in a book by Susan Shirk, who as US Deputy Assistant Secretary of State for East Asian Affairs was then directly in charge of US–China relations. She writes that at the time of the bombing, the Chinese leadership was in a state of high alert because two weeks earlier, Zhongnanhai, the main compound of the ruling elite, had been surrounded by a surprise peaceful sit-in of Falun Gong, a Buddhist-inspired sect of yoga-type meditation and health exercises. Shirk quotes an insider source as saying that President Jiang stayed up on the night after the bombing to write a long memo, not on how to deal with the United States, but how to crush Falun Gong by means of ludicrous over-reaction. Media reporting about the bombing demonstrated how much control the Communist Party had lost over Chinese society since the proliferation of semi-independent commercial newspapers and the internet, which both sensationalized dramatic news events for higher circulation figures and profits, adding extra pressure on the government to adopt a hardline stance towards the United States.

An investigation coordinated by Susan Shirk blamed the *'horrific blunder'* of the bombing, as she called it, on the CIA, using the wrong method to locate a targeted Yugoslav military agency and using outdated databases. Still, very, very few Chinese believed the Americans could make such a stupid mistake. In the minds of many, it must have been some lower-level anti-China conspiracy. Anyway, the Chinese domestic pandemonium had further complicated US–China relations: China no longer only perceived itself as an on-and-off adversary or 'enemy of the future' of the United States, but also the victim of today. In New Delhi, an academic security consultant with access to military intelligence also dismissed any American account of errors or blunders as a cover-up and is absolutely convinced that it was a premeditated attack on Chinese electronic devices and technicians, hidden in the embassy to help the Milosevic regime's air defences against American bombing:

Why did they, the Americans, bomb the embassy? Only those two rooms were targeted. I have very concrete information [about] what these two rooms were doing, what the people in those rooms were doing.

The Yugoslavs brought down a B-117 stealth bomber and transferred it to the Chinese. The Chinese were developing a stealth bomber. Stealth technologies you get nowhere. Russians refuse to part with any of these technologies. There is no way they can get it from the EU because of the arms' embargo. So the only way to get it is through 'stealth!'

So, after eight years of volatility but with regular improvements, US–China relations under President Clinton ended on a sour note, and it would get worse. US President George W. Bush and his coterie of neo-con warriors were in no mood to continue the sweet-and-sour tactics that Clinton had played with the Chinese – and the Russians. Bush downgraded America's tentative 'strategic partnership' for the 21st century with China – agreed by Presidents Clinton and Jiang Zemin in 1998 – to one of *'competition'*, and talked of upgrading Taiwan and supplying it with any arms that it needed to defend itself.

Before '9-11' the Bush administration's policy towards China was one of 'congagement' – a blended strategy that transcends both containment and engagement and should embrace neither but should contain elements of both.

The Bush administration continued Clinton's policy of ending India's isolation by lifting the remaining sanctions for its 1998 nuclear tests. This conformed to the administration's de-emphasis of non-proliferation in favour of 'counter-proliferation' by means of the National Missile Defence. Interest in India had grown considerably in the US Congress against the backdrop of the 'rise of China', the spy-plane crisis and new escalating tensions over giant arms' sales to Taiwan. The Bush administration's public assertion that its new fervour for India had nothing to do with any anti-China strategy was dismissed by most observers as just diplomatic talk.

Nevertheless, Chinese Foreign Minister Tang Jiaxuan rejected the 'Primakov Triangle' and said that time had not yet come for a strategic alliance between the three countries: 'We are for discussion on issues of mutual interests, but it is premature to set up any mechanism at the government level'. By May 2001, China had just gone through its first crisis with the Bush administration over the EP 3 spy-plane incident near Hainan and the rearmament of Taiwan, but it chose to avoid confrontation with the new US president. A senior scholar, Sun Shihai, Deputy Director of the Institute of Asia-Pacific Studies under the Chinese Academy of Social Sciences, said that the trilateral partnership should not become a strategic triangle with military components that could be aimed at a third country, especially the United States. But he did emphasize the countries' convergence of interests on issues like the establishment of a multi-polar world, a just and equitable international political and economic order, as well as opposing neo-interventionism in the name of human rights.

The most important factor that kept the idea of an 'India–Russia–China triangle' alive was the broader *'Bush Doctrine'* – the embodiment of neo-conservative determination as divulged in their bible, the 'Statement of Principles' of the The Project of the New American Century. The manifesto advocated a

'Reaganite' foreign policy of military strength and moral clarity, more specifically a significant increase in defence spending and the need to strengthen ties with democratic allies and to challenge regimes that were hostile to American interests and values. Translated into action at the outset of the Bush administration, this meant a series of unilateralist priorities such as missile defence, withdrawal from the Anti-Ballistic Missile (ABM) Treaty, creation of a high-tech rapid-reaction military with overwhelming scope and power and a revitalization of the American nuclear weapons' industry. Bush first made his intentions firmly clear and then expressed willingness to talk, but as consultations, not as negotiations – in other words, you can express your opinion and we will listen but it will not affect our plans.

Renewed Russia–China Friendship Treaty

After US President Bush met with Russian President Putin in Slovenia on 16 June 2001, Russia and China signed a fully fledged bilateral friendship and cooperation treaty in July 2001, which stressed that its aim was not to recreate the old Cold War military alliance while also insisting that it was not directed against any country. Since the Mao–Stalin Pact of 1950, which had so scared the West, had quietly lapsed in 1979, it was the first time that Russia and China had concluded a major bilateral treaty. Yet analysts on both sides acknowledged that they saw the current relationship as a counterweight to the United States' status as the world's only superpower. Liliya F. Shevtsova, an analyst at the Carnegie Moscow Centre think tank, viewed Moscow's recent moves towards Beijing – at least in part – as a message to the Bush administration: 'The Kremlin is sending Washington a warning that if there is no change for the better in relations between Moscow and Washington – now at their coolest in years – Russia is quite ready to strike a closer alliance with Beijing', she said. India was not part of the project at that time because it had shown early enthusiasm for Bush's 'new concepts of deterrence, moving beyond the constraints of the 30-year-old ABM treaty and work[ing] toward deploying a ballistic-missile-defence system'.

According to one analysis, Putin mulled over China during his visit: whether to strike some kind of loose alliance with Beijing – and India? – to counter US supremacy. 'There was a month or two when it could have gone either way', one senior US official said during the negotiations about a new treaty to be signed by Putin and Bush on 24 May 2002, 'until Putin figured out that the Chinese didn't have a lot to offer'.

After the airborne assaults on the World Trade Centre and the Pentagon on '9/11', Putin was the first foreign leader to get through to Bush on the telephone. Condoleezza Rice, then National Security Adviser, conveyed to Washington Post columnist Jim Hoagland that there had been a steady evolution towards a strategic Russian choice that this crisis seems to have confirmed: 'That Russian choice is seen at the White House, as I understand it, to be one of pursuing alliance with and integration into the West rather than flirting with a Third Way strategy built on partnership with China and others who want to reduce American influence abroad'. The US design was clearly to bring Russia into a unidirectional – that is, subservient – partnership with the United States so as to lessen China's leverage on global questions, including missile defence. Sensing that Russia had a special role to play in Bush's 'war on terror', Putin seized the opportunity to recast US–Russia relations after ten years of decline and succeeded in reclaiming Russia's place at the big table. When Bush formally abrogated the ABM Treaty on 13 December 2001, Russia's response was to state pragmatically that it was no longer bound by the 1993 accord known as Start II, which outlawed multiple-warhead missiles and other especially destabilizing weapons in the two nations' strategic arsenals. Putin realized that it was better to accept grudgingly, rather than to resist NATO expansion as Yeltsin had done, and then later to back down.

Beijing responded in a very different way to Bush's ABM announcement. The Chinese considered it as targeted at them, not at the Russians. The Russians would under any subsequent missile agreement always retain enough warheads to overwhelm any future US National Missile Defence, whereas the Chinese only had a very small nuclear arsenal.

China said that the US plans to develop a multi-billion dollar defence system that would shoot down incoming missiles would undercut the deterrent value of its own small nuclear arsenal – about two dozen missiles capable of reaching the United States – and a successful missile umbrella could be stretched to protect arch-rival Taiwan.

The United States, however, has told China repeatedly that it is developing the missile shield to counter surprise attacks from 'rogue states' like North Korea and Iraq [sic!] and that the policy was not being pursued with China in mind. Beijing also feared that the Bush administration's action will mean that nations will no longer agree to any nuclear disarmament control treaties. This could push China into a regional arms race with India and Pakistan. "We have enough domestic concerns. An arms race is only a rich man's game. A poor man cannot play", said Professor Niu Jun, US foreign policy expert at Beijing University's Institute of International Studies. In the end, China's muted response showed that it had decided that there was nothing that it could do and that it was intent on maintaining stable relations with the United States.

While Russia's new Friendship and Cooperation Treaty with China, which was signed in July 2001, seemed to set both on a new strategic course, '9/11' had clearly turned Russia's priorities around. Despite Bush's initial ABM shock, Presidents Putin and Bush in May 2002 opened an entirely new relationship with the signing of a treaty that committed both countries to reducing their nuclear arsenals from about 6,000 warheads each to no more than 2,200 by the end of 2012. With the renewed Russo-American rapport, China appeared to be the loser, as reflected in Chinese President Jiang Zemin's reminder of the first anniversary of the new Sino-Russian strategic partnership, which should have paved the way towards a multi-polar world. China was the leading member in the newly founded Shanghai Cooperation Organization (SCO), and now in the wake of '9/11' US military bases were at China's doorstep in Uzbekistan and Kyrgyzstan, with Russia's approval.

'China–Russia Relations Remain Better than Russia–US Ties'

In December 2002 Russian President Vladimir Putin visited China to reassure the Chinese about the relevance and validity of the Russian-Chinese strategic partnership (first agreed in 1996 and consolidated by their Friendship Treaty in 2001). Despite recurrent frustrations about US hegemony, Putin wanted to maintain good relations with the United States while disagreeing with US President Bush's approach to terrorism. On the day of Putin's arrival in Beijing, the People's Daily published an article under the headline 'China–Russia Relations Remain Better than Russia–US Ties'. The Pravda newspaper explained that Putin himself had complained to Chinese journalists about NATO expansion, which under the current global situation of terrorism and nuclear issues was a negative development. Another new cloud above the US–Russia relationship was the imminent Anglo-American invasion of Iraq, which Russia energetically and China ephemerally tried to block.

After Beijing, Putin went to India where he again tried to sell the idea of a strategic partnership or 'strategic triangle' in Asia for Russia, China and India – with Moscow taking the lead. Putin tried to convince India of the compatibility of the triangle with good bilateral cross-relations between all involved, defining the triangle not as an anti-US coalition but just as a *'counterpoint'* to the US. Putin's aim, analysts say, is traditionally Russian – to centre Moscow solidly between East and West, Atlantic and Pacific, NATO and China.

Putin defined terrorism's main danger as secessionist movements that challenge state sovereignty. While Russia's main concern was Chechnya, China viewed the Muslim separatists in its western Xinjiang region as terrorists, and India maintained that the core problem of Kashmir was Pakistani-based terrorism. Putin supported the Indian view, but the United States viewed Pakistan as an indispensable ally in its wider 'war on terror' and China would also never renege on its key geostrategic alliance with Pakistan. From its defeat of India in the 1962 Border War, Pakistan was China's tool for keeping Soviet ally India off-balance and, more recently, China's back door to the Indian Ocean, Arabian Sea and the Persian Gulf.

The heart of Indo-Russian relations is defence cooperation and it embraces the joint production of Brahmos cruise missiles and the joint manufacture of advanced submarines. The SU-30 project is engaging almost all of the production capacities of Hindustan Aeronautics. Consequently, the aviation industries in both India and Russia have acquired the capacity to undertake the joint development, production and marketing of medium-range transport aircraft.

After the Anglo-American invasion of Iraq there were – not surprisingly – renewed calls for a 'Moscow–Beijing–New Delhi triangle', a potential alliance of three nuclear-armed countries of some 2.5 billion people that would theoretically be able to balance US power in coming years. Indian Prime Minister

Atal Bihari Vajpayee had just concluded a successful visit to China and the two countries had expressed similar views on the American war on Iraq. All three countries were disturbed by the blatant disregard of the United Nations and protested against what they viewed as a rejection of the rules of the international game.

Russia, China and India still back the primacy of the United Nations Security Council in solving crises, and support the principle of non-intervention in the internal affairs of sovereign states. Apart from shared concerns over US dominance, the three have other common interests and mutually reinforcing needs. All three are weary of militant Islamic groups and want stability in Central Eurasia. The main weakness in the triangle, however, comes from China's and India's competitive relationship, with both holding conflicting visions of regional dominance, with China so far the winner. While Russia and China are opposed to US Theatre Missile Defence (TMD), which is in clear violation of the ABM Treaty, India offered its enthusiastic support to the United States. China, too, has a stake in Kashmir in the areas bordering Xinjiang and is a major arms' supplier to Pakistan. In short, Sino-Indian relations would continue to remain a stumbling block for materialization of the strategic triangle for which Russia had been canvassing.

But the arms' sale relationship between Russia and the two Asian countries was growing steadily. The trade provides Moscow with billions of much-needed dollars and important arms' export markets, while Beijing and New Delhi get sophisticated armaments ranging from combat aircraft to submarines. In 2003, Russia and India held their first joint naval exercises in the Indian Ocean, when a large task force of Russian surface ships and nuclear attack submarines simulated attacks on aircraft-carrier groups. The naval exercise was coordinated with a mission by long-range bombers. On 13 May 2003, several Russian strategic bombers – Tu-95 Bears and Tu-160 Blackjacks – flew from a base in Central Russia to the Indian Ocean to simulate an attack by long-range cruise missiles.

It has, however, been argued that the trilateral axis could hardly be feasible because the Indian nuclear and missile programme is not so much aimed at Pakistan, but is in fact deterrence against Chinese nuclear warheads. The would-be triangle is also seen as implausible because India and China also happen to be competing economies. Moreover, Russia and China have already solved their border disputes, while China and India are still divided by a chunk of barren terrain and the granting of asylum to the Dalai Lama and thousands of his followers. There have also been warnings that a well-armed and strong China may one day not just make Russia its junior partner, but even pose a threat to Russia's resource-rich Far East.

The 'Trialogues': No 'Equilateral' Triangle

On 3 September 2003 the first *'trialogue'* of the foreign ministers of Russia, China and India took place in New York. The three countries together represent the vast majority of the global population and theoretically could be able to balance US power in coming years. After the US invasion of Iraq, there was again more shared opposition to US policies than in previous years. India had new doubts about a closer relationship with the United States. As a counterweight to Islamic terrorism and at the behest of the United States, India had growing military ties with Israel, which were a very divisive issue in a country with the second largest Muslim population in the world after Indonesia. Bush had failed to condemn or even to mention terrorism in Kashmir in his UN speech earlier in the week. At the official level 'the dialogue between Moscow, Beijing and New Delhi will continue', said Russian Foreign Minister Igor Ivanov, adding that the three nations have a shared interest in a 'multi-polar and just world'.

Russian President Vladimir Putin had been particularly insistent upon the triangle during his December 2004 visit to India. But China had so far resisted, and it is unlikely that India will be a party to overt anti-American actions in Central or South Asia, even though it will clearly collaborate more with China on trade and energy issues and for anti-terrorism purposes may even liaise with the Shanghai Cooperation Organization (SCO) now that China has offered it such an opportunity.

In April 2005, when China's major cities were shaken by violent anti-Japanese demonstrations, Chinese Premier Wen Jiabao was on an official visit to New Delhi. Wen used the occasion to pledge Chinese 'support for India's aspirations to play an active role in the UN and international affairs'. Part of the Indian media 'over-interpreted' this as Chinese support for Indian permanent membership of a reformed United Nations Security Council. Wen and his Indian counterpart Manmohan Singh signed a broad-based 'India-China Strategic and Cooperative Partnership for Peace and Prosperity', of which the main content was a five-year pact for cooperation in five high-tech sectors, in which these two fastest growing 'elephant economies' (that is, mammoth versions of 'tiger economies') have optimal synergy: India in software; China in hardware. The hope of China's Prime Minister Wen Jiabao was that an India–Russia–China axis will 'democratize international relations', a pointed indictment of US hegemonism. India, for its part, wanted improved cooperation with the dynamic economies of East Asia, a bigger regional role and a counterweight to Chinese and US sponsorship of Pakistan. Indian Prime Minister Manmohan Singh observed: 'India and China can together reshape the world order'.

The April 2005 Sino-Indian strategic partnership followed less than one decade after the establishment of the Sino-Russian strategic partnership, which was triggered by the United States dispatching two carrier-led task forces to the Taiwan Straits in 1996 in response to Chinese missile tests, and as a warning to the Taiwan electorate not to vote for independence. (Then) Chinese Premier Li Peng stated that the strategic partnership between the two countries would help to correct the 'balance of forces' in the world. This went in tandem with the 'Shanghai Declaration', to set up a security body of China, Russia and three former Central Asian Soviet republics, initially named the 'Shanghai Five', which aimed to counter further inroads by the US and NATO into the region and which in 2001 was renamed the Shanghai Cooperation Organization.

India and Russia had also concluded a strategic partnership in 2000. Under the accord, the two countries agreed to develop a common strategy in dealing with Afghanistan. Both New Delhi and Moscow were concerned that the radical Islamic agenda of the Taliban was having an impact on areas such as India's Kashmir and Chechnya in Russia. President Putin stressed Russia's unqualified support for India's bid for permanent membership of the UN Security Council, something that China was ambiguous about in 2005 and explicitly opposed in subsequent years as India moved closer to the United States. Nevertheless, China, India and Russia were now tied together by three bilateral strategic partnerships, of which two, Russia–China and Russia–India, had a robust arms' supply relationship as the strongest component, and the third, the Sino-Indian, had the least military–strategic content.

Vladivostok: Russia's Far Eastern Metropolis

Soon after this promising improvement in India–China relations, the new Russian Foreign Minister Sergei Lavrov met with his Chinese and Indian counterparts, Li Zhaoxing and Natwar Singh, in June 2005 in Vladivostok, their first meeting outside of a multilateral forum. They discussed security and this time also energy security and especially regional stability, considering the waves of instability that were engulfing Uzbekistan and Kyrgyzstan, which were allegedly instigated by Western-inspired *'orange revolutions'*. The symbolical event, the signing of a China–Russia border agreement that had been negotiated for four decades and that concerned two per cent of the 4,300-kilometre border, should set an example for China and India. China and Russia had fought a short border war on an island in the Ussuri River in 1969 but were reaching a final settlement now. Why couldn't China and India ? In terms of concrete results, the meeting produced a communiqué that did not mention the term 'strategic triangle' but stressed that it is in the interests of the three countries to strengthen their trilateral partnership, and that the mutually beneficial cooperation will contribute to the consolidation of peace and stability in Asia and the world at large. The selection of Vladivostok as the venue can be viewed as emphasizing Russia's status as an Asian power along with India and China.

A commentator in the Russian magazine Kommersant wrote that former Russian Prime Minister Yevgeny Primakov's dream had come true, as his 1998 'triangle' was designed to curb US influence, specifically the 2005 fight against 'colour revolutions' in former Soviet Republics:

In fact, yesterday's meeting in Vladivostok witnessed that Russia and China agree to create their own alliance to fight 'colour revolutions' in Central Asia. Lavrov stated that the uprising in Andijan was nothing else than 'the operation of Islamic extremists, Taliban leftovers and some Chechen terrorists'.

By putting responsibility for the Andijan events on international terrorists, Lavrov expressed solidarity with Beijing's official position. China is a most ardent supporter of Uzbek President Islam Karimov's 'fight with terrorism', including the slaughter in Andijan. This means that Russia is ready to share responsibility with China for everything that goes on in the region. This would be the first step to create a joint military bastion of Moscow and Beijing, which would be protecting Central Asian regimes from 'colour revolutions' and excessive American penetration into the region.

It would soon be clear, however, that Lavrov's and the commentator's rhetoric were too premature and way over the top. India was improving its relations with China, but far more substantially with the United States. The US is a huge trading partner for India and China, and Russia will not be able to compete at this point, at least not for the foreseeable future. Moreover, the Bush administration had in the meantime lifted restrictions on arms' deliveries to India, which was going to cause problems for Russian defence exports to India, and Washington did not have intentions of making such a concession to China. In addition, Sergei Karagonov, the Chairman of the Presidium of the Russian Council for Foreign Defence Policy, was convinced that Primakov's idea was not viable. He emphasized that none of the three countries would want to join a coalition in direct opposition to the United States.

Nevertheless, the 'Vladivostok Trio' had given some other substance to Primakov's triangle. The trio stressed the primacy of the United Nations, which the United States is sometimes inclined to bypass, and the need to reform it. The demand for 'consistent, sustained and comprehensive opposition to terrorism without any double standards' was a warning that India, Russia and China consider murderous secessionists in Kashmir, Chechnya or Xinjiang as dangerous as the US considers Osama Bin Laden and al-Qaeda. They also wanted the global oil economy to recognize Russia as one of the world's largest fuel producers, and India and China among the biggest consumers. To that end, India, which has put US$ 1 billion in Russia's Sakhalin-I project and might invest more, would host a meeting in October 2005 of Asia's principal oil producers and buyers. This would be another feather in the cap of India's Minister of Oil, Mani Shankar Aiyar.

In the energy sector, China and India for a long time seemed to become rivals that might get into armed conflict over oil and minerals. In January 2006, India and China put aside their energy rivalry. The two states' oil majors – CNPC and ONGC – signed a mega-pact for joint bidding in Central Asia, the Caspian Sea Region, Africa and Latin America.

Indian Minister of Oil M.S. Aiyar explained that fierce Sino-Indian competition had driven prices up further: "Wherever the Indians have gone, the Chinese are already there", wrote Madhu Nainan, chief editor of Petrowatch, a market intelligence newsletter in India. "Mostly, it is India that needs cooperation with China – and not the other way around." The biggest energy issue between the US and India is the construction of a 2,775 kilometres (or 1,725 miles), US$ 7.5 billion gas pipeline from Iran through Pakistan to India, which has already been under negotiation for fifteen years. India adamantly rejects any US pressure over its millennia-old relations with another ancient Asian empire: Persia, or Iran.

When Indian Prime Minister Manmohan Singh announced in March 2006, with the visiting US President George Bush at his side in New Delhi, that the two had reached agreement on a 'historic' civilian nuclear pact, China and Russia felt that their reluctant triangular partner was compromising its 'independent foreign policy' and that India felt that it had to reinforce its credentials that it was not a second Japan and would not subordinate its foreign policy autonomy to Washington. The countries' three leaders – Manmohan Singh, Hu Jintao and Vladimir Putin – met in a so-called 'outreach session' during the G8 summit in St. Petersburg in July 2006, which underlined that the latter two had now been accepted as crucial players in the world. But the three also held their first trilateral summit, the first of its kind among the three countries. The current G8 have 45 per cent of the world's GDP, whereas inclusion of China and India would move this to the 60 per cent level, thus enhancing the forum's ability to influence global political and economic relations. "Our approaches to key international problems are very close or, as the diplomats say, they practically coincide", Putin said in his opening remarks. Putin threw his support behind proposals to expand the G8 by including India, China and other outreach countries that Russia had invited to attend the summit: "Without such countries as India and China it is impossible to solve global economic and financial problems", he said. Putin outlined a new political agenda for the G8 to help mould a new multi-polar world. "Our world has not become safer after the collapse of the bipolar world", he said. "On the contrary, it has become less predictable. [...] We do not have the tools and instruments to address the challenges of today". An expanded G8 may become such a tool: "What mankind is concerned with today, what we are doing in G8 is to try and work out a new architecture of international relations", Putin concluded.

New Delhi

The foreign ministers of the three (re-)emerging giants met again in Delhi in February 2007 to further discuss ways to build a more democratic 'multi-polar world'. The three – Pranab Mukherjee, Li Zhaoxing and Sergei Lavrov – emphasized that 'they were not setting up an alliance against the United States, but on the contrary, intended to promote international harmony and understanding', a joint communiqué stated. The latter was a euphemism for blocking the launch of another US war against Iran. 'The key to building a multi-polar world order based on the principles of equality of nations – big or small – respect for sovereignty and territorial integrity of countries, international law and mutual respect', the communiqué routinely stated, required a 'democratization of international relations'. Thus the United Nations represented the 'appropriate instrument' for dealing with world problems. One Indian commentator, N.V. Subramaniam, compared the India–China–Russia triangle with the Six-Party Talks on North Korea: "Because the US wouldn't talk directly to North Korea, their bilateral [meeting] had to be upgraded by including four other parties, with China hosting it".

The 'Triangular Three' all had long agendas to discuss with the United States, but since they would not get far bilaterally, they conveyed their common demands trilaterally to Washington, foremost on Iran. Russia and China were vehemently opposed to Bush's war-mongering in the Gulf and so was India, but India was also negotiating a civilian nuclear deal with Washington. It did not want to anger Washington bilaterally, but through the triangle it could convey its opposition in a more circumspect way. Subramaniam referred to the Cold War game of the US, playing off China against the Soviet Union. At the 43rd Munich Conference on Security Policy from February 9-11, 2007, Russia's President Vladimir Putin attacked US unipolarity and NATO's eastward expansion with a clear intimation of the emerging importance of the India–China–Russia 'strategic triangle'. Putin found himself still too weak to take on the US alone, but splitting Europe and pushing the triangle with India and China might, according to his logic, have more chance of registering with Washington.

Harbin

In October 2007, the three foreign ministers of the triangle met once again – for the first time in China – in the northeastern (Manchurian) city of Harbin, built as a Russian railway hub on Chinese soil in the early twentieth century and acting as a sanctuary for White Russian émigrés after the Bolshevik revolution and for Jews during the Second World War. The Harbin Communiqué reiterated the principal elements of Delhi that: "the development of China, Russia and India is a major contribution to peace and development of the region and the world and is beneficial to the process of global multi-polarity". But the reality was that India had been increasingly veering away from Russia and China and closer to the United States and Japan. It was participating in a 'strategic dialogue' with a new 'military–political triangle' in the Asia-Pacific region involving the US, Japan and Australia. In September 2007 India held a large-scale naval exercise with them in the Bay of Bengal –its first-ever military exercise in a multilateral format – involving US aircraft carriers and submarines. It was named the *'Quadrilateral Initiative'* and described by analysts and commentators as a 'democratic coalition to contain China'. The exercise had been preceded by an appeal by former Japanese Prime Minister Shinzo Abe to the Indian Parliament during his August 2007 visit to create a 'broader Asia' or 'the arc of freedom and prosperity', based on common values of democracy, which would eventually incorporate the United States and Australia and specifically exclude China. Before Abe's departure, Japan's Defence Minister Yoriko Koike and the Commander of US Pacific Command, Admiral Timothy Keating, arrived in Delhi to finalize the details of defence cooperation and the Malabar 07-02 manoeuvres. Ironically, one day after the manoeuvres ended, Abe resigned as prime minister after just one year in office. Difficulty in passing the special bill – which allows Japan to refuel US and other allied ships in Afghanistan-bound operations – was the ostensible reason for Abe's surprise resignation, but the sudden resignation called into question the ability of Japanese leaders to pursue what Mr Abe called 'assertive diplomacy', a stance welcomed by Washington, which wants Japan to shoulder more of a global burden. Abe, a right-wing nationalist, was succeeded by Yasuo Fukuda, a moderate with a non-ideological and far more accommodating stance towards China.

Lavrov strongly criticized the emerging 'East Asian NATO' without any direct reference to India, although the import of his statements could not be lost on New Delhi. Never before, perhaps, in the saga of India–Russia relations had such a serious contradiction appeared in their respective perceptions over Asian security. In recent years, India had also been critical of US policy towards Iran, both on sanctions and a multi-billion dollar gas pipeline, linking Iran with India, but during late 2007, India had calculated that finalization of the long-stalled nuclear deal with the US was more advantageous to India. So, when the Bush administration announced a regime of unprecedented sanctions against Iran immediately after the Harbin meeting, branding Iranian security bodies as sponsors of international terrorism and virtually making Iran an enemy country under US law, Russia and China lost no time in criticizing Bush's move, but India kept mum. Later, at a joint press conference with his Russian and Indian counterparts, Chinese Foreign Minister Yang Jiechi criticized US plans for deployment of the missile defence system in Central Europe, saying that this would not only not ease global security concerns, but would undermine the global strategic balance. In contrast, Indian Foreign Minister Pranab Mukherjee simply maintained that India had no plans for cooperation with the US missile defence system. He stonewalled. He would not be drawn into any criticism of US plans.

China was obviously concerned about India's drift into the US camp, but the Chinese still liked to believe that 'India's DNA doesn't allow itself to become an ally subordinate to the US, like Japan or Britain'. And they were right. Left-wing opposition against the deal in India had reached a climax and many on the right accused the left of doing China's bidding. Then, in October 2007, Ai Ping, Director-General of the Chinese Communist Party's International Liaison Department, stated that China had nothing to do with this and that the nuclear deal was entirely India's internal matter. Ai said that China highly cherishes its sovereignty and independence, "so we must respect other people's sovereignty and independence". India's leftist parties oppose the deal because they see it as a way of bringing India into the US strategic orbit and of compromising sovereign decision-making on foreign policy, security and nuclear matters. Even the Hindu nationalist BJP, which has been traditionally pro-American and which negotiated a nascent alliance with the Bush administration in early 2004, says that the nuclear deal sacrifices national sovereignty. "A strategic partnership is not a synonym for strategic subservience, and that's why we are opposed to it", said Jaswant Singh, chief nuclear negotiator with the Clinton administration from 1998–2000, foreign minister in the last BJP administration and now a Member of Parliament.

Yekaterinburg

Interestingly, the 'Triangle's' foreign ministers held their most recent trilateral meeting on 15 May 2008 in the Russian city of Yekaterinburg (from 1924–1991 named Sverdlovsk) in the Urals, on the border of European Russia and Siberia, again emphasizing Russia's dual nature as a Eurasian country. The focus this time was on the need to fight terrorism and the drug threat. The three foreign ministers – Sergei Lavrov, Pranab Mukherjee and Yang Jiechi – 'supported the international community's efforts to improve the situation around Afghanistan and believe that in addition to these efforts, the establishment of drug security belts around the country would be useful'.

The ministers also focused on economic and military cooperation, touching on topical international matters, including the unilateral declaration of independence by Kosovo in February 2008. Lavrov said that Russia, India and China insist that talks between Serbia and its breakaway province, Kosovo, should be resumed. Unilateral secession is a common concern that the three share with Serbia, the common analogy being: China's Taiwan question; Russia's Chechnya; and India's Kashmir.

'Primakov's Arms' Sales Triangle'

Parallel to the triangular volleys of the Sino-Indian-Russian troika and the marathon dance around the Indo-US nuclear deal, another showdown was looming between the two biggest military export machines in the world: the battle between the 'Bear and Eagle' for the Indian arms' market. American arms' dealers made no secret of their desire to break Russia's domination of the Indian market, one of the most lucrative in the world, because India still imports much more of its hardware than China. Russia's Vladimir Putin working assiduously and methodically to rebuild Russia's position as a top player in the so-called

'Near Abroad' and the world at large during his final years in office as president. After the loss of so many rounds of arms' contract negotiations in East Europe, the Caucasus and Central Asia to the US and NATO, Putin and the Russian generals are in no mood to let India end up in the American orbit. William Cohen, former US Defence Secretary under President Clinton, who was leading a large delegation of American arms' dealers to India in February 2007, said that India was a US$ 30 billion opportunity over the next five years. American nuclear power companies hope that they will also get US$ 30 billion of a total market of US$ 100 billion, but there are many competitors.

The supreme prize for which all of the world's fighter aircraft manufacturers will contest is a replacement deal for 126 planes for the Indian Air Force. Will India buy Russian MiGs (or Sukhois) again as it has done for decades, or will it go for US, French or other European planes. Putin was the guest of honour on Indian National Day in January 2007 and he signed a deal for the Indo-Russian co-production of MiG engines and joint development of a transportation plane. Whether India in the end opts for US F-16s, F-18s or Russian MiG-35s or Sukhois is a step that will have long-term implications for the strategic orientation of India as a potential partner in the newly emerging regional economic–strategic triangle of Russia, India and China and the possible accession of India to the Shanghai Cooperation Organization. Russia has a long history as the main arms' supplier of both India and China – to India from 1962 all the way through the Cold War and to China (re-)starting in the early 1990s. The two giant Asian nations bought 70 per cent of Russia's global arms' sales throughout the 1990s.

New Delhi has managed to purchase everything from tanks to fighter aircraft, to submarines. The biggest, but still incomplete, deal is the transfer of the Soviet-era aircraft carrier *'Admiral Gorshkov'* (launched in 1982) 'for free' (!) but on the condition of major refitting and additional aircraft deals. Under the deal, worth US$ 2 billion, the 'Gorshkov' is currently being refurbished by Russian shipbuilders. India would also take updated versions of 50 Mikoyan MiG-29K naval fighter aircraft, along with a training package for Indian sailors and aircrews. India would have to pay US$ 700 million for a refit of the vessel, plus it would have to purchase the MiG-29Ks and eight naval helicopters for another US$ 800 million. India was also offered options for upgrades to Indian port facilities in order to dock and service the 'Gorshkov' for a total of another US$ 1.5 billion.

In order to accommodate the upgraded MiG-29K, the 'Gorshkov' requires an extension to its flight deck, installation of an arrested landing system like that used on US and French carriers, plus a replacement of its maintenance-intensive steam propulsion system with a diesel power plant. All of this has proven to be too much to do for the originally agreed price. The Russian naval shipbuilder Rosoboronexport (ROE) is now demanding an additional US$ 1.2 billion to finish the job. The Indian naval command is appalled by this 'blackmail', but hardly has an acceptable alternative. This is where the United States came in.

America's 'Gift' for India: 48-year old 'Kitty'?

According to reports in the Indian and US media – apparently based on official leaks – US Secretary of Defence Robert Gates, on his visit to New Delhi in February 2008, carried with him a letter from US President George W. Bush offering a better deal for India than the one that it has now been struggling to get out of Moscow for four years. The Indian Navy will reportedly be offered the soon-to-be decommissioned USS *'Kitty Hawk'* aircraft carrier – also for free – provided that the Indian Navy will foot a big refitting bill and agree to purchase 65 of the newest model Boeing F/A-18E/F Super Hornets to be operated off the 48-year-old carrier, which is 22 years older but twice as big as the 'Gorshkov'. The 'Hawk' has made its last voyage and is waiting to be decommissioned, but the rumours that India is still interested in buying it persist on the internet.

The US is unlikely to win this 'dumping-contest' with the Russians. The Indian defence establishment has serious complaints over US equipment and unsatisfactory sales' methods. The Indian Navy recently bought the 36-year-old landing ship dock (LSD) 'Trenton' for US$ 50 million, the first-ever Indian naval ship purchase from the US. According to Indian navy standards, the service life of an aircraft carrier is 40 years and twenty for an LSD. A report to the Indian Parliament by the Comptroller and Auditor General (CAG) of the Indian Navy asserts that the USS 'Trenton', built in 1968 and rebaptized INS 'Jalasha', was purchased without undertaking a proper physical assessment, but with only a 'visual inspection' and an 'over-reliance' on – inadequate – information supplied by the US Navy. Furthermore, the ship was only delivered in a 'safe-to-steam' condition and would require upgrades and modifications, aspects that the Indian Navy kept hidden from competent financial authority. In February 2008, six Indian Navy sailors died aboard the 'Jalasha' following a toxic gas leak. In more alarming revelations, the CAG says that New Delhi had signed restrictive clauses assuring Washington that it would not deploy the INS 'Jalasha' for offensive purposes and would allow regular US inspections of the ship. Observers say that this is against established policy and bound to raise a political stink and accusations of New Delhi buckling under US pressure and possibly financial muscle.

While in New Delhi in February 2008 at the head of a large delegation of defence contractors, US Secretary of Defence Robert Gates welcomed the recent Indian decision to buy six Lockheed Hercules C-130J cargo aircraft, valued at US$ 1 billion. His main purpose was to help Lockheed Martin sell 126 F-16s and/or Boeing its F/A-18 Super Hornet, worth US$ 10 billion.

The importance of the deal is not only commercial, but that the new-generation aircraft will be in use with the Indian Air Force for the next 40 years, and clinching the deal therefore becomes absolutely vital for the US if it is to aim at 'inter-operability'. Gates knew that it is the sort of deal that will ensure that US–India military-to-military cooperation will become irreversible and will pin India down as the US's strategic ally in the region. Stung by the strong opposition against the US–India nuclear deal and the Jalasha scandal, Gates modestly said: "We're not looking for quick results or big leaps, but rather a steady expansion that leaves everybody comfortable".

Russia (and the United States) Favour India and 'Discriminate' against China

The US and Russia have been engaged in a cut-throat competitive bidding spree in India. This had already started with talks on the purchase of P-8i Poseidon long-range maritime reconnaissance patrol aircraft with antisubmarine war capabilities to replace Russian-made Tu-142M bombers. The deal could be worth US$ 2 billion, the biggest defence deal so far between Russia and the United States.

Some of the Russian transfers to India include weapons and technology that Moscow refuses to supply to China. Moscow and Delhi agreed to begin the joint development of a new, so-called fifth-generation fighter. This aircraft would be a potential rival in performance to the US F-22 Raptor, defence analysts in New Delhi said. India also agreed in 2007 to buy another 40 Su-30MKI fighters from Russia for US$ 1.5 billion, in addition to an earlier order for 140 of these aircraft. Some military experts say that this versatile, twin-engined jet is probably the best fighter and strike aircraft in the world. But Russia has not offered it to China while Moscow is also offering to sell India its latest fighter: the MiG-35. In nuclear submarine technology, Russia has also been more generous with India than with China. The unspoken rationale behind this is obvious: Russia – not unlike the United States – considers China an emerging *'global peer rival'* and potential long-term threat, while India – at best – is deemed a secondary regional power.

China has become a top importer of Russian military equipment and systems, which is ironic given the historic antagonism between Beijing and Moscow from the late 1950s until the Soviet demise. Nevertheless, Russia, out of frustration with the United States' 'winner-takes-all triumphalism' and humiliation of the Yeltsin presidency by the Clinton administration, and for cash, during the 1990s agreed to sell China its sophisticated Sovremenny-class destroyers (now the flagships of the Chinese Navy), 'Sunburn' anti-ship missiles, and advanced Sukoi Su-30 MKK fighter aircraft.

Both nations have also agreed to cooperate on the joint development of new military technologies, including so-called 'asymmetrical' warfare (cyber-warfare) technology aimed at curbing US dominance in this area. During the 1980s, Israel was – dodging US objections –a 'covert' supplier of advanced military technology to China, estimated at US$ 4 billion. When Israel wanted to supply the Falcon, an airborne radar system equipped with advanced Israeli-made aeronautics on board a Russian-made plane, to China in 2000, the US Congress threatened sanctions against Israel. Only when Congress moved to cut the US$ 2 billion aid that it gives Israel annually did Israel buckle and had to pay US$ 350 million in compensation to China. The US did not, however, oppose Israel's supply of the Falcon to India.

Russia's arms industry is suffering a near collapse in exports to China as the Russian top brass agonizes over which technology can safely be sold to China, as well as Beijing's desire to receive licences to do the work itself, the independent newspaper Nezavisimaya Gazeta reported on 28 January 2008. The main issue is indecision: 'Russians feel genuinely concerned, in the medium to longer term, that Russian and Chinese interests may collide again', said Alexey Muraviev, a strategic analyst at Curtin University of Technology in Perth, Australia.

'There is this debate about whether we should arm the Chinese when they may eventually turn against us'. Nezavisimaya further reported that Moscow's willingness to deliver cutting-edge technology to India – another major importer of Russian weapons – had 'embittered the Chinese generals'. After orders peaked at more than US$ 2 billion a year earlier this decade, Chinese arms' deals with Russia shrank to almost nothing in 2006, and no major new contracts are in the pipeline, according to Russian, Chinese and US defence experts. Still, with the EU–US arms' embargo on China still in place, most analysts expect that Moscow and Beijing will eventually negotiate compromises that clear the way for future contracts: 'Russia still provides what the US and the EU will not supply'.

Russia 'Strong-Arming' India

As a logical next phase in its ambitions as a major power, India in 2002 undertook to establish its own military outpost in Tajikistan and spent over US$ 1 million to renovate a former Soviet airbase, Ayni, 10 kilometres from the Tajik capital Dushanbe. Ayni's value to India stems from Tajikistan's geographic location, as it shares borders with China, Afghanistan, Uzbekistan and Kyrgyzstan. A narrow strip of Afghan territory – the Wakhan corridor – separates Tajikistan from Pakistan. The Russians recently started to pressurize the Tajiks to deny India deployment and even access to Ayni, allegedly because of increasing Russian unease about India's new closeness to the United States. The Russian message was that if India wanted to have a strategic beachhead in Central Asia, it has to keep its distance from the US. It also served as a warning to India to decide in Russia's favour in a host of big-ticket defence deals that are on the agenda:

'Don't buy too much American, or else!' There is another irritant in India–Russia relations, for which Russia itself is at fault: the endless delay in delivery of the aircraft carrier 'Admiral Gorshkov' and the steep hike in costs of the Sukhoi fighter aircraft.

On top of that, there is the China factor. What impact will the US and Russian arming of India have on Sino-Indian relations, while the United States maintains its arms' embargo on China and maintains pressure on the divided European Union to fall in line. The US has in recent years rejected a policy of containment of China, at least publicly. Only the short-lived former Japanese

Prime Minister Shinzo Abe openly advocated 'value-based diplomacy' (democracy and human rights) and containment, and appealed in a speech to the Indian Parliament in August 2007 for India to join, which India never did. Under its former inward-looking Prime Minister John Howard, however, Australia did, but the new Prime Minister Kevin Rudd, a Chinese-speaking former diplomat, cancelled Australia's participation in the 'Quadrilateral Dialogue', a coalition of democracies aimed at 'furtively' containing China, immediately after taking office. Indian Prime Minister Manmohan Singh, on his January 2008 visit to China, also reiterated the theme that India will not be part of any 'contain China scheme'.

Does the Triangle have a Future?

The 'Trio' of Russia, China and India was triggered by three events:

- The American sanctions against India over its May 1998 nuclear tests;
- The December 1998 Clinton–Blair bombing campaign against Iraq, a country with which Russia maintained close relations;
- The *'erroneous'* US bombing of the Chinese Embassy in Belgrade in May 1999.

The three countries had deeply shared grievances about – perceived – American/Western neo-colonialist arrogance, hypocrisy, double standards and deception, etc. US unilateralism provided a basis for continued – but just intermittent – solidarity, as the three of them had their own national bilateral agendas in pursuing better relations with each other and with the United States. While Russia and China shared opposition against the US-sponsored democratic 'colour revolutions' in former Soviet republics in 2005, India was more interested in expanding its relations with the United States. In 2006 the themes of their consensus were the democratization of international relations, multi-polarity, respect for the United Nations, which the United States often tended to bypass, and opposition to Bush's sabre-rattling against Iran. In 2007 the focus was on joint opposition against an emerging 'East Asian (!) NATO' – four democracies, including Australia and the United States – for the containment of China. After some confusion about its orientation, India dropped out this time, and in 2008 Australia as well. India would also not participate in the US-sponsored missile defence, at least not now, and the Indian communists succeeded in derailing the US–India nuclear deal. In 2008, the 'Triangle' also expressed opposition against the unilateral declaration of independence of Kosovo, but it remains to be seen whether they can hang on to this against the United States and the European Union. Opposition against further NATO expansion will probably be more effective, because the European Union itself is divided over this. China is neutral on the issue of Ukraine's and Georgia's accession to NATO and still resists Russia's request for closer military cooperation, such as in the Shanghai Cooperation Organization (SCO). Russia advocates collective security for SCO, but China advocates only cooperative security – anti-terrorism, anti-extremism and special dialogues on energy security.

The question is, will the Russia–China–India triangle survive as a viable grouping in Asian and global diplomacy, or will the inherent contradictions in the triangle render it marginal or irrelevant? There is a vast asymmetry in the countries' actual and potential power. The US design was to strengthen India against a much stronger China and to lock the fellow democracy into the position of an ally and military client state with restrictions on its sovereignty, similar to the formerly defeated Asian great power of Japan. It is now clear, however, that this is not going to work as Washington envisioned. India practises democracy, not based on crusading Bushist ideological zealotry but out of sheer pragmatism: it is the natural way to manage the internal dynamics of such a culturally diverse country. But India will never base its foreign policy on an agenda of spreading democracy or show prejudice against countries that are not Western/American-style democracies.

An accumulation of factors – foremost of which is the realization that negative relations with the United States during the Cold War have held India back, plus the recognition that China's normalization of relations with the United States in 1972, combined with Deng Xiaoping's reforms from 1978, have facilitated and accelerated China's rise – have convinced India that it must optimally expand its relations with the United States for reasons of geopolitics, economics, trade and investment, particularly high-technology integration. For reasons of history and internal divisions, however, it cannot do so on American terms. India needs stable relations with China and in recent years it has achieved significant improvement in its relationship with China, but this is not sustainable without a broader Asian 'balance of power' with outside participation of the United States and, perhaps in the longer term, the European Union/OSCE. At the same time, India wants to continue its close relationship with its Cold War ally Russia, perhaps in a diluted form but still substantial. As Sujit Dutta, a senior analyst with the Institute of Defence Studies and Analyses in New Delhi, puts it:

India is not going to be a junior partner of China. No question. If Russia accepts to be a junior partner of China because of this vast asymmetric power relationship and its contradictions with the West, then the only way that scenario will play out is India becomes a junior partner with China or alternately that China accepts an equal status for India. Much will depend on whether China's nationalism becomes what it says: accepting multi-polarity as a basis for the new world order. Multi-polarity doesn't seem to be the essence of it, though, as we observe Chinese foreign policy.

In other words, India will need the United States and Japan to balance against China, and in the longer term something similar may apply to Russia. It is interesting to note what former US National Security Adviser Zbigniew Brzezinski said about this: 'In the longer run, I happen to think that Russia really has no choice but to become gradually more associated with the Euro-Atlantic community. Because if it isn't, then it's going to find itself essentially facing China all by itself'.

The 'trio' was not an alliance and will not be one, but just a *ménage à trois* of intermittent *'one-night stands'*, with the three countries taking common positions on selected, but not the most important, issues.

The endgame for the three countries in the mid-to long term may very well be that China will enter into a bipolar superpower relationship with the United States; India will become one pillar in an Asian and global multi-polar balance of power, underpinned by the United States; and Russia will return to Europe for the fourth time in its history, after three failed precedents since Peter the Great.

RUSSO-CHINESE RELATIONS ELEVATED

Despite the declaration and reputation of the "strategic partnership" between Russia and China established in 1996, relations developed at snail's pace. The promise to boost trade ties between the two countries to the $20 billion level by 2000 was not realized. Border negotiations were deadlocked over a couple of remaining disputed points: Heixiazi Island near Khaborovsk and Abagaitui Island on the Argun River.

The 1991 agreement, excluding the two points above, was juristically reconfirmed in 1999. In September 1999, when Russian sinologists began to emphasize a would-be "strategic triangle" between Russia, China and India during a symposium session held at the Institute of the Far East in Moscow, a correspondent from a Chinese newspaper did not take their reports very seriously, and a Russian diplomat criticized the idea for its impracticality. A prestigious Chinese academic journal on Russia mentioned that Russo-Chinese relations are on a second axis that is easily influenced by Russo-US and Sino-US relations. The better the latter becomes, the worse the former becomes, and vice versa.

Just after his inauguration, Russian President Vladimir Putin was eager to visit to Europe in early 2000. He welcomed US President Bill Clinton in

Moscow in early June, while waiting until July to visit Beijing. The joint statement published there on missile defence unveiled a different approach between Russia and China. China was afraid that the new Russian president was overly pro-western at China's expense. Even when President Putin paid his first visit to India in October 2000, a high-ranking Chinese correspondent suggested in an internal report that this trip may have been held to counter China as a part of Russia's "balance" foreign policy.

Emerging problems in relations were, however, worked out through bilateral cooperation, particularly over the border region, which kicked off during the later years of the Yeltsin period. Successful enforcement of the 1991 agreement, strict management of Chinese migration, joint control of the border regime and other border cooperation had a positive effect in stabilizing the border region. It was undoubtedly shown that border cooperation had moved forward, regardless of any divergence of opinion or disputes between governments. Then, Putin urged the conclusion of a "neighbourly friendship and cooperation" treaty, which Jiang Zemin had proposed to Yeltsin earlier, in order to solidify the basis of Russo-Chinese relations. On the eve of signing of the treaty in July 2001, it was reported that Putin, wanting to bring the border dispute to an end, repeatedly argued for a compromise on the remaining border disputes, although it was unrealized.

After both of them successfully completed the treaty and played up the "partnership," new challenges emerged in the aftermath of "9/11." Russia and China immediately responded to US President George W. Bush's call for a "united front" against "international terrorism." If the Chinese view on the Sino-Russian axis mentioned above were true, Russo-Chinese relations had again hit another stumbling block.

In fact, bilateral relations were neither disturbed nor worsened. In addition to border stability and cooperation, economic relations gradually developed: $8 billion in 2000, $17.7 billion in 2001, and $11.0 billion in 2002. Russian arms sales to China were also progressive, with the sale of A–50 AWACS going through in November 2000, while deals over an upgraded SU–27K jetfighter and six submarines were finalized (the total amount is said to have been around $1.5 billion). It went beyond the estimated arms sales of $1 billion, at that time. Since 2000, energy issues have been at the top of their agenda. China's urgent demand for oil and gas made possible the close cooperation over the construction of a pipeline through Siberia and the Far East. The move was put forward during a Mikhail Kasiianov-Zhu Rongji meeting in September 2001. The Russo-Chinese treaty provided the full basis for further cooperation, and was not influenced by outside factors.

President Putin, just after his meeting with Jiang Zemin in June 2002, praised Russo-Chinese relations: "The recent improvement in Russo-US relations never ignores Russo-Chinese relations, and the latter reaches a higher level than the former because of the existence of the friendship treaty." Nevertheless, problems soon emerged between Russia and China: China's unfriendly attitude toward Russia's entry into the WTO (China countering it with a demand that Russia lift its "barrier" policy against "Chinese migration" as a condition for Chinese support), problems over Russia's "dumping" of Russian exports, such as steel and chemical fertilizer, and Khabarovsk's severe reaction and propaganda over the Heixiazi Island issue. By the end of 2002, Putin was describing Russo-Chinese relations as "friendly but businesslike."

Breakthrough: The New "Partnership"

In March 2003, Hu Jingtao was selected as the new president of China. For his first trip abroad, he chose Russia. To say that Russia and China were somewhat irritated by Bush's unilateral approach would be an understatement; the presence of the US army in Central Asia for an undetermined period of time, and the US invasion and its subsequent occupation of Iraq being the most obvious irritants.

Nevertheless, Russia and China did not closely coordinate against the US-UK "collation" on Iraq. Russia leaned upon a French initiative to soften the UN resolution on sanctions against Iraq. China cautiously watched the process but did not make its position clear at first.

For the most part, rapid economic interactions between the two countries started in 2003. In 2003, the trade volume hit $15.6 billion (up $4.6 billion from 2002) which, if the negative effects of the SARS epidemic on the economy in May of that year are considered, is a tremendous achievement. It reached $21.2 billion in 2004 and $25.2 billion in 2005. Meanwhile, some twenty-four SU–30 jetfighters (at a cost of almost $1 billion) were sold in 2003, while the total amount of arms sales reached $2 billion. Defence Minister Sergei Ivanov visited Beijing and concluded the sale of six S–300 missiles. Nevertheless, when economic issues were internationalized, the Russo-Chinese "partnership" remained "businesslike." Problems related to the proposed Siberian pipeline illustrate the realities of Russo-Chinese relations. Despite repeated Chinese calls for a route to go through China, Russia did not finalize it, and in September 2003 put its final decision on hold. Instead, Russia emphasized the importance of a direct route to the Pacific Ocean. A drastic push for better "relations" was brought about by the border arrangement. In October 2004, Russian President Putin and Chinese President Hu Jintao declared that Russia and China had successfully resolved the remaining border dispute by cutting each disputed island, Heixiazi and Abagaitui Islands, in half. The two presidents were proud of the results and declared it a "win-win" compromise. They also strongly suggested that it could potentially be applied as a model to other border disputes around the globe.

The present condition of Russo-Chinese relations would not have been possible without defusing and resolving the border issue first, with little chance of bilateral cooperation in the vital areas of energy and arm sales. Who would have imagined an oil and gas pipeline crossing over the Amur River or a joint military exercise prior to the border dispute being resolved?

With regional stability enhanced, mutual trust between the two countries has grown. As shown in this article, basic challenges to Russo-Chinese relations originated mostly from border disputes. The better the situation of the border, the better the relations. Lessons gained from Russo-Chinese relations suggest that they have not been a secondary axis, and have been affected little by the US. It is a considerably independent variable, basically controlled by bilateral factors, and has been particularly modified by border politics in the aftermath of the Cold War.

THE WAY AHEAD IN INDO-RUSSIAN TIES

Russia is one country that India cannot afford to sideline, as it is the only trusted partner with whom India has mutual compatibility and a close political, military and economic partnership for decades. Russia (and the Soviet Union) contributed to creating India's key strengths and capabilities in the nuclear, defence, space and heavy industry sectors when no other country was willing to support India's endeavours to modernise.

Even today, despite the hype surrounding the visits of other members of the P-5, India's relationship with Russia has brought it greater benefit than its ties with other major countries. With hopes high the questions now are: What has been achieved so far? What are the priorities? What we can expect from our trusted friend? What should we do to further consolidate this relationship?

The Path Covered

The Indo-Russian relationship has evolved over time. Russian foreign and security policy is based on the concept of a "multipolar" world, first formulated by former Foreign Minister and Prime Minister Yevgeni Primakov. It is in this context that Russia has its interest in the South Asian region where it gives primary importance to India. In October 2000 the "Declaration of Strategic Partnership between India and the Russian Federation" was signed in New Delhi since when there has been an all-round development in bilateral cooperation. In this declaration the system of Annual Summits was institutionalized. The previous or tenth summit was held in Moscow in December 2009 between Indian Prime Minister Manmohan Singh and Russian President Dmitry Medvedev. This year would be a very important stage in the development of bilateral relations, as it marks the tenth anniversary of the signing of the Declaration on Strategic Partnership between India and Russia.

During Prime Minister Putin's visit in March 2010, deals worth US $10 billion were signed to further strengthen defence and economic relations. In addition, five agreements were also signed. Prime Ministers Manmohan Singh and Putin held comprehensive and in-depth discussions on bilateral, regional and global issues.

Cooperation in the area of atomic energy production for peaceful purposes and a roadmap for the construction of Russian designed nuclear power plants was agreed upon. A memorandum of understanding (MoU) for the production of satellite navigation equipment and services for civilian use and cooperation in the mineral fertilisers sector, 14 supplementary pacts on the Gorshkov aircraft carrier deal, and an additional agreement on military aviation ties were also signed.

During Putin's visit, Information technology and telecommunications were also identified as focus areas for future economic cooperation between New Delhi and Moscow.

According to Indian Defence Minister Mr. A.K. Antony, Indo-Russian relationship has moved beyond buyer-seller to co-producer in the field of design development and scientific research.

Almost 70 per cent of Indian military hardware is of Soviet/Russian origin. Russia is the only country with which India has established an institutionalized defence cooperation mechanism operating at the Defence Ministers level. In 2008 India and Russia agreed to extend the terms of the Indo-Russian Inter Governmental Commission for Military Technical Cooperation for another ten years till 2020. India and Russia are all set to sign their biggest ever defence deal pegged at $30 billion with the Cabinet Committee on Security giving a go ahead to a mega proposal for joint development and production of the fifth-generation fighter aircraft (FGFA).

In the field of Nuclear Energy, Russia is a long standing partner for India. Currently two nuclear power reactors are being supplied by Russia in Kudankulam and two more are planned. In 2009, India designated Haripur (West Bengal) as an additional site for the construction of nuclear power plants with Russian cooperation. An Inter-Governmental Agreement on broad based cooperation (cooperation in the field of use of atomic energy for peaceful purposes) and a Road Map for future cooperation was signed during the visit of Prime Minister Putin to India in March 2010.

Russia is the second most potent space power in the world. Russia's cooperation in India's Unmanned Space Flight project (Chandrayaan 2), the Human Space Flight Project and the development of Youthsat to be launched by India's GSLV are ongoing projects. In March 2010, a new area involving the joint manufacture of satellite navigation equipment for civilian users based on the Russian GLONASS system, commenced.

The sixteenth session of the India-Russia Inter-Governmental Commission on Trade, Economic, Scientific, Technological and Cultural Cooperation (IRIGC-TEC) held in New Delhi on 18 November 2010 expressed satisfaction at the continuation of high level bilateral contacts.

They welcomed the holding of the first-ever India-Russia Business Dialogue within the framework of the prestigious St. Petersburg International Economic Forum in June 2010 and expressed confidence that the MoU entered into by CII and SPIEF Foundation would pave the way for regular institutionalized B2B interactions and exchanges.

The Working Group on Science and Technology (S&T) under the aegis of IRIGC-TEC, and the "Integrated Long Term Program (ILTP) are the two principal institutional mechanisms for S&T cooperation with Russia. The ILTP was recently extended for a further ten years beyond 2009 with a renewed mandate for "Innovation led technology growth". The 'Working Group' focuses on collaboration activities in mutually agreed priority areas. The ILTP programme focuses on collaborative research in basic sciences and in Inter-Academy exchange programmes.

There is great interest in Indian studies, dance, yoga and music in Russia. An India Cultural Festival will be held in Russia in 2011 and a Russian Cultural Festival will be held in India in 2012. The Russian side has also suggested timing the event with the 150th birth anniversary celebrations of Rabindranath Tagore which are scheduled for 2011.

The Priorities

With Chinese defence procurements on the decline following the creation of its strong defence industrial base, India constitutes a major portion of Russian defence exports. Russia is also ready to supply India strategic platforms and technology that no other country will - such as nuclear submarine on lease.

India and Russia have intensified their R & D collaboration and joint production. It is important that this spills over into other economic sectors in order to assist economic development and technological upgradation in both countries.

Trade and investment ties also need to be enhanced as these are very low. While India's imports from Russia in 2010 are US$ 1.642 billion, its exports are $0.399 billion (State Customs Committee of the Russian Federation: first quarter of 2010).

There is a need to diversify the trade basket, both import and export. The business community in both countries is sceptical about its counterpart. The combination of Russian potential in high technology and availability of 30 per cent of world resources with India's standing in the fields of industry and engineering could result in major achievements. Economic cooperation is extremely important which if not strong would weaken the mutually beneficial ties.

Space exploration is another major priority area for India since it is a long term and ambitious endeavour and no state can embark upon it alone. The geopolitics of the 21st century dictate that there is a need to take Indo-Russian collaboration to greater heights and space collaboration could play a key role towards this end. Civil Nuclear Cooperation is another area of importance where there is vast scope for India-Russia cooperation.

Russia is not happy about India diversifying its sources of arms procurement. The issue of timely delivery of orders placed by India (for instance, aircraft carrier INS Vikramaditya or Gorshkov) is being addressed. Russia would have to resolve the internal issues that arise from its military industrial exports centring on Rosoboronexport. The two sides need to deepen their cooperation in this area and expand it to the more dynamic civilian sector.

India should participate in the Russian initiative to create a counterpart to Silicon Valley in Skolkovo, outside Moscow. The Russian IT and innovation sector is competitive and Russia enjoys enormous depth in scientific studies. India should enter into collaborative arrangements which would help the cause of innovation in both countries and their translation into concrete economic benefits.

India and Russia need to discuss how to enhance India's participation in Central Asia and benefit from the China-India-Russia initiative. Russia has reached out to Pakistan at the Sochi Summit and strengthened its relations with China.

India's participation in forums like SCO, RIC and BRIC needs to be strengthened, through which India and Russia can work to maintain regional security as well as enhance cooperation in the sector of environment and disaster management, in pharmaceuticals, metallurgy, biotechnology as well as in tourism.

India should promote a greater focus on Russia, and launch initiatives for the study of Russia in India. There should be greater effort in publicising the benefits of bilateral cooperation in both countries, for which there is very little visibility.

SCO AND STRATEGIC PARTNERSHIP BETWEEN CHINA AND RUSSIA

China and Russia share similar positions and close views on important international issues. The strategic partnership between China and Russia is based on high-level political trust, on the common interests of the two countries.

All kinds of relations between countries are influenced from the outside, and relations between China and Russia are not an exception. But thanks to close ties and high-level confidence between the two countries the strategic partnership between China and Russia is already developing to a certain extent according to its internal logic.

Absent external pressure, relations between China and Russia would have advanced anyway. Maybe they would have evolved in other directions. Of course, in current conditions, relations between China and Russia are more important for the recovery and balance in international relations, which are undergoing radical changes.

The projects of Belt and Road and the EAEU were underway before Donald Trump came to power. The two projects envisage the development of infrastructure for the sake of progress and prosperity of the peoples of the concerned countries, and are not directed at sowing violent conflicts between peoples and disorder in the world.

It is necessary to judge not by words, but by deeds. The implementation of the Belt and Road and the EAEU benefits economic cooperation between the participating countries in accordance with accepted international rules and promotes understanding between peoples.

After its membership expansion, the SCO acquired even more opportunities to implement economic cooperation in the Eurasian region, including cooperation within the framework of the Belt and Road and the EAEU projects.

STRATEGIC PARTNERSHIP BETWEEN CHINA AND RUSSIA

The friendship between Russian President Vladimir Putin and Chinese President Xi Jinping is turning back in the centre of global powerful relations.

Russia and China have strengthened their cooperation and proved their partnership has been getting stronger during this year.

China's shift in strategic focus from the Soviet Union to the United States seems to be the most important geopolitical realignment of the last several years.

In addition, Beijing is now proud of having great relations not only with Washington, but also better relations with Moscow than does Washington. The relationship between China and Russia is seen as a mutual and beneficial partnership. Moscow claims that this is the greatest Russian foreign policy achievement during the post-Soviet period.

In May 2016, Boris Titov, co-chairman of the Russian-Chinese Friendship committee and Russia's ombudsman for entrepreneurs' rights commented on the conference titled 'Russia and China: Taking on New Quality of Bilateral Relations', "together we can become a centre that can influence global processes."

The sanctions, which have been a major issue in the European-Russian relations, do not pose a great challenge for the cooperation between China and Russia. According to Titov, they do not affect mutual projects where businesses of middle or small size play a role. China creates huge markets and opportunities for the Russian products.

"Politics always contradicts economic interests, business is far away from politics, we need honest and direct relations," the co-chairman stated, drawing the attention to the main obstacles of closer cooperation which comes with excessive bureaucracy and adherence to official rules and formalities of both countries. However, considering China's extent of living experience under sanctions, Russia and China "will be able to go through this period significantly better together."

During Putin's visit to Beijing in June 2016, which was his fourth visit to China since 2013, both countries highlighted the importance of their bilateral relationship.

"President Putin and I have unanimously decided that the more complicated the international situation, the more determined we should be, guided by the spirit of strategic cooperation and the idea of eternal friendship," Xi said in a press statement following their talks. "Russia and China stick to points of view which are very close to each other or are almost the same in the international arena," Putin added.

After successful joint naval exercises in the South China Sea in September, the 21st (2016) regular meeting of the Russian and Chinese heads of government, which was held in November 2016, came with the usual agreements and memorandums in St. Petersburg. The major topic of discussion was trade, in particular free trade, the World Trade Organization (WTO), and protectionism. Dimitry Medvedev, Russian's prime minister disagreed with the statement as if the WTO should be destroyed and replaced with something else.

He encouraged Chinese premier Li Keqiang to develop integration projects between China and Russia without the other countries of the WTO. Following a new way of a 'Chinese-Russian path', Russia and China would develop their relation in creating bilateral economic projects and integration strategies. Russia has aspirations to increase trade turnover with China to $200 Billion in the next three to seven years, by 2020 as a target.

That said, the two countries have made no small show of trying to expand ties. Nevertheless experts argue that the relationship between China and Russia is imbalanced and fraught: the two countries hold significant cultural prejudices about each other and have different interests that are probable to diverge even more in the next years. Moreover, the Chinese-Russian relationship is an inherently restricted partnership conditioned on its power to rise both parties' interests.

"The reality is that Russian and Chinese relations are probably the best [they've been] in modern history... They're both opposed to a world dominated by a source of power that isn't one of them," said Roy J. Stapleton, founding director of the Kissinger Institute for Chinese-U.S. Studies, and a former U.S. ambassador of Singapore, China and Indonesia.

"They both feel threatened by U.S. unilateralism." Stapleton raises the issue of the complicated and winding diplomatic relationships between the U.S., Russia and China. The three countries together represent the largest geographic area.

They constitute the most economically powerful and militarily significant states. Furthermore, they hold a quarter of the world's population and an account for 41 percent of its gross domestic product. If all three can agree with one another they could vastly benefit. However, 'two is company and three is a crowd'. Bearing in mind the close proximity of China and Russia, rumours suggest that a two-vs.-one scenario is arising.

At one time, the Soviet Union and China were close to starting a war against each other. Nowadays Russia and China tighten their strategic relations and are seen as building the world's second and third biggest military powers. History seem to suggest that enemies can become friends but as the old saying goes, "keep your friends close and your enemies even closer". Both China and Russia realize the importance of partnership with each other, while remaining suspicious and cautious.

What if Russia's relations with the United States are about to change? What happens if Vladimir Putin and Donald Trump, the currently elected president of the United States of America, follow the rapprochement as both parties claim they want? What if America limits Putin's powerful position in Europe?

All those issues have an impact on the strategic partnership to China as well. When talking about the meaningfulness of the renewed strong partnership between China and Russia, we cannot extract one alliance out of the global context but need to see the international cooperation as a whole. Events from the history between those two countries can serve as a reminder that there is no escaping the fundamental tension between Russia and China when it comes to the need for economic ties with rising powers and developing their world position as leaders. This should be considered in analysing the questions in order to project what the future of China-Russia relations could mean for the regional politics of Asia in an emerging multipolar order.

2

Evolution of Russian-Chinese Strategic Relations

TOWARDS A BILATERAL PARTNERSHIP

The first years of transition in Russia were dominated by radical economic reforms and desire to integrate rapidly the occidental community. However, this period soon left the place for a more auto-centric approach, which meant a retreat of radical economic reforms and a more equilibrated foreign policy between its Western and Eastern axis. Since the normalization of Soviet-Chinese relations announced by M. Gorbachev in 1989, the Presidents B. Yeltsin and Jiang Zemin announced for the first time "constructive partnership" in 1994, and "strategic partnership" in 1996. Strategic relations between Russia and China should be seen as a part of the triangle including both countries and the US. Promoting a multipolar world and the desire to counteract the dominance of the US in the post-cold war world are among the common objectives of Moscow and Beijing.

Another element is the refusal of interference in internal affairs, notably for the human rights and local separatism issues. So, Russian policy towards China (and *vice versa*) is inversely correlated with the policy towards the US. Consequently, the political or strategic factors play a dominant role in the conception of Russian policy in Asian-Pacific region.

The Russian-Chinese Treaty of Good-neighbourliness, Friendship and Cooperation between Russia and China was signed in 2001. It partially repeats the Sino-soviet treaty expired in 1980, precisely, concerning the respect of territorial integrity and sovereignty, Russian engagement for the "one-China" policy (non-recognition of Taiwan independence), and expansion of links in numerous domains (of which the military one).

Further, two articles of the new treaty indicate the military alliance, even if the parties deny this fact and the Treaty doesn't contain a clause of mutual defence. Finally, the treaty mentions actual problems related to countries economic inequality issues revealed especially at the regional level. So, Russia and China should renounce any form of pressure and facilitate cooperation in frontier regions (art.14), and cooperate to combat illegal immigration (art.20).

The bilateral Treaty (2001) consolidated the basis for Russian-Chinese political partnership. However, in spite of the proclaimed strategic partnership, Russian and Chinese interests diverge on several aspects of regional policy in Central Asia.

Convergence and divergence of interests at the regional level

In Central Asia, China and Russia interact in the framework of the Shanghai Cooperation Organisation (SCO). The SCO was formally created in 2001 by Russia, China, Kazakhstan, Kyrgyzstan, Tajikistan and Uzbekistan. In reality, the SCO is the continuation of the Shanghai Forum, created in 1996 by the above-mentioned countries except Uzbekistan aiming to stabilize the post-soviet Central Asia.

The main goals were the demarcation and protection of the common border and also, for China, solution of ethnic minority problems in the frontier zone. So, regional security is the first objective of the SCO.

However, one can note that Shanghai Forum was founded in 1996, a period of tensions in both Russian-American and Chinese-American relations. Later, the regional preoccupation of the SCO will not exclude the orchestrated action of the organization against the US. Moreover, the acceptance of Mongolia, Pakistan, India and Iran as observers reinforces the international role of the SCO.

At the same time, the SCO reveals the conflict of interests between Russia and China as both countries are searching to increase their presence in Central Asia. On the one hand, China demonstrates a growing interest towards this zone which was submitted to its influence in the past. The SCO is the only structure at China's disposal to promote its interests in the region, rich in hydrocarbons. In this way, China and Russia become rivals for access to oil and gas reserves of Central Asia.

On the other hand, the SCO is one of several organizations serving to promote Russian interests in the region. Russia is present through the CIS and panoply of sub-regional blocs and treaties concluded between different CIS states. In this context, the activation of the Eurasian Economic Community (EurAsEC, regrouping Russia, Belarus, Kazakhstan, Kyrgyzstan, Tajikistan and, since 2006, Uzbekistan) can be viewed as an attempt to oppose the growing influence of China in Central Asia (Facon (2006)). The reinforcement of EurAsEC arrives when China stresses the importance of economic issues within the SCO. More precisely, the Framework Agreement to enhance economic cooperation (signed in September 2003; and also the action plan approved in September, 2004) fixes the main orientations for 2020 aiming to establish a SCO free-trade zone.

However, the economic mission of the SCO remains weakly defined, while the non-coordinated accession of its members to the WTO puts into question its emergence as a trading bloc.

Moreover, the growing competition of Chinese goods in such a case could have negative effects on Russian producers. The latter puts a strong limit for the development of regional trade integration within the SCO. In this context, the Russian Ministry of Economic development and trade officials propose to limit the scope of economic partnership within the SCO. Russian economic interests should be promoted through the EurAsEC while the SCO should be limited to security issues only.

Nevertheless, in spite of numerous discrepancies, the global framework of Russian-Chinese relations creates a favourable context for the development of economic cooperation and the creation of costly energy exports infrastructures.

RUSSIAN-CHINESE RELATIONS: A STUDY IN CONTEMPORARY GEOPOLITICS

The disappointment which a number of Russian politicians feel over the way their country's relations with the West evolved in the decade following the end of the Cold War, has led many of them to discuss various „eastern options". Since 1994, one hears the talk of new axes, alliances and partnerships with countries ranging from India to Iran to Iraq, but above all, with China. This harkens back to a traditional adage of Russian diplomacy: when checked in the west, look for opportunities in the east. This largely self-contained elite discussion received much wider attention in December 1998 when then Prime Minister Evgenii Primakov casually mentioned the need for creating a „strategic triangle" consisting of Russia, China and India.

The offer found no immediate takers and was subsequently downplayed by Primakov himself, but it left a trace. Never before had a senior Russian leader been so explicit about the idea of counterbalancing the global domination of the West, led by the United States, by means of a Eurasian alliance. A few months later, during the Kosovo crisis, Russia and China moved even more closer together in their opposition to U.S. "hegemonism".

Symbolically, as the Russian military forces were holding their first major exercise dubbed „West-99" which for the first time in a decade again designated NATO as the enemy, a visiting high-level Chinese military delegation was given unprecedented access to Russian nuclear bases. Moscow and Beijing are beginning to live up to the notion of a strategic partnership through taking a common position on the issue of theatre missile defenses in Asia, which they oppose. There are signs that Moscow is relaxing its self-imposed restrictions regarding the quality level of the arms and technologies it sells to China.

Only recently, the Sino-Russian relationship was carefully analysed and found to be of rather limited nature. Is this changing now? Is a new geopolitical realignment in the works? Will the current Moscow-Beijing entente eventually lead to an alliance? Or, conversely, are the inherent constraints in the bilateral relationship strong enough to keep China and Russia from forming an anti-Western bloc?

Or, to completely reverse the discussion, can it be that the present improvement in the Moscow-Beijing ties is only a short-term phenomenon, and in the medium and long term the two countries will collide again, as China becomes more powerful and assertive? What, in short, are the prospects and limitations of the geopolitical relationship which is likely to be among the most important and complex anywhere in Eurasia?

Geopolitics, of course, is only one aspect of the broader Russo-Chinese interaction. Economic relations, cross-border migration, contacts at regional and local levels, and not least among ordinary people, the impact of information technology and the exponential growth of communication, leading to cross-cultural influence, i.e. everything which is usually associated with the world of the future, is not covered by geopolitics.

A narrowly geopolitically-focused perspective is not just deemed to be old-fashioned and plainly obsolete, it can be distorting and misleading. Still, it is highly useful for a number of important reasons.

First, much of the government-to-government bilateral relationship between Beijing and Moscow today is about geopolitics.

There is little else, at least for the moment, to back the claim of a „strategic partnership". Second, the bulk of Chinese and Russian elites are keen students or at least admirers of geopolitics, which informs many of their actions. Third, for much of the outside world it is the prospect of a geopolitical realignment of China and Russia – and not, say, the chances for their economic cooperation-which evokes the most intense interest.

This article starts with an assessment of the new status quo between Russia and China, the vaunted correlation of forces between them, which has undergone dramatic changes in the last ten years. It then proceeds to take stock of the geopolitical gains resulting from the improvement in the bilateral relations. Lastly, it examines the potential for geopolitical cooperation and conflict between the two countries in the future.

Role Reversal

The starting point for any discussion of contemporary Sino-Russian geopolitics is recognizing and assessing the new standing of the parties vis-a-vis each other. The first fundamental change concerns the position that Russia and China hold in Asia.

Most Russians lamenting the passing of the Soviet Union usually compare their country's decline with the apparent new omnipotence and omnipresence of their erstwhile global rival, the United States. Still, the change of fortunes between Russia and China is only slightly less dramatic. In 1989, when President Gorbachev came to Beijing to repair the 30-year old Sino-Soviet rift, the USSR still included the five Central Asian republics; Mongolia was a loyal Moscow ally, and home to some 75,000 Soviet military personnel; so was Vietnam, with its strategic naval and air facilities. Laos and Cambodia were Soviet clients. India was a quasi-ally, under the 1971 treaty. In Afghanistan, even after the Soviet withdrawal, a pro-Moscow Najibulla regime continued to hold Kabul. As long as Soviet aid flowed, Moscow retained a measure of influence in Pyongyang.

Ten years later, along the former Soviet border, China has four neighbours, and Russia is only one of them. The others, Kazakstan, Kyrgyzstan, and Tajikistan, the new Moslem states, are engaged in a careful balancing act between Russia, China and the West. The Commonwealth of Independent States (CIS), a most useful framework for the dismantlement of the Soviet Union, has turned out to be virtually useless as a tool for post-Soviet integration. Mongolia, having shaken off Moscow's tutelage, has for the first time in its recent history adopted an independent foreign policy posture. Vietnam and its neighbours in Indochina have gravitated toward the ASEAN.

Ironically, Russia was constrained to become a supporter of the Afghan coalition which had ousted Najibulla, but the coalition has been defeated by the Taleban forces which now control at least three quarters of the country, including the capital. In 1997, many Russian political leaders and top military commanders sincerely feared that the Taleban would march across the former Soviet border and take over the entire region up to the Volga delta. These fears have since been proven false, but even without the Taleban, Russia finds it increasingly difficult to help maintain stability in the once dormant Central Asia. To add insult to injury, Moscow has found itself excluded from both the

Korean nuclear energy (KEDO) project and the Korea peace talks. The ties to India have grown stale and deteriorated. In short, Russia has ceased to be a political superpower in Asia and it faces a hard task of asserting itself even as a major regional player.

China, by contrast, has gone some way to becoming a regional power in Asia-Pacific. The „gathering of Chinese lands" has achieved important results. In 1997, Beijing achieved a historic reunification with Hong Kong, to be followed by reabsorption of Macau at the end of 1999. After this, only Taiwan will remain on Beijing's reunification agenda. China's claims to the South China Sea have been repeatedly reasserted. Beijing's diplomatic stature has also grown. From Kashmir to Korea, its influence is acutely felt and often sought by the local and regional forces. Whether it is nuclear proliferation in South Asia or the stand-off on the Korean Peninsula, Beijing is a key outside player. In Central Asia, it is quietly supplanting Russia's waning influence as it moves to diversify its sources of energy supply and to protect its rear. Beijing diplomats have been issuing statements on the conflicts in the Persian Gulf and the Balkans. In a symbolic recognition of its new role, China has evidently become the single most important country from the perspective of the world's only superpower, the United States.

The change in the relative economic weight between Russia and China is equally, if not more drastic. In 1989, the U.S.S.R. was still the world's third largest economy, after the U.S. and Japan. It produced substantially more goods and services than China. Ten years later, Russia has been demoted to the 16th place, in terms of its GDP. By contrast, China, due to its phenomenal growth rate since the start of Deng Xiaoping's reforms, has been able to surpass its former mentor several times over. Even if Russia starts to grow again at a decent annual rate of 3-4%, which is not yet in sight, its relative decline vis-a-vis China will continue. By 2010, the margin of difference between them can be tenfold. Even in per capita GDP terms the gap is fast closing. Thirty years ago the Soviet Union dominated China in this respect by approximately seven to one. Currently, China accounts for about 60% of Russia's level, and some of its coastal provinces have surpassed Russia's national average. Russia's technological lead over „backward China", historically the source of Moscow's pride, is also becoming history.

In 1989, the Soviet army was the most potent military force in both Europe and Asia. In the following years, it has gone through unprecedented decline. In 1997, e.g., it was officially admitted that the Russian military did not possess a single army division that was combat-ready. The quantity and quality of the forces deployed in the Far East have gone down significantly. Their power projection capabilities have been drastically reduced, and problems with the discipline abound, as weapons arsenals catch fire and blow up, and conscripts take to the taiga to escape hazing. The defeat of Moscow's attempt to subdue rebellious Chechnya by military force has become an emblem of a thoroughly new phenomenon – Russia's military weakness. By and large, Russia has missed on the revolution in military affairs. As a result, many have become convinced that, in any hypothetical major military conflict Russia would probably lose if the war remained conventional. Consequently, reliance on nuclear weapons for national defence has never been more pronounced in the Russian military doctrine and strategy. Clearly, this has implications not only for the West, but for the East-i.e. China – as well. Some Russian military officers privately admit that in a conflict with China the main Russian defenses along the border, including all the principal cities, will be overrun in a matter of days, leaving the General Staff with few options other than going nuclear.

China, for its part, has been steadily, if slowly modernizing its vast, although still primitive armed forces. Since 1992, it has been able to do this with the help of steady Russian transfers of arms and military technology, at the average annual rate of about $1 billion. In a pathetic symbol of the changed fortunes of the two states in the defence area, Russian military enterprises have been constrained to sell their products to China – or face closure. Recently, the People's Liberation Army has been buying more Russian-made combat aircraft than the Russian Air Force itself. Even in the nuclear field, there are projections that China may get even with Russia in the next 10-15 years if the latter continues on its path of decline and Beijing adopts an ambitious nuclear build-up policy.

In 1989, the last year of the Soviet census, the country's population reached 282 million, which made it the world's third largest. In 1999, when Russian census was cancelled due to the lack of funding, the country's population dropped to 146 million – two million less than when the USSR was dismantled. This figure roughly equals the combined population of China's three northeastern provinces which border on the Russian Far East. As to the Far East itself, its population has been declining faster than the national average, about 9% in the last decade of this century. Across the Amur and the Ussuri rivers, some 5 million Russians are facing around 130 million Chinese. Even if the entire population of Russia were resettled along the Chinese border, that would redress the imbalance with North-East China only temporarily. The population decline in Russia will continue unabated, and the country may lose as much as 10% of its current population in the next three or four decades. China's population will continue to grow from the current 1.2 billion, and Beijing's family planning policy will only moderate that growth, not arrest it. It has become commonplace in Moscow and Vladivostok to refer to the huge Chinese demographic „overhang" in the border area as a prime security concern. Thus, the collapse of the Soviet Union, which itself was a result of a quarter of a century long decline, has dramatically reversed the geopolitical dynamics of Eurasia as a whole. Long an assertive and expanding centre, Russia has been on the defensive all around, losing ground to the historical rivals and to the new states which for centuries were its provinces.

It strives to project an image of a still great power, to win time and restore the status quo, but it has found this increasingly difficult. China, by contrast, is not a status quo power. In the past 150 years it has suffered from too much humiliation at the hands of Europeans, including the Russians. It is now looking forward to coming back to the world stage as a strong independent force to be reckoned with. In the Sino-Russian relationship, roles have been reversed. Never since the two countries have established permanent contacts three hundred years ago, has Russia been the weaker, the less dynamic and the less confident of the two. This new distribution of power and influence, this newly prevailing „wind from the East" is more than a passing phenomenon.

Even assuming that Russia's economic crisis will be eventually overcome, and allowing for inevitable and increasing difficulties in China as its transformation deepens, it is unlikely that the traditional geopolitical relationship between the two countries – i.e., Russia's preponderance – will be restored. Russia's relative decline vis-a-vis China will probably continue well into the 21st century. This change in stature has wide-ranging implications for both countries, and for the outside world. For the time being, however, the reversal of roles has helped to establish a more equitable relationship from which both Russia and China have been able to draw important benefits.

Positive Gains

It would be absolutely wrong to argue that the new geopolitical environment in Asia, in the short to medium term, is inherently inimical, or even threatening to Russia. The end of the 25-year-long cold war between Moscow and Beijing has brought both countries important benefits. This concerns above all the 4,400-kilometer long common border, once the scene of bloody armed clashes. Since 1991, a series of agreements have been signed which led to the delimitation, demarcation and the partial demilitarization of the border. Of its entire length, only three river islands currently controlled by Russia remain contested. Beijing is no longer raising claims to some 1.5 million square km of territory annexed in the 19th century by Czarist Russia through „unequal treaties". The border which for three decades had been a source of tension and a likely site for large-scale conflagration has become a zone of tranquillity. Both governments have felt confident enough to decrease and dealert their military forces facing each other. Confidence-building measures are in place. The nightmare of a Sino-Russian conflict has become remote. In fact, both countries' General Staffs have designated different risks and opportunities. Beijing's main axes of strategic interest run to the south and southeast; Moscow feels the pressure of NATO enlargement and NATO interventionism in the west and the heat of instability in the south. Instead of confronting each other face to face, as they did in the past, Russia and China are actually standing now back to back to each other and feel so much more secure.

What is more, the border agreements and the military detente have been extended to the three former Soviet republics in Central Asia. Together with Mongolia, from which all Russian forces were withdrawn in 1992, they now form a huge buffer zone between Russia and China in Inner Asia, limiting their direct contact to Chinese Manchuria and the Russian Far East. The rise of the new states lowers the prospect for the resumption of a Cold-War type confrontation, though it could revive the traditional schemes of the struggle for the zones of influence. For the time being, however, both China and Russia abstain from this kind of competition.

Beijing and Moscow are concentrated on the domestic needs rather than outward expansion. Another major change is linked to the emergence of regionalism in both Russia and China. For the first time in 500 years, centralized political control in Russia is no longer absolute.

Popularly elected provincial governors, legislators and city mayors are wielding real power and occasionally challenge the federal authorities. In a parallel development, China's provinces have been becoming more assertive vis-a-vis Beijing, eager to preserve their particular interests. As on the Russian side, these interests have much more to do with gaining (or preserving) economic advantages than with power politics.

Thus, although this may appear paradoxical, the dramatic reversal of geopolitical roles between Russia and China has resulted in a more peaceful and equitable relationship which is mutually satisfying and valued by both. Whether this relationship will continue depends on how the longer-term interests of the two countries will interact.

Convergence of Interests and Its Limitations

In their rhetoric, Moscow and Beijing employ many like-sounding formulae. However, a geopolitical tour d'horizon allows one to see both convergence of interest and important differences which limit cooperation and may even point to conflict.

Multipolar world

Both Russian and Chinese leaders use the concept of multipolarity as the shorthand for the desired state of international relations in the post-Cold War era. Yet, taken on its own merit, the concept in the longer term can probably suit Beijing much more than Moscow. China is on the way to become a regional power, whereas Russia's fortunes continue to decline. Having ceased to be for the first time in history a self-contained and self-sustained universe, Russia will soon discover that its territory falls within the zones of attraction of several power centres, and, moreover, that some of Russia's own regions start to gravitate in different directions.

The North-West from Kaliningrad to Karelia to Kola, e.g., would move to „meet" the European Union, whereas Khabarovsk and Primorie would become part of China's „near abroad". It will require more than an average effort on behalf of the Russian leadership to respond to this new challenge creatively, and work out a new geopolitical model for the Russian state-both in terms of its domestic structural organization and its relation to the outside world.

This, however, is yet a task for the future. For the time being, Moscow and Beijing continue to use the rhetoric of multipolarity as a code word for their opposition to what they see as the domination of the world arena by the United States. This reminds one of the anti-hegemony platform that Washington and Beijing used to characterize their alignment in the late 1970s-1980s, when both perceived the Soviet Union as an adversary.

The United States

The Cold War-era triangular relationship has undergone a fundamental change, both in structure (with the diminishing of Russia's role) and in meaning (America no longer has a better relationship with China and Russia than these two have between themselves). In the early 1990s, when it briefly appeared that Moscow could become Washington's strategic ally, the Chinese grew concerned – for such a change would have meant, to them, a U.S. – engineered encirclement of the People's Republic. The failure of the Russo-American strategic partnership, which became evident in the dispute over NATO enlargement, brought relief to the Chinese government. By the mid-1990s, Sino-Russian relations reached the level of public cordiality which is no longer present in the U.S.-Russian case. In 1996, Moscow and Beijing agreed on a formula for a long-time partnership.

Having started with verbal expressions of opposition to „hegemonism", Russia and China have found it useful to work together on specific issues, such as Iraq, the Balkans and theatre missile defenses, in an attempt to contain U.S. assertiveness, or at least to get some leverage vis-a-vis Washington. In general, this has not worked, but has increased the self-confidence of both governments. After the Kosovo crisis, both countries' militaries have come to see themselves on the receiving end of American-led international interventionism. The NATO operation against Yugoslavia has resulted in the intensification of political and military contacts between Moscow and Beijing. The UN Security Council has become de-facto split with China and Russia routinely teaming up against the United States and its allies.

Still, all this cooperation, or even strategic alignment is likely to fall far short of an anti-American bloc. China, by culture and tradition, prefers to act alone; Russia would probably reject the role of a junior partner that it would be offered in any hypothetical coalition; most important, both countries, whatever their current differences with the United States and their opposition to the „unipolar world", need good relations with America for a host of economic, financial and other reasons. For Moscow, the most vital foreign policy issue is debt restructuring and relations with the international financial institutions, where Washington plays a paramount role. Russia's economic development is doomed without access to Western technology and capital investment. For Beijing, suffice it to mention that China's trade with America is worth ten times its trade with Russia.

Japan

It is still too early to speak about a „triangle" with Beijing, Moscow and Tokyo as its three corners: the level of mutual dependency among the three is far too low. However, from the Russian point of view a solid relationship with Japan is a necessary second pillar of Moscow's Asian policy, which otherwise would be too slanted toward China – to Russia's disadvantage. No meaningful economic integration of Russia into Asia-Pacific is possible without Japanese participation in the development of the Russian Far East. As for Japan, the rise of China is displacing it from the long-held position as the number one nation in Asia. From Tokyo's perspective, an active and successful policy of engagement toward Russia would serve as a hedge against a too dominant China.

Russia finds itself in a situation where the natural Sino-Japanese rivalry presents Moscow with an opening. It needn't make a choice between the two; rather, developing ties with one would strengthen its position with respect to the other, and vice versa. Even though both Beijing and Moscow remain suspicious of a resurgent Japan, China's fear is much stronger. Even though Russia and China expressed concern over the expansion of Japan's role in the bilateral defence relationship with the United States, China is more worried. Russia, by contrast, has acknowledged the stabilizing effect of the U.S.-Japan security relationship which effectively places Japan's defence policy under American control– something which the Chinese are yet to recognize.

Moscow and Beijing have voiced their objection to the U.S.-driven plans for a theatre missile defence system in East Asia, but Beijing's interests are more directly implicated than Moscow's. Interestingly, however, China shares the Japanese view on the status of the Kurile islands – a vestige of the times when the USSR was regarded its chief adversary.

Korea

China and Russia, no less than America and Japan, are clearly interested in the successful management of the situation on the Korean Peninsula – both the stand-off between South and North Korea and the incipient crisis within the North. The two countries, however, are able to exercise very different degrees of influence on the situation on the Peninsula. Whereas Beijing is the only international player with a real access to the Pyongyang leadership, Russia can only watch the situation from the sidelines. China, unlike Russia, is also party to the Korea peace talks – by virtue of the 1953 armistice agreement. Moscow's pleas to broaden the talks to include itself (and Japan) have fallen on deaf ears in Washington as well as in Beijing. China is reluctant to give up its exclusive position as one of the two outside powers – alongside with the U.S. – involved in the peace process.

The Chinese hope that Korea, which historically used to gravitate toward China, will once again assume this familiar posture. In the future, however, a reunified Korea may indeed see its ties with Russia, the weakest major power in North-East Asia, as a natural and relatively benign counterweight to the domination by the two regional hegemons and historical overlords, China and Japan. If this happens, Moscow's relations with Beijing will become more delicate.

CHINA-RUSSIA SPECIFIC INTERACTION

As noted, a number of very practical issues affect the Chinese-Russian relationship in various ways. Most significant among these are economics, security, and shared and/or competing interests in Central Asia.

Economics

The most important economic exchange between Russia and China involves energy. Russia is a major energy exporter, while China's imports grow each year. Moreover, China has become a profitable market for Russian oil. Nevertheless, creating the necessary energy infrastructure and reaching concrete agreements on energy supplies and pricing has not gone smoothly, exacerbated by infighting among Russian energy companies and mutual mistrust and misunderstanding between China and Russia. This has led to frustration, especially in China. After years of negotiations and Russian efforts to play off China against Japan, in January 2011, Russia began shipping oil to

China through the East Siberia–Pacific Ocean (ESPO) pipeline. This was enabled by a 2009 agreement that provided a $25 billion Chinese loan to Russia's oil and pipeline companies, Rosneft and Transneft, with an agreement for Russia to provide China with 300 million tons of crude oil over a 30-year period. However, in the first two months of the pipeline's operations, Russians charged the Chinese National Petroleum Corporation (CNPC) with underpaying for oil by $100 million. The dispute was settled the next year. Moreover, when Chinese president Xi Jinping visited Moscow in June 2013, China and Russia signed an additional crude oil deal worth $270 billion.

Natural gas, however, has yet to flow from Russia to China, in spite of a 2006 memorandum between Gazprom and CNPC that pledged 30 billion cubic meters of gas to China via a western route and 38 billion cubic meters across a route in the east, as well as an additional 2009 agreement. Russia and China have been sharply divided on the price of gas, and as a result, the necessary pipelines have not been built. This is due, in part, to issues in Chinese politics related to CNPC. Some analysts speculated that a loan deal with Gazprom would eventually lead to a resolution, similar to the oil deal. However, it seems that gas exports will no longer be a monopoly of Gazprom. Rosneft now has plans to sell liquid natural gas (LNG) to Japanese companies from a terminal on Sakhalin, while Novatek, an independent gas producer, has partnered with CNPC to sell China LNG from the Arctic. Finally, at the May 2014 summit between Vladimir Putin and Xi Jinping, China and Russia agreed to a 30-year gas deal that will begin delivering gas from Russia to China in 2018 after the necessary infrastructure is completed. The price of that gas is referred to as a "commercial secret."

In a related issue, Russia has clear economic and political interests in further developing the RFE, where it needs to reassert its control over the region and form a stronger basis for international influence in the

Asia-Pacific region. Energy plays a role in these goals, but there are other aspects to this challenge as well. After the fall of the Soviet Union, the RFE was virtually ignored while the new leaders of Russia attempted to put the state back together. Since 1991, the population in the area has shrunk by 20 percent, to 6.28 million, and is projected to drop further to 4.7 million by 2025.24 However, in recent years Russia has paid new attention to the RFE, due in part to the growth of China and dimming prospects for economic growth based on European trade and investment. Thus, in 2009 the Russian government approved the "Strategy for Socio-Economic Development of the Far East and the Baikal Region until 2025 (Strategy 2025)" to promote the development of its eastern regions. The 2012 Asia-Pacific Economic Cooperation (APEC) summit in Vladivostok also served as a catalyst for Moscow's attention, with the Russian government reportedly spending over $20 billion to upgrade Vladivostok's infrastructure.

Russia has a dilemma in developing the RFE. On the one hand, it needs the assistance of China and other Asia-Pacific powers to spur economic growth. The Russian government does not have the resources itself, and corruption and bureaucratic inefficiency stymie much of its efforts.

On the other hand, Russia does not want the RFE to become an appendage of China. It is uncertain if Russia will be able to successfully walk this line. In August of 2013, the Chinese State Development Bank announced that it may spend $5 billion in the RFE to finance Russian development programs. Moreover, Chinese workers reportedly now farm 40 percent of arable land in the Jewish Autonomous Region of the RFE, while Chinese farmers grew 90 percent of vegetables sold in the RFE in 2012.26 In sum, the RFE provides numerous opportunities for economic cooperation that would benefit Chinese and Russians. However, these opportunities also provide a potential liability to the Russian state as it seeks to establish a firm grip on its eastern regions.

China and Russia are also finding areas of cooperation on trade and investment. In 2010, China became Russia's biggest trade partner, and Russia's Micex exchange began trading the yuan and ruble as China and Russia sought to reduce dependence on the dollar in international trade. Nevertheless, Russia's place in China's overall trade is still modest. According to Chinese data published by the IMF, Chinese exports to Russia rose from $13.21 billion in 2005 to $44.07 billion in 2012, more than tripling. Nevertheless, calculations show that Chinese exports to Russia as a percentage of total exports only rose from 1.7 percent in 2005 to 2.2 percent in 2012. For sake of comparison, Chinese exports to Russia in 2012 were only 12.5 percent of Chinese exports to the United States. From 2005 to 2012, Chinese imports from Russia rose from $15.89 billion to $43.95 billion, although the percentage of total imports remained at 2.4 percent.

Russian data provided to the IMF shows that Russian exports to China grew from 5.4 percent of its total in 2005 to 6.8 percent in 2012. Russian exports to the United States in 2012 were only 36 percent of exports to China. Russian imports from China grew more than fivefold from 2005 to 2011, rising from 5.2 percent of the total in 2005 to 14 percent of the total in 2012.27 Thus, Russia is more dependent on mutual trade than China. In 2013, total trade rose only 2 percent from the previous year to $90 billion.

While increasing trade is beneficial for both states, the nature of trade is of concern to Russia. Russia fears becoming a provider of natural resources to

China and little else, and in 2006 Putin made a political issue of unbalanced trade. Chinese observers tend to complain of structural issues. For example, writer Qiu Huafei notes that Sino-Russian trade is largely focused on the needs of border communities, involving too few advanced technological goods. Qiu also points out that trade is hindered by contract violations, lack of institutionalized channels for resolving disputes, poor treatment of Chinese business personnel in Russia, the prevalence of a "China threat" mentality in Russia, and unsettled Russian debts. Other Chinese analysts, however, are more optimistic, pointing to the potential for Russian high-technology exports to China and foreseeing a Chinese move toward more of a domestic consumption-based economy that will provide greater export opportunities for Russia.

Security

Following armed clashes in 1969,31 both sides' desire for border security became a major factor leading to rapprochement in the late 1980s and early 1990s and continues to be a key issue. Russia looks defensively at the United States and NATO and also sees a major contemporary threat in terrorism coming from its south. At the same time, China is embroiled in disputes with Japan and Southeast Asia and seeks to suppress minority unrest within its borders. Each side needs assurance that their joint border will not create problems.

One fascinating aspect of the security relationship is the recent change in relative power positions. During the Cold War, the Soviet Union was the dominant power in the political, economic, and military arenas. Today, apart from nuclear forces and the technological sophistication of some major weapons systems, China is ascendant in the relationship. In fact, the rapid buildup of the PLA might lead one to expect that Russia would shift to a more defensive posture toward China.

There is some evidence that this is occurring, although for the most part, Russia does not see China as a major security threat at this point. China's rise makes the world more multipolar, giving space to Russia. Moreover, Russia sees China as focused on its east and south and understands that China has many domestic problems that take up resources and the attention of its leaders. For Russia, good ties with China are important for Russian security. From China's perspective, strong ties with Russia help prevent closer Russian ties with NATO in a manner that would isolate China. Likewise, Russia's annexation of Crimea was seen by many in China as a welcome defeat of the West. Taking various factors into consideration, one Chinese analyst suggests that the United States, Russia, and China are all hedging against each other. Arms sales are one important component in the Sino-Russian security relationship. China has been engaged in a sustained, long-term buildup of high-tech arms since the

1990s. With the United States and Europe refusing to sell China most types of military equipment since 1989, Russia has been China's most important source of foreign weapons. From 2006 to 2010, 84 percent of Chinese arms imports came from Russia.

From the Russian perspective, the period since the collapse of the Soviet Union has been marked by severe economic difficulties, moderated now by energy exports. As a result, military sales to China have been a welcome and at times industry-saving source of funds, and Russia has sold China a large variety of weapons. These include Su-27 and Su-30 fighter aircraft, surface to air missile (SAM) systems, *Sovremenny*-class destroyers, helicopters, transport aircraft, antiship missiles, torpedoes, radars, and jet engines. Nevertheless, Russian arms sales to China peaked in 2005 and have declined since then. Sales have dropped from $3.13 billion in 2005 (in constant 1990 prices) to $679 million in 2012. While sales to China comprised 60 percent of Russian arms exports in 2005, by 2012 the figure had fallen to only 8 percent. Most major weapon system deliveries from Russia to China were completed by 2009, and since 2006, major arms exports have been limited to jet engines, fire control radars, transport aircraft, and helicopters.

There are a variety of explanations for this drop in arms sales. From China's perspective, its own defence industries are capable of producing many of the weapons previously purchased from Russia. Additionally, there was some dissatisfaction with Russian arms sales. Russia often refused to sell China its highest-technology equipment, even though it was willing to sell more-advanced items to India. This has been an irritant to China. China hoped for more licensed production of systems within China and technology transfers, and was unhappy with delivery delays and the quality of Russian arms.

The Russian perspective is more complex. On the one hand, there is consternation about China reverse-engineering Russian technology and then using it in its own weapons exports, beating Russia on price in the process. Russians claim the Chinese J-11B fighter plane is a copy of the Su-27, while China is heavily marketing the JF-17 fighter, developed with Pakistan. In 2011, the Russian government commissioned a report entitled "The Strategies and Tactics of Chinese Exporters of Arms and Military Equipment," and the head of the Mikoyan (MiG) and Sukhoi design bureau sent a letter to Roxoboronexport asking that it not sell large numbers of RD-93 engines to China because the MiG-29 competes against the JF-17 for export sales and the JF-17 uses that engine.

Various Russian officials are also concerned about the strategic implications of China's growing military power. In this regard, there are differing opinions among Russian elites. Kevin Ryan notes that "the view from Moscow of military relations with China varies depending on the organizational viewpoint of the individual." Arms manufacturers have a different perspective from strategic planners. Russia faces the conundrum that China wants more and more sophisticated weapons, which might decisively affect the balance of power in the Asia-Pacific region (alienating the United States), as well as the balance of power between China and Russia itself.

The arms sales relationship between Beijing and Moscow will require careful observation as a barometer of their defence cooperation. Recently, there has been discussion of renewed Russian arms sales to China, especially the 400-kilometer-range S-400 SAM system and the Su-35S fighter, Russia's most advanced weapons. In December 2012, *Jane's 360* reported that Russia will also sell four *Lada*-class diesel submarines to China. Nevertheless, these deals are not firm. Another indicator of Sino-Russian defence ties is joint military exercises. The first military exercises were Peace Mission 2005, held under the auspices of the SCO with the publicly stated aim of combating terrorism. This exercise was conducted in the RFE and China's Shandong province and involved naval and amphibious operations. Ten thousand troops participated, as well as submarines and strategic bombers. This led to speculation that the exercises were about much more than terrorism, with China hoping that they would be seen as simulating an invasion of Taiwan. Various other Peace Mission exercises have been held as well. However, the level of actual coordination in such exercises is usually low.

Recent naval manoeuvres demonstrated greater coordination in military cooperation. From 5 to 12 July 2013, Russia and China conducted joint naval exercises of unprecedented size, named Joint Sea 2013. China sent seven naval vessels, including a guided-missile destroyer and frigates, while Russia provided 11 warships, including the Pacific fleet's flagship *Varyag*, a guided-missile cruiser, and a Kilo-class submarine. The exercises focused on surface warfare, antisubmarine warfare, air defence, and the rescue of a kidnapped vessel. Apart from the military aspects of the drills, the political message was also important. China would like the exercises to be seen as a warning to the United States and Japan, with an implication that Russia stands beside China in its various maritime disputes, especially the Diaoyu/Senkaku Islands. Russia, however, has taken a neutral position in these disputes, thus the exercises may misrepresent Russia's actual position.

As if to balance these exercises, shortly after the Chinese departed, Russia began its own unilateral military drills. In the largest military exercise since the fall of the Soviet Union, it reportedly conducted manoeuvres involving 160,000 troops, 500 tanks, 130 combat aircraft, and ships from the Pacific fleet. The exercise involved the rapid reaction of Russian forces deployed to the RFE.

It was designed to demonstrate the power of the Russian military to its Asian neighbours and its ability to quickly move forces to defend its eastern domains. Thus, while the naval exercises in early July showed tight cooperation with the Chinese military, the exercises later in the month demonstrated Russian independence and the ability of Russia to defend itself against any potential Chinese encroachment.

Central Asia

Central Asia (defined here as Kazakhstan, Kyrgyzstan, Tajikistan, Uzbekistan, and Turkmenistan) is an arena of relatively weak states with small populations attempting to govern vast areas. The region has large energy reserves and is strategically located between China, Russia, and the Middle East. Moreover, it can contribute to stability in Afghanistan but is also vulnerable to radical ideology and violence spilling over Afghanistan's borders. Thus, it is a region where Russia, China, the United States, India, Pakistan, Iran, and Turkey all seek influence. The Central Asians themselves, of course, strive for autonomy and room to maneuver, playing the various powers against each other. They also have squabbles with each other. In this setting, Russia and China engage in both conflict and cooperation. So far, their common interest in regional stability and keeping US influence out of the area has led the cooperative element of the relationship to dominate. Charles Ziegler notes, "Surprisingly, these two powers have found their interests coincide remarkably well in Central Asia, at least in the short term."

Zbigniew Brzezinski noted in 1997 that Russia's dilemma in Central Asia is that it is too weak to dominate the area politically and too weak economically to develop the region. This still holds true today. Central Asia is part of Russia's "near abroad," a strategic part of the former Soviet Union. Russia sees Central Asia as being within its sphere of influence. The security of Central Asian states, and the form of government they adopt, is particularly important to Russia. However, it also has economic interests. Russia has attempted to control the energy infrastructure of Central Asia, purchasing energy at cheap prices and then reexporting it to Europe at a profit. It further uses its influence to protect ethnic Russians left in the area after the disintegration of the Soviet Union.

China has three major interrelated goals in Central Asia. The first is to ensure stability in its northwestern Xinjiang Uyghur Autonomous Region. China does not want Central Asia to be used as a base for promoting separatism in Xinjiang. Second, China desires closer overall economic and infrastructure linkages with Central Asia. This will further its overall goal of rapid economic development and, in Beijing's view, stabilize Xinjiang. Third, China strives to increase energy imports from Central Asia by winning energy contracts and developing the infrastructure to deliver oil and gas to China. China sees this as an essential part of an energy diversification strategy. Moreover, it sees pipeline routes across Central Asia as more secure than sea lanes from the Middle East that are susceptible to disruption by the US Navy.

Russia and China both want to eliminate the "three evils" of "terrorism, separatism, and religious extremism" from the region. They work to reduce as much as possible the influence of the United States in Central Asia by seeking to limit US military basing in the region and preventing new "colour revolutions" that might bring stronger democratic governance to the states of the area.

China has been active in developing infrastructure in Central Asia. For example, the China Road and Bridge Company won a contract to build a road from Osh in Kyrgyzstan to the Irkeshtam Pass with China, funded in part by the Chinese government. China is developing rail links to connect Xinjiang with Afghanistan via Tajikistan, while Chinese telecom and internet companies are tying the region together electronically. China has been active in the Asian Development Bank's (ADB) Central Asia Regional Economic Cooperation (CAREC) program, designed to accelerate economic growth and reduce poverty. Moreover, China is systematically attempting to increase its soft power and "people to people" understanding in Central Asia through Confucius Institutes, government-funded organizations that promote Chinese language and culture outside China. Russia has lost ground to China here, although there is still suspicion of the latter among residents of the region due to China's size and potential influence.

Chinese president Xi Jinping's visit to Central Asian states in September 2013 illustrated the success of China's strategy when he sealed economic deals in what he called the "Silk Road Economic Zone." President Xi visited Turkmenistan, Uzbekistan, Kyrgyzstan, and Kazakhstan.

In Kazakhstan, Xi and Kazakh president Nursultan Nazarbayev signed $30 billion worth of agreements and symbolically opened a 700-mile gas pipeline that, in conjunction with other pipelines, will take gas from the Caspian Sea to the Chinese coast. China, through CNPC, also purchased an 8.4 percent stake in Kazakhstan's Kashagan oil field in the Caspian Sea, joining a consortium of international oil companies. In Turkmenistan, Xi opened the world's second biggest gas field, Galkynysh, which will lead to a tripling of Chinese gas imports from that country. In Uzbekistan, he signed $15 billion in energy deals.

With China's major economic investments in the region and establishment of new "strategic partnerships," Russian deputy foreign minister Igor Morgulov felt it necessary to assert, in a not entirely convincing manner, "Our Chinese friends recognize the traditional role our country continues to play in this region, so we do not see any regional rivalry problems." The institutional body that ties Russia and China together on Central Asian issues is the SCO. The SCO consists of China, Russia, Kazakhstan, Kyrgyzstan, Tajikistan, and Uzbekistan. Established in 2001 with a history rooted in successful border negotiations, the SCO provides a mechanism for Russia and China to cooperate on issues relevant to Central Asia, and, as mentioned earlier, is the institution through which China and Russia conduct military exercises. The SCO is a unique organization for China in that China took the initiative in its founding and considers itself a leader of the organization. Chinese analysts proudly point to the SCO as a key example of China's "new diplomacy" based on trust, equality, respect for diversity, and an emphasis on development.

In some ways, the SCO has been very successful from the perspective of its founders. One Chinese analyst notes that the SCO has been able to maintain stability through the world economic crisis that began in 2008, and there was no "Arab Spring" in the region. There have been no major terrorist attacks in the area, Chinese and Russian relations are good, and the Central Asian states are cooperating. Moreover, other regional actors have been eager to join the SCO as observers. However, Russia and China do have differences over the SCO. Russia demonstrates some ambiguity toward the organization. It would prefer that the Collective Security Treaty Organization or the Eurasian Economic Community, both of which Russia dominates and do not include China, take the lead security and economic roles in Central Asia.

Moreover, Russia prefers that the SCO primarily focus on security cooperation and strategic issues, while China's emphasis is on economic cooperation. From a Chinese perspective, Russia is not very active in cooperating with China in the SCO but does not block Chinese initiatives. There has been disagreement on additional members, too.

One Chinese analyst claims that while Moscow has reportedly supported the membership of Iran, India, and Pakistan, China believes that this would move the focus away from Central Asia and give the SCO an anti-Western character, which China does not want. Furthermore, the SCO has challenges in actually implementing its cooperative agreements, due in part to the lack of capacity in Central Asian member states. Yet, in spite of these differences, the SCO remains a relevant organization in structuring ties between Beijing and Moscow.

Implications for the United States

The United States does not and should not oppose good relations between Russia and China. A peaceful relationship between these two nuclear powers leads to stability in Eurasia. The time period in the 1960s and 1970s when China and the Soviet Union were close to war was very dangerous. Washington also views closer ties between Russia and China as helpful to US interests in a variety of areas. For example, energy cooperation between Russia and China can, in the long run, make China less dependent on Iranian oil supplies, possibly loosening China's ties with Iran's government. Chinese and Russian cooperation is useful in developing Central Asia while preventing any one power from dominating the region, while greater coordination between Russia and China may help in efforts to stabilize Afghanistan after the US withdrawal.

Nevertheless, the relationship between the United States, Russia, and China also has a competitive, triangular aspect to it, with each side adapting hedging strategies. One analyst in Beijing explicitly stated that, despite much of the rhetoric coming out of Beijing to the contrary, the US pivot to China is a hedging strategy rather than a containment strategy. China, similarly, is hedging against the United States through its relationship with Russia. Russia hedges against both China and the West. Each state worries about the other two countries getting too close, although arguably the United States is less susceptible to this worry than China or Russia. For example, Russia strongly objects to the concept of a G2 between the United States and China, as this would deny Russia a seat at the table in making decisions on world order. In fact, Russia is overshadowed by more powerful states in most multilateral forums, including the G8 and BRICS gatherings. Similarly, China is worried about the potential for closer Russian ties with NATO, and in particular does not want to see joint missile defence cooperation between the two sides. At the same time, China does not want the United States to believe that it has entered an alliance with Russia that would threaten US interests. Similarly, Russia looks to the West for modernization and development and does not want a relationship with China that would isolate it from Europe or the United States.

How can the United States best manage this foreign policy triangle? First, it needs to understand the dynamics of this triangle and consider how policy decisions on issues important to Russia or China affect the triangle. When the United States supports policies that Russia and China oppose or commits to policies targeted at China or Russia, it drives those two states closer together. This does not mean the United States cannot oppose Russia and China on any given issue, but it must understand that closer Russian-Chinese cooperation on world order issues will result. One example is Syria. We can debate whether the US decision to back away from a military strike on Syria was correct in terms of Middle East policy. However, the decision to compromise with Russia did defuse a world order question that was pushing Russia and China closer to each other and further from the United States. Another example is the Ukraine conflict. Recent Western economic sanctions on Russia have created stronger economic links between China and Russia. Policymakers should assess regional policies both in light of their regional impact and a broader strategic perspective.

Second, Russia wants to again be an important player in the Asia-Pacific region. The historic US interest has been to ensure that no single country dominates the region. A stronger Russian role in Pacific affairs, bolstered by a more prosperous RFE, can be good for the United States once the Ukrainian crisis is resolved. Therefore, the United States should in the long run encourage better relations between Japan and Russia and between South Korea and Russia. This means encouraging energy exports from Russia to South Korea and Japan and encouraging a resolution of the dispute between Japan and Russia over the Kurile Islands.

The United States should provide incentives for US companies to invest in the RFE to the extent it is profitable. The US Pacific Command has engaged Russia through port calls and Russian participation in RIM-PAC exercises, but more might be done to develop military-to-military cooperation.

Third, the time may soon come to press for three-way nuclear negotiations. China's historic policy has been to maintain a small nuclear deterrent whose numbers are a tightly controlled secret, claiming that the United States and Russia must substantially reduce their forces before China will enter into arms control negotiations. However, the United States and Russia have reduced their deployed nuclear weapons, while China has been presumably increasing its weapons. Thus, Alexi Arbatov and Vladimir Dvorkin assert that "it can be speculated that the real motives behind China's complete secrecy about its nuclear forces lie not in their 'weakness' and 'small size' but in the much larger strength of China's actual nuclear arsenal than can be construed from observing the weapons deployed on its surface. In addition, China's economic and technical potential would allow it to build up its nuclear arms rapidly."

This is more threatening to Russia than the United States because of Russia's greater reliance on nuclear weapons for defence. Thus, it may finally be time to push for trilateral arms control negotiations, although at this point there are still serious obstacles to such negotiations. These include new strains in US-Russian ties, continued Chinese secrecy over the size of its arsenal and its nuclear doctrine, as well as Chinese insistence that Russia and the United States further disarm before China engages in meaningful nuclear reduction talks.

Fourth, the US withdrawal from Afghanistan opens new possibilities for three-way cooperation to work for stability in Afghanistan and all of Central Asia. While the United States was criticized by both Russia and China for having troops in Afghanistan, they now fear the results of a US withdrawal.

China feels it lacks the resources to deal with Afghanistan, and many Chinese analysts feel the Afghan government will fall after 2014 when Washington withdraws combat troops. China, which is heavily concerned with its own domestic stability, is worried about the implications of potential chaos in Afghanistan for what it sees as its Uyghur problem.

Thus, it is clearly in the interest of all three states to have a strong Afghan government after 2014 that can minimize the level of violence within Afghanistan and prevent the spread of extremism and terror outside its borders. The United States, Russia, China, and perhaps the SCO can coordinate policies to produce an outcome that will be in the interest of every state. In other words, the struggle in Afghanistan and its environs is one of organized states against nonstate actors, and the states have incentives to cooperate.

In conclusion, the Chinese-Russian relationship is strong and has been building momentum for close to two decades. Russia and China are bound together by a desire to bring about a world order that is marked more by a concert of great powers than US hegemony, an order that is defined by classical Westphalian values as opposed to liberal concepts that degrade the sanctity of state sovereignty.

The relationship is also built on practical cooperation in the realm of economics, energy, security, Central Asian issues, and the SCO. Nevertheless, this is not an anti-US alliance. For their own development goals, Russia and China need the United States and Europe. China feels that its developmental accomplishments are fragile and domestic unrest is a threat, while Russia has failed to substantially expand its economic base beyond energy production.

A certain degree of cooperation between Russia and China can be in US interests. Moreover, each of the issue areas discussed in this article has arenas of conflict. If in the long run Chinese power continues to grow relative to that of Russia, these conflicts will become more intense as Moscow resists being identified as a junior partner of Beijing. With smart policies, Washington can work the strategic triangle to ensure that its core interests are maintained.

THE SINO-SOVIET RAPPROCHEMENT IN THE CONTEXT OF STRATEGIC TRIANGLE

It is rarely disputed that enmity and mistrust toward the Soviet Union brought China and the United States together in the 1970s. American diplomacy, actuated in accordance with Henry Kissinger's realist ideals, sought to play the "China" card in its fight against the Kremlin. The China factor in U.S. foreign policy thus played an important role in calculations about how to manage the United States' adversary relationship with the Soviet Union (Talbott, 1981: 82). China, for its part, was seeking to pursue normalization with the United States in order to counterweight the Soviet Union. Galenovich (2001) noted that China's posture vis-à-vis the Kremlin in the 1970s was openly aggressive. Beijing called for creating a joint front against the USSR, ceased to recognise the 1950 treaty of Friendship, Solidarity, and Mutual Assistance, and repeatedly demanded the Soviet Union withdraw its forces from Mongolia, halt assistance to Vietnam, and reduce the troop presence along the Sino-Soviet border (Galenovich, 2001: 1). Beginning in 1979, the first talks between China and the Soviet Union were terminated when the Soviet Union conducted the invasion of Afghanistan (Hyland, 1981: 138).

In the early 1980s, a shift in the power balance occurred. The Soviet Union's deteriorating relations with the United States, troubled economy, and declining defence capabilities made the Kremlin seek ways of invigorating its relationship with China. At that juncture, the Chinese leadership was discontented with U.S. foreign policy toward the Taiwan issue (i.e. increased contacts and arms sales), U.S. criticism of the human rights situation in China, and Washington's unwillingness to provide industrial technology so coveted by Beijing. The above-mentioned factors played a key role in bringing China and the Soviet Union together after 1985 when the Sino-Soviet rapprochement commenced.

In March 1982, the then Soviet leader, Leonid Brezhnev, in his Tashkent speech opined upon China as a "socialist state" and strongly criticized the U.S. "two China" policy, thus sending a signal to Beijing that Moscow was ready for renewing a dialogue (Wishnick, 2001a: 75). In response to Brezhnev's appeal, the Chinese leadership subsequently announced its determination to conduct "independent foreign policy" aimed at improving relations with both the Soviet Union and the United States without attaching itself to any big power (Goldstein, 1990: 122). As a consequence, the Soviet Union and the People's Republic of China began a round of talks devoted to the normalization of Sino-Soviet relations and resolution of border disputes.

The results of negotiations, albeit not as fruitful as parties had envisioned, had a significant impact on the increased levels of trade between the two nations. The volume of trade, for instance, skyrocketed from $300 million in 1982 to $1.2 billion in 1984 (Voskressenskii, 1999: 244).

However, three crucial challenges, the so-called "three obstacles," which had been thwarting rapprochement between Moscow and Beijing since the beginning of the 1980s, remained. Beijing still expressed its dissatisfaction with the deployment of Soviet troops along the Sino-Soviet border, the Soviet Union's support for Vietnam's occupation of Cambodia, and the Soviet invasion of Afghanistan in 1979. The Soviet leaders Andropov and Chernenko fell short of achieving any substantial progress on these issues largely due to the short tenure of their offices. It was Mikhail Gorbachev who gave impetus to the normalization of Sino-Soviet relations after ascending to the Communist Party's leadership in 1985.

The Soviet response to addressing the "three obstacles" in Sino-Soviet relations was reflected in Mikhail Gorbachev's speech in Vladivostok on July 28, 1986. In his speech, the new Soviet leader signalled his willingness to resolve the main points of contention between Moscow and Beijing. Gorbachev announced his decision to reduce the number of troops along the Sino-Soviet border and withdraw a considerable part of the Soviet contingent from Mongolia and Afghanistan by the end of the year. The Soviet leader, however, stopped short of giving concessions on the Soviet support of Vietnam's occupation of Cambodia. Only two years later when the Soviet Union began withdrawing forces from Afghanistan, Moscow suggested Hanoi should follow suit (Su, 1989: 115), and in December of that year Vietnam withdrew its troops from Cambodia. Thus, by the end of 1980s China and the Soviet Union made significant progress in overcoming the impasse in the relationship and were gradually moving toward full normalization.

Nevertheless, the two countries had different motives underlying their pursuit of better relations. While China was seeking to establish a peaceful milieu within the strategic triangle in order to focus on its economic development, the Soviet Union sought to restore the ideological nexus between the two communist countries (Voskessenskii, 1999: 247) with an intent to avert a possibility of a two-front conflict, and boost the Soviet economy. During Gorbachev's first visit to China in 1989 for the Sino-Soviet summit in Beijing, Chinese and Soviet leaders reached a mutual understanding on how to improve the Sino-Soviet relations. Accordingly, Mikhail Gorbachev and Deng Xiaoping agreed that the new relationship would be based on the principles of peaceful coexistence and mutual respect, would not be aimed against any third country, and the ideological factor would not play any role in the normalization of Sino-Soviet relations. The aforementioned goals were reflected in the joint Sino-Soviet communiqué of 1989. According to the document, the Soviet Union and People's Republic of China agreed to develop their relations on the basis of the five principles of peaceful coexistence, including respect for international norms such as sovereignty, noninterference, and peaceful resolution of disputes (Wishnick, 2001a: 105). Further, any attempt or action by any country to impose its own will on others and seek "hegemony in any form" would be discarded by Moscow and Beijing.

The end of Sino-American confrontation following the decay of the Soviet Union removed the main rationale behind U.S.-Chinese cooperation, and the image of an opening China was replaced overnight by an image of a defiant

China ruled by dictators (Zhu, 2006: 90). A month after the Sino-Soviet summit, the Chinese leadership witnessed a hitherto unseen degree of public discontent. The Tiananmen crackdown sparked harsh criticism from the United States which imposed sanctions against China. The Soviet Union, on the contrary, issued a response stating that the events in China were an internal affair, and suggested political dialogue as a means to resolve social problems. Besides, it was not in Gorbachev's interests to undermine the overwhelming progress in Sino-Soviet relations achieved during the previous four years of his tenure. Socio-economic problems in the Soviet Union (mass protests in Tbilisi, Georgia and other Soviet republics) also made Gorbachev refrain from open criticism of China's violent quelling of the protests in Beijing.

In the final analysis, the events in China made the Soviet leadership consider the consequences of liberalization that had been gaining momentum since the beginning of *perestroika*, while a fragile rapprochement between the two countries after two decades of confrontation dissuaded Gorbachev from taking a more assertive stance towards Beijing.

The Soviet Union soon became embroiled in painful process of disintegration, and Sino-Soviet relations were no longer atop the Kremlin's agenda. The Soviet Union and the communist bloc in Eastern Europe subsequently began to unravel.

In sum, the Sino-Soviet rapprochement in the second half of the 1980s was caused by important power shifts within the strategic triangle between the USA, USSR, and PRC. The United States under the Reagan administration was determined to economically exhaust the Soviet Union, thus eliminating it as a major geopolitical threat, while engaging China in order to maintain a strategic advantage in containing the USSR. In light of the worsening economy and political stagnation, the Soviet Union began to reverse its course toward China in the early 1980s for economic, political, and security reasons (Tucker, 1995-96: 518). China, for its part, was also looking forward to resolving disputes with the USSR because of the security threat emanating from the troop presence along the Sino-Soviet border and around China (i.e. Vietnam and Afghanistan). Although the "three obstacles" constantly stymied negotiations between the Soviet Union and China under Brezhnev, Andropov, and Chernenko, Sino-Soviet relations began to mend after Mikhail Gorbachev's ascension to power, and by the end of the 1980s most disputes were resolved.

The normalization of Sino-Soviet relations did not have a long-lasting impact, however, for the Soviet Union and China failed to achieve substantial progress in their economic cooperation. Because Sino-Soviet trade was markedly lower than trade between China and the United States, China considered U.S.-Chinese relations more important. The volume of Sino-Soviet trade amounted to $2 billion by 1985, whereas Sino-U.S. trade had already reached $6 billion by 1984 (Mills, 1986: 543). Thus, although the strategic triangle by and large lost its military component after the end of the Cold War, its political and economic implications remained important well into the following decades.

SINO-RUSSIAN RELATIONS IN A CHANGING WORLD ORDER

The nature of the relationship between China and Russia is a major determinant of stability in Eurasia and the Asia-Pacific region. Sino-Russian relations also shape the broader world order and, hence, are important for the security of the United States. Because China, Russia, and the United States have a degree of influence in nearly all major regional and strategic issues, the US-Russian-Chinese triangle is a complicated game, and Washington must take this triangle into account when formulating policy. In light of the Snowden affair, some commentators saw a greater willingness of Russia and China to snub the United States. Leslie Gelb and Dmitri Simes wrote in July 2013 that "Russia and China appear to have decided that, to better advance their own interests, they need to knock Washington down a peg or two." This is due to Moscow and Beijing's common interest in reducing the influence of the United States in world affairs. While the Chinese-Russian strategic partnership is substantive and productive, it is based on both dissatisfaction with a US-led world order and very practical considerations. The relationship is not grounded in a shared long-term positive vision of world order, and the conditions that have given rise to the partnership will also limit it and perhaps even erode it in the long term, as seen in disagreements over energy, weapons sales, and Russia's annexation of Crimea. This article examines the Chinese-Russian strategic partnership, focusing on the drivers of this relationship as well as its points of friction. It then examines Chinese-Russian interactions in the realms of economics, security, and Central Asia and considers the implications of the Chinese-Russian partnership for the United States.

CHINA, RUSSIA, AND WORLD ORDER

In 1996, China and Russia proclaimed a strategic cooperative partnership, which was subsequently anchored in the Treaty for Good Neigh-borliness, Friendship, and Cooperation signed in 2001. In 2008, both countries ratified an action plan to implement the treaty. In 2011, the nature of the relationship was raised to a "comprehensive strategic and cooperative partnership," the highest level of cooperation from China's perspective. Since the 2001 treaty, Chinese and Russian leaders have signed more than 50 additional bilateral agreements.

When Russian president Dmitry Medvedev attended the Shanghai Expo in 2009, he proclaimed that Russian-Chinese relations had achieved their "highest point in history." This partnership has been characterized by frequent visits between high-level leaders, growing cooperation in energy, expanding trade, Russian arms sales to China, expanded people-to-people contacts, and some level of diplomatic cooperation over the Middle East and other issues.

The partnership between China and Russia is motivated by two broad factors: common views on what they object to in the contemporary world order and practical concerns. Regarding world order, both countries hope to end what they have seen as US hegemony and institute a more multipolar system. This would involve a stronger role for the United Nations Security Council (UNSC), where Russia and China both have a veto, in dealing with pressing security issues. There is, of course, some irony in the fact that the "liberal" United States has reservations regarding the United Nations while China and Russia embrace this institution. A more multipolar world order where China and Russia had greater influence would raise their status and better protect states that raise the ire of the West but where China and/or Russia have important interests, such as Iran, Syria, and North Korea. In March 2014, Russia used its veto in the UNSC to defeat a draft resolution condemning the referendum by which residents of Crimea voted to join Russia.

Another element of the current world order that China and Russia wish to undermine is the liberal emphasis on human rights and minority self-determination and the resulting erosion of sovereignty that these entail. Russia and China believe that human rights are primarily an issue for state governments, not the world community. This view stems in large part from domestic politics. Russia wants freedom to do what it sees as necessary with Chechnya, the Caucasus, and most recently, Ukraine. China is determined to suppress all dissent in Tibet, Xinjiang, and other restive regions, as well as recover Taiwan. Moreover, both China and Russia believe in maintaining geographic spheres of influence. For Russia, this means having decisive influence in the foreign policy of the states of the "near abroad," or republics of the former Soviet Union. For China, this means a privileged position for its territorial claims in the South China Sea and the maintenance of a friendly government in North Korea. For both China and Russia, preventing revolutions in Central Asia or other former Soviet republics that would bring democratic, pro-Western governments into power is a priority.

Another relevant world order issue for Russia and China is reform of international institutions. Interestingly, this does not include the UNSC. Neither country is eager to see an expansion of the Security Council or loss of its veto power there. However, it does include reforms to financial institutions such as the World Bank and International Monetary Fund (IMF), giving a greater share of authority in those institutions to non-Western states. It also includes the development of multilateral organizations that exclude the West, such as the BRICS (Brazil, Russia, India, China, and South Africa) and the Shanghai Cooperation Organization (SCO).

Nevertheless, Russian and Chinese views on world order diverge in important respects as well. It is unclear what kind of world order China ultimately will seek, but there are numerous voices on foreign policy being heard in China today with multiple views on the proper direction of foreign policy. While Hu Jintao insisted that China's development is peaceful, recent aggressive policies in the East and South China Seas lead China's neighbours to doubt these assurances. Some in China, including some People's Liberation Army (PLA) officers, push for a triumphalist foreign policy that seeks Chinese hegemony. Other thinkers envision a return to an "all under heaven" system consisting of a hierarchical world order led by a benevolent Chinese imperialism. Most of these views of world order envision a more powerful international position for China that could undermine important Russian interests.

Putin's view of world order is more limited, but also challenges the status quo. Putin demands that Russia be treated as a great power. While attempting to build closer ties with Europe, Russia still insists on keeping the former Soviet republics in its orbit, a policy some compare to the Monroe Doctrine and others describe as imperialism. While this has mainly disrupted the international system in Europe, with Russian military force used in Ukraine and Georgia, it also confronts Chinese interests in Central Asia.

The Chinese-Russian relationship is also built on very practical issues. The first is economics. Both Russia and China place a high priority on domestic economic development. One result is that mutual trade and investment are important to both sides. As Russia has an abundance of oil and other natural resources while China is an importer of such products, the energy trade is a practical way in which both sides benefit. In addition, the Russian Far East (RFE) has an undeveloped economy that Moscow cannot afford to expand alone. Economic growth in the RFE has been a goal of Russian-Chinese cooperation, although one that has been less successful. Overall, the levels of trade and investment outside the energy sector have been disappointing.

Security is another important issue. Threats and border clashes led perilously close to war in the late 1960s and early 1970s. By the 1980s, both China and Russia were absorbed with domestic concerns. A secure Russian-Chinese border was imperative for both sides. After a series of negotiations, the last border dispute was resolved in 2008 and the border demilitarized. In addition, throughout the 1990s and early 2000s, the Russian defence industry was desperate for orders and cash. China wanted advanced weapons systems, and both sides benefited from Russian weapons sales to China, including fighter planes and submarines.

In politics, economics, and security, the Sino-Russia "comprehensive strategic and cooperative partnership" is driven by mutual interests, not mutual affection. Dmitri Trenin, a well-regarded analyst of Russian politics, observes, "There has never been a spirit of camaraderie about Russo-Chinese summits. The leaders do not take off their ties or use first names. And there have been few truly strategic conversations. But the summits arc invariably business-like and results-orientated."

In a similar vein, Andrew Kuchins asserts that Russia has "profound ambivalence" toward China, but acts in a pragmatic fashion. Trenin's conclusion from his study of Chinese-Russian relations is that "while both countries need each other and would benefit from a stable political relationship and close economic ties, both Moscow and Beijing lack the long-term strategies to create such a bond."

The foundations of the Sino-Russian partnership may not be stable for the long term. As China rises in power, its conception of the ideal world order is likely to diverge from Russia's viewpoint.

For example, Leszek Buszynski argues that Russia has been eclipsed by China in the Asia-Pacific region. Russia is being marginalized, and its partnership with China has not been in Russia's best interests.

Moreover, there may be increasing conflict between China and Russia over spheres of influence that overlap, especially in Central Asia. In sum, world order is driven by values but also power, and as China's power increases relative to Russia's, there will be a divergence of views on such an order.

Even practical issues change character over time. Growing Chinese military capabilities may make Russia rethink its border security. Russian concerns about being primarily a provider of resources to China may dampen economic ties, as may Russian fears about Chinese dominating the RFE. Thus, it is worth exploring issue areas to understand where China and Russia cooperate and where they have conflicts.

Russia's annexation of Crimea in March 2014 illustrated tensions between the Chinese and Russian worldviews which also affect practical issues. Russia's move put China in an uncomfortable position. China's foreign policy declarations (if not always its actions) have long rejected outside interference in the internal affairs of any state. China has often criticized the United States for violating this principle, and Russia clearly violated the noninterference principle in Ukraine. Moreover, China has important interests in Ukraine.

It imports Ukrainian weapons and military technology, it has agricultural interests in Ukraine, and Ukraine is the linchpin for Chinese investment plans in Eastern Europe. Most seriously, the Crimean referendum provides an unwanted precedent that residents of Taiwan, Tibet, or Xinjiang might refer to in calling for similar referenda.

On the other hand, Russia is an important strategic partner of China, and Putin clearly counts on Chinese support. The Chinese government saw advantages in a Western setback, while the Chinese press went further in praising Putin for being strong and poking the West in the eye.

Moreover, China had much to gain in a confrontation between Putin and the West that make Russia more dependent on China for energy purchases and economic growth.

In the end, China refused to commit to either side. It abstained on a UNSC draft resolution condemning the Crimean referendum. It issued bland statements that were fairly noncommittal and tried to muddle through in a way that would not offend Ukraine or Russia. However, clearly practical considerations and realpolitik overrode a firm stance on principles.

CHINA'S PERSPECTIVE ON ITS STRATEGIC PARTNERSHIP WITH RUSSIA

China has used the deterioration of Russia's relations with the EU and U.S. to strengthen its position within a strategic partnership with the Russian Federation. The PRC's goals are to counterbalance the U.S., secure its own economic interests in the post-Soviet area, increase border security and obtain Russian support for Chinese international initiatives. In exchange, China supports Russia by abstaining from open criticism on its annexation of Crimea and by importing raw materials. The partnership brings more benefits to China, which is positive for the EU. The PRC, unlike Russia, is concerned about destabilisation of NATO's Eastern Flank and favours European integration.

China responded positively to Russia's Far East policy after the latter's deterioration of relations with the EU and U.S. in 2014. China has cautiously made Russia economically dependent on it, for example, by importing gas and investing in Central Asian states. Through these instruments, China tries to stabilise the situation in states located in Russia's traditional sphere of interest in exchange for its support of Chinese international initiatives and security along its western borders.

Since Chairman Xi Jinping rose to power, and specifically since 2014, there has been a visible intensification of bilateral contact, confirmed in 2014 by the establishment of a new intergovernmental committee at the vice premier level.

On the Chinese side, it is chaired by Zhang Gaoli, a member of the Chinese Communist Party's (CPC) Politburo Standing Committee and Xi's trusted associate. The Chinese leader, as well as Russian President Vladimir Putin, exercise strong leadership of their countries, which eased the establishment of personal relations between them.

After his ascension to chairman of the CPC in May 2013, Xi choose Russia for his first foreign trip. Both leaders meet every few months—15 times since 2014. Under previous chairman Hu Jintao, high-level meetings between China and Russia took place less often.

Common Interests?

From a political perspective, China considers it essential to build a multipolar global order as a tool of U.S. containment. That is the vision behind new regulations and ventures for which China seeks Russian support, such as the Asian Infrastructure Investment Bank and "Belt and Road" initiative (BRI). China counts on Russia's assistance on these and emphasises the complementarity between Russia's Eurasian Economic Union and China's BRI. At first, Russia viewed the Chinese concept with distrust. Today, though, after its pro-China pivot, Russia is presented as China's most important partner, for example, during the Belt and Road Forum in Beijing in May. China is also trying to push other common initiatives, such as Internet legal regulations. In 2015, the PRC, together with Russia, Kazakhstan, Tajikistan and Uzbekistan, submitted to the UN General Assembly a revised draft of a 2011 resolution on the International Code of Information Security.

Both China and Russia accuse the U.S. of inspiring the Arab Spring and Ukraine crisis. The PRC also cooperates with Russia on UN Security Council votes, for example, vetoing draft resolutions on Syria six times. Western support for the overthrow of the Libyan regime in 2011 is another binding factor. China has taken an ambivalent stance on Russia's annexation of Crimea and its actions in eastern Ukraine, hoping for a similar Russian position on Chinese territorial disputes.

Economically, the Russian pivot to Asia enabled China to strengthen its presence in Central Asia, which is especially important from the BRI perspective. China makes use of Russia's low capability to generate capital and actively invests in states in the region by providing them a measure of economic stability. China has expressed interest in buying shares of Russian companies and energy projects located on Russian territory. Until 2014, such actions were blocked by Russian authorities afraid of Chinese domination. In

2015, the Silk Road Fund acquired 9.9% of the Yamal LNG project. Chinese enterprises already have around 30% of the shares of that project and construction works are financed by Chinese state-owned banks. The cooperation between Russia's Rosneft and the China National Petroleum Company is also growing. The PRC's collaboration with Russia is also helpful in internationalisation of the yuan and the establishment of non-Western credit card payment systems and separate rating agencies.

China also finds cooperation with the Russian Federation important in the context of security of its western border and internal stability. The PRC is guarding against terrorism, particularly by radicals amongst the Uyghur ethnic minority living in Xinjiang province and across the border in Kazakhstan.

The danger of terrorism is intended to be counterbalanced by the capabilities of thc Shanghai Cooperation Organisation as well as Russia's military presence in Central Asia.

The Russian Federation has finally consented to sell China modern military equipment, including 24 Su-35 fighters and four S-400 surface-to-air missile systems, which will probably be deployed to the South China Sea region. China also uses Russia's objection to the U.S. THADD anti-missile system being deployed in South Korea as international confirmation of its own objections.

SINO-RUSSIAN RELATIONS AFTER THE COLD WAR

The period from March 1999 to September 2001 was marked by new, hitherto unseen challenges in the international environment for Moscow, Beijing, and Washington alike. During this period, China and Russia had the strongest common interests and the greatest need for cooperation (Cheng, 2009: 152). Accordingly, two crucial factors paved the way for the Sino-Russian rapprochement at the beginning of the new millennium: (1) U.S. aggressive foreign policy and (2) political change in Russia. First, U.S. military strikes against Iraq and increasing American presence in the Central Asia; plans for creation of U.S.-Japanese Theatre Missile Defence (TMD) and National Missile Defence (NMD); NATO expansion into the Baltics; and, ultimately, bombing of Yugoslavia, during which the Chinese embassy in Belgrade had been destroyed. All these developments reflected Moscow and Beijing's concerns over growing American influence, inasmuch as many of the above-mentioned events directly affected Russia and China's spheres of national interest. Second, Russia's new leader, former Prime Minister Vladimir Putin, started to pursue a course aimed, *inter alia*, at working towards a multipolar system of international relations and creating a favourable environment for Russia's economic development upon assuming the presidency in 2000. One of the main tenets of Putin's foreign policy, delineated in the Foreign Policy Concept of June 28, 2000, was maintaining good-neighbourly relations with the country's neighbours, and Russia's relationship with China (on a par with India) was defined as "one of the most important" directions of Russian foreign policy in Asia (Leksyutina, 2010).

In July 2000, Vladimir Putin paid his first official visit to Beijing, where Russian President and his Chinese counterpart issued a joint communiqué, "the Beijing Declaration," on the Anti-Ballistic Missile problem. In light of Washington's plans of withdrawing from the ABM Treaty signed between the United States and the Soviet Union in 1972, Vladimir Putin and Jiang Zemin China confirmed their strong opposition to the U.S. plans of deploying missile systems and agreed upon the essence of the U.S. National Missile Defence and Theatre Missile Defence programs, which, according to the parties, was to seek "unilateral military and security advantages" (Wilson, 2004: 161). One year later, during Jiang Zemin's visit to Moscow in July 2001, Russia and China signed a historical agreement, the "Treaty for Good Neighborliness, Friendship and Cooperation," under which Moscow and Beijing agreed to develop long-term relations of friendship and equal partnership. Furthermore, the Treaty prioritized strengthening confidence in the military area and enhancing security between countries, while providing framework for moving towards a more stable regional and international environment. Under the pact, Moscow and Beijing expressed their will to uphold the strict observance of generally recognized principles and norms of international law against any actions aimed at exerting pressure or meddling in the internal affairs of the sovereign states. In addition, Russia and China agreed to develop mutually beneficial cooperation in trade, military, energy, transportation, scientific and technical spheres, and other fields. Ultimately, the parties to the Treaty voiced their determination to fight terrorism, separatism, extremism, organized crime, drug trafficking, and illegal migration in the following twenty years.

Another significant achievement in Sino-Russian relations during this period was the establishment of the Shanghai Cooperation Organization, in June 2001. Building upon the Shanghai agreement of 1996, China, Russia, Kazakhstan, Tajikistan, Kyrgyzstan along with the new member, Uzbekistan, further consolidated their relations by setting up the Shanghai Cooperation Organization with the declared objectives of strengthening mutual trust and good-neighbourly friendship among the member states; encouraging effective cooperation among the member states in political, economic and trade, scientific and technological, cultural, educational, energy, communications, environment and other fields; devoting themselves jointly to preserving and safeguarding regional peace, security and stability; and establishing a democratic, fair and rational new international political and economic order (Bailes et al., 2007).

Despite increasing cooperation between Moscow and Beijing resulting in the new Sino-Russian Treaty and the establishment of the Shanghai Cooperation Organization, both agreements lost their tremendous significance, albeit for a short period of time, in the wake of the post-9/11 realignment in global politics (Kutchins, 2010: 41). After the collision of U.S. and Chinese planes in April 2001, increased arms sales to Taiwan, and U.S. President George W. Bush's remarks about defending Taiwan by all means, Sino-U.S. relations reached their nadir prior to the 9/11 events. Likewise, U.S.-Russian relations exacerbated after the "espionage" scandal in early 2001, and were further damaged by plans of the NATO enlargement and U.S. withdrawal from the ABM treaty. For these reasons, the improvement of relations with the United States was on top of China and Russia's foreign policy agendas in the aftermath of the terrorist attacks on the United States. Accordingly, both countries sought to take advantage of the momentum in order to improve their relations with Washington during this period, but Russia even more so.

After Vladimir Putin supported the United States in its efforts to combat the Taliban in Afghanistan, Russia's President expected Washington to provide more room for negotiation on such divisive issues in bilateral relations as the second round of NATO expansion and termination of the ABM Treaty. However, just like at the beginning of the 1990s, Russia's "honeymoon" with the United States appeared to be short-lived: the Bush Administration provided too little in return for the Kremlin's support. China, for its part, also sought to resuscitate its relations with the United States after September 11. During the informal summit of the Asia Pacific Economic Cooperation (APEC) in Shanghai in October 2001, President George W. Bush and Jiang Zemin reiterated that both countries attached great importance to Sino-U.S. ties, vowed to work together to build a constructive relationship, and agreed to establish long and medium-term mechanisms for combating terrorism (Mao, 2003: 85). Nonetheless, the U.S. invasion in Iraq in 2003, spread of the "color revolutions" into the post Soviet states, and the third round of NATO expansion in Europe made Moscow rethink its approach to relations with the United States and focus on further developing of the "strategic relationship" with China.

During Vladimir Putin's visit to Beijing in October 2004, Russia and China concluded the supplementary agreement on the Eastern section of the Sino-Russian border, which was subsequently ratified by the countries' parliaments in 2005. Furthermore, during this summit, Vladimir Putin and Hu Jintao approved the implementation guidelines of the Sino-Russian Treaty of 2001 for the next four years (Cheng, 2009: 161). Subsequently, in July 2005, the Chinese and Russian leaders issued a joint communiqué on the "International Order in the 21st Century," which reaffirmed the common goals of working toward a multipolar world previously stated by Moscow and Beijing.

During the Shanghai Cooperation Organization's Astana summit in 2005, Russia and China along with four Central Asian states released a declaration, which declared that "a rational and just world order must be based upon consolidation of mutual trust and good-neighbourly relations with no pretense to monopoly and domination in international affairs" (Bailes et al., 2007). Russia and China participated in joint military exercises under the SCO's Peace Missions in 2005 and 2007, which were aimed at combining efforts at preventing a possible ethnic conflict in a third country and countering terrorism (Wishnick, 2009: 20). However, in light of the Georgian crisis and ensuing split of Abkhazia and South Ossetia in 2008, China did not express support for Russian policy toward Georgia due to dangerous ramifications of the of the republics' cessation. During the presidential meeting in Dushanbe following the Russian-Georgian conflict, China's Hu Jintao expressed his concern to Russia's President Dmitri Medvedev about the conflict and voiced his hope that the disputing parties would be able to resolve the conflict through dialogue and consultation (Yuan, 2011: 12). Nonetheless, Moscow's recognition of the breakaway regions was not welcomed by Beijing due to its concerns over the Taiwan issue and separatist movement in Xinjiang.

THE SINO-RUSSIAN RELATIONSHIP IN THE 21ST CENTURY

Since the end of the Cold War, Russia and China have been the only permanent U.N. Security Council members, whose political systems are undemocratic (Grant, 2012: 16). This is one of the main reasons why China and Russia cooperate on a wide range of international issues in an effort to counterbalance the United States and other Western countries. However, there is one important difference in these countries' statuses in global affairs. China's increasing role in world politics is widely associated with its extraordinary economic growth, whereas Russia's assertive posture in the international arena stems from Moscow's nostalgia of its former superpower status and relatively high energy prices, which allowed the Kremlin to salvage its faltering economy after 2000 (Larson and Shevchenko, 2010: 64). Thus, internal weaknesses and fears of U.S. power make Russia and China hold similar positions on many global issues. Moscow and Beijing remain strongly committed to the principle of noninterference in internal affairs of sovereign states mainly due to domestic problems and regional separatism. Further, both countries maintain relations with the pariah states, including North Korea, Iran, Cuba, Myanmar, and Syria, and object to Western sanctions against these regimes. For instance, in 2005,

China and Russia blocked U.S. sanctions against Myanmar the Security Council, labeling such efforts as "meddling in internal affairs." The same held true for China and Russia's position on sanctions against Burma (2007), Sri Lanka (2009), Zimbabwe (2008), and, most lately, Syria (2012). With regard to regional affairs, Russia and China cooperate on trade and security issues within the Shanghai Cooperation Organization, but the latter is far from being considered a substantive body, in part, due to disputes between Moscow and Beijing over leadership in the organization (Scheineson, 2009).

The economic partnership between Moscow and Beijing remains the weakest aspect of bilateral relations. Although the volume of bilateral trade has been growing steadily throughout the previous decade reaching $60 billion in 2010, it is still far below its potential. One of the reasons underlying slow progress in establishing closer economic ties between Russia and China is the difference in patterns of economic growth. Accordingly, the strengthening of Russian national currency and a rise in international energy and raw material prices fuelled Russia's economic growth in the 2000s. These developments had a positive impact on Sino-Russian economic relations (Moshes and Nojonen, 2011: 43). However, bilateral trade during 1996-2010 was marked by the decrease in Russia's exports of machinery and transport equipment from 17.7 per cent to 1.3 per cent, whereas exports of raw materials to China increased from 7.1 per cent to 20.6 per cent. By contrast, China's exports of machinery and transport equipment increased from 5.7 per cent in 1996 to 35.4 per cent in 2010, while manufactured goods started to constitute 18.6 per cent of China's exports to Russia as opposed to 7 per cent in 1996. Despite the fact that Sino-Russian trade has been growing remarkably in the last decade (Itoh and Kuchins, 2011), the above-mentioned economic disparity in trade capacities raises grave anxieties that Russia is gradually becoming a "junior partner" in Sino-Russian economic relations, or a natural resource appendage (*pridatok*) to China (Kutchins, 2010: 33). Russia's exports of energy resources to China are likely to either remain on the same level or may even increase in light of Russia's inability to reform its economic structure and China's growing demand for natural resources.

Conclusions

The strategic triangle among the United States, China, and the Soviet union has undergone a host of vicissitudes throughout the last four decades of the Cold War, culminating in a unipolar world order based on U.S. dominance in international relations. The collapse of the power balance within the triangular system in 1991 had a consequential impact on Sino-Russian relations and U.S.-Chinese relations alike. As regards the U.S.-Russian relationship in the new millennium, both powers attempted to forge closer ties with China, albeit not simultaneously, when relations between Washington in Moscow deteriorated. By the end of the 1990s China and Russia began to express their dissatisfaction with U.S. unilateralism, and such a stance was reflected in the countries' shared vision of a multipolar world and the concept of the "strategic relationship directed towards the 21st century." Despite grandiose proclamations of the "strategic partnership," shared vision of a multipolar world, and increased diplomatic cooperation, Sino-Russian relations are utterly lacking in substance. Much like during the Cold War, the relationship between Moscow and Beijing is based upon counterbalancing the United States in global politics, for cleavages within the strategic triangle among the three powers have generally led to the reorientation of China and Russia's foreign policies in the 1990s and late 2000s.

In so far as economic relations between Moscow and Beijing are concerned, notwithstanding increased economic interaction, neither country truly regards another as a strategic partner. Russia still considers its relations with the European Union indispensable, while the United States remains priority for China (Kotkin, 2009). This configuration is unlikely to change in the future: besides military hardware and natural resources, there is little Russia can offer to its "strategic partner." Likewise, most joint projects between Russia and China are aimed at enhancing energy cooperation through building oil and gas pipelines in Central Asia. Given the resource-oriented model of Russia's economy, Moscow will likely remain China's resource and weapons supplier for decades to come. China, for its part, has been using its "strategic" alliance with Russia as "strategic" leverage vis-à-vis Washington. Diplomatic cooperation with Moscow has helped China promote the idea of multipolarity as it relates to Beijing's national interests. It can be assumed that China's relationship with Russia will become irrelevant as soon as China becomes an independent power in global affairs.

This, in all likelihood, will mark the end of the "strategic" partnership between the two powers, paving the way for U.S.-China rivalry.

3

Russia's Tilt Towards Asia and its Implications for India

Geographical transcontinentalism and dualism in Russia's self-perception have played an important role in shaping its identity and engagement with Europe and Asia. Russia was geographically and politically associated with both continents in the days of the country being an empire; these associations continued even as it became a modern nation-state.

Historically, the seat of Russia's imperial administration was located in Kiev (before its shift to Moscow in the 16th century), resulting in Russia's active involvement in European politics. In the 19^{th}century, the Russian Empire expanded its geographical boundaries up to the Pacific Ocean. Within its ambit were Eastern Siberia, Caucasus and Central Asia, which deepened its engagement with Asia.

While incorporating new landmass, Russia embraced new people along with their cultures and religions. The subsequent imperial expansion of the Russian state incorporated substantial Muslim communities, most notably in the Caucasus and Central Asia. During the latter stages of the Soviet era, Russia expanded more in Asia; this played an important role in shaping the identity of the Russian state and society. However, its political elites continue to identify Russia as an integral part of the European political and cultural setup, considering its Asia policy to be only secondary.

This duality in Russia's approach has a bearing on Asia, in general, and India, in particular. The old Soviet Union's engagement with Asia benefitted India, both in terms of economic development and its interests in the international arena. Following the disintegration of the USSR, Russia attempted to integrate with the transatlantic political and economic system. However, this caused a rift within its political elites regarding the benefits of such a policy.

The resulting "Eurasianism vs. Atlanticism" debate articulates the dualism in Russia's self-perception as either a European or an Asian entity. The Eurasian approach received a fillip in the post-Soviet phase, when engaging with Asia was a practical question, not a theoretical one. Led by the then Foreign Minister Yevgeny Primakov, Eurasianism re-emerged as Russia's renewed de-ideologised outlook towards the world, particularly Asia.

While the concept of 'Eurasianism' is centuries old, it resurfaced as a foreign-policy option only in the post-Soviet era during the 1990s. This directional tilt was a result of its desire to benefit from the economic rise of Asia, and not only due to a rift with the transatlantic system.

The Nature and Scope of the Tilt

It is important to first define the "tilt" that Russia has taken towards Asia, to understand the factors that are driving it. During the 1990s, the leaders of the post-Soviet Russia realised the importance of developing relations with its Asian neighbours for various reasons. It should not be perceived as Russia's attempt at finding an alternative to the west, but rather as the political elite's acknowledgment that Russia's goals of domestic development and modernisation cannot be achieved without cooperating with the rising economies of Asia. "Thus, by pivoting to Asia, Moscow is not turning away from Europe, but giving Asia a level of attention commensurate with Russia's practical interests and the realities of the 21st century."

The tilt is not merely a political dialogue, but a primacy accorded to the rising economic powers of the region and its various groupings. Russia's Asia strategy has been to further its engagement with the region by forging new multilateral regional platforms and deepening engagement with the existing ones. According to Russian Foreign Minister Sergei Lavrov, "It is our clear commitment to ensure strength, stability, security and prosperity of the Asia Pacific. Intensification of the 'Eastern' track policy, development of regional bilateral ties, participation in inter-governmental structures are among Russia's foreign policy priorities." In the last decade, Russia has deepened its engagement with countries such as China and Vietnam, along with multilateral platforms such as the Association of South-East Asian Nations (ASEAN), East Asia Summit, and the Asia Pacific Economic Cooperation (APEC). It also actively broadened the ambit of the Shanghai Cooperation Organisation (SCO) by adding India and Pakistan as members. Several neighbouring countries are in negotiations to become full members. Moreover, Russia has developed its relations with Pakistan to diversify its defence-exports policy and gain more leverage over the situation in Afghanistan. Certain factors call for Russia's increased involvement with Asia.

1. A "tilt towards Asia" opens up an ideological space for Russia to construct its own norms of international engagement. It provides a platform to further its agenda of a multipolar world order, which is necessary to secure its rise and re-emergence as a global power. Several developing and developed economies of Asia and the Pacific, too, prefer a polycentric world order that allows them to negotiate their models of economic development through their respective political structures. This common ground leads to increased cooperation which, in turn, provides economic and geopolitical opportunities for Russia in its strategic competition with the West.
2. The Russia–Asia cooperation offers opportunities in the energy sphere, since Russia is currently heavily dependent on Europe for its oil and gas exports. Russia is the largest supplier of natural gas and petroleum oils, with Gazprom contributing to 40 percent of Europe's gas imports. Russia aims to retain its monopoly over these exports to Europe, while also reducing and diversifying its dependency on the same. Russia's oil and natural gas industry is crucial to its economy, making up 36 percent of Russia's federal budget revenues. Diversification is, therefore, a strategic necessity for Russia. Energy-hungry countries of Asia, such as Japan, South Korea, China and India, which are in the process of diversifying their energy imports, can find a viable alternative in Russia. China has already accelerated the process by becoming the second-largest destination for Russia's energy exports, following Europe. On 21 May 2014, Gazprom and China National Petroleum Corporation (CNPC) signed the 'Purchase and Sale Agreement' to supply Russian gas for 30 years, via the Eastern route. It is the biggest purchase and sale contract in the history of the global gas industry. South Korea requested Gazprom to resume the decade-old 1,200-km Trans-Korea gas pipeline project that would bring Russian gas through North Korea to the South's industrial hubs. The project is now part of South Korea's "New Northern Policy," as President Moon Jae-in mentioned during his 21 June 2018 address to the Russian Parliament Duma, the first-ever by a South Korean president. South Korea, along with Japan, has also invested in utilising Russia's Arctic deposits of gas and oil. South Korean entity Daewoo Shipbuilding and Marine Engineering is constructing three ice-breaking vessels for the Japanese Mitsui OSK Lines and China's COSCO shipping, which are set to sail under a long-term charter deal

to transport Liquefied Natural Gas (LNG) from the Russian Yamal LNG project to the Sabetta Port on the Kara Sea.

3. Russia has been making efforts to integrate its sparsely populated region of Eastern Siberia with the Asian system, with the intention of developing the region. Geopolitical development of Siberia has been neglected and the region remains a weak link in Russia's Asia policy. The establishment of the Eastern Economic Forum by Russian President Vladimir Putin is one of the ways to develop Siberia – the icy expanse that spans across much of Eurasia and North Asia. The Forum, organised annually in Vladivostok since its establishment in 2015, has been set up with the aim of accelerating development of the economy of Eastern Russia and expanding international cooperation in the Asia-Pacific region. Over the years, the forum has served as a platform for a gathering of regional heads of states, with the Chinese, South Korean and Japanese leaders attending the 4 annual session. Developing the region also yields benefits to Russia from the perspective of utilising its potential as a transit hub connecting East Asian countries with Europe. Both their leaders have also shared their interests in linking the Inter-Korean railway to the Trans-Siberian railway. Both Japan and South Korea have expressed their desire to utilise the Trans-Siberian railway to tranship their goods to Europe. Thus, Russia's growing potential as a transit state, coupled with its Arctic energy deposits has provided a platform for Japan to increase its engagement with Russia. Bilateral relations with Japan have matured to a level where foreign ministers of both countries have now been tasked by their respective heads to oversee negotiations for signing a peace treaty that would end their World War II-era hostilities and settle competing claims over a group of islands in the Pacific.
4. The Greater Eurasian Partnership (GEP), announced by Putin at the 2016 St. Petersburg International Economic Forum, proposed including India, Turkey, Iran and the ASEAN states. This project, though still in its early stages, is Russia's attempt to utilise its potential as a transit state between the rising economic powers of Asia and the technologically advanced Europe. According to Russian scholar Sergey Karaganov, the Greater Eurasia is a common economic and security space, with the geopolitical capacity to transform the world order into a bipolar system, comprising two macro-geopolitical blocs: the Trans-Pacific Partnership (TPP) and the Greater Eurasia. The project, while appreciating Asia's economic and geopolitical rise, intends to integrate Eurasia's development with the East Asian growth by making Russia the fulcrum

of such an exercise. Institutions such as SCO and Eurasian Economic Union (EaEU) can help achieve this goal and are already in their phases of expansion. Finally, the GEP project reclaims Russia's status in the Eurasian region, which is currently economically dominated by China.

5. China plays a key role in Russia's tilt and serves as a strategic partner. After all, the two countries share a border of 4,300 km, making China an important part of Russia's Asia policy. Regionally, a shared approach on the security and political stability of Central Asia is key to improving bilateral relations. It is also crucial to ensure the security and stability of the Asia-Pacific region, especially with regards to their concerns over the deployment of the US global missile defence system in the region. The two countries share an aversion to a US-led exclusive grouping in the Asia-Pacific region, which also has implications for India.
6. The process of 'de-dollarisation' has evolved to be part of the tilt, following sanctions by the West. As American sanctions on Russia's sectors increased in scope—over the latter's alleged meddling in the 2014 US elections and its involvement in the Ukraine crisis—the head of the state-owned bank VTB, Andrei Kostin, devised a plan for banks and companies to convert dollar settlements into other currencies. Russia prefers local currencies in its dealings with Asian economies, with respect to deals involving billions of dollars. The idea is to wean off Russia's biggest industries off the US currency as sanctions on its defence exports industry have affected its dealings with countries such as Turkey, China and India, with which it has strong defence ties. Russia has already signed the S-400 deal with India, which will be transacted in Russian currency, Roubles. While the process would progress at a snail's pace and may continue only for the period of sanctions, it would impact Russia's economic engagement with which it has strong economic ties. Russia is also engaged in an ongoing dialogue with China to draft a joint-action plan to deter US sanctions.

Implications for India

The realignment of Russia's policy towards Asia presents opportunities for cooperation between India and Russia, diversifying and broadening the nature of their strategic partnership. However, it can also create some friction in the time-tested Russia–India bilateral ties.

There is some congruence in the way India and Russia perceive the world order. For one, both countries uphold the centrality of the United Nations in international affairs and reject the unipolar world order. India perceives Russia as a strategic partner in achieving a polycentric, stable and balanced world order. For Russia, India is one of the most important financial and political powerhouses of the world.

The renewed and broadened nature of Russia's engagement with Asia will have several implications for India. These are the following—

- Russia's continued focus on the Eurasian region is perhaps the most beneficial aspect of its tilt. The tilt is the result of concerns such as security, terrorism, political and economic stability, drug trafficking, and social-sector development. By including India as a member of the SCO and initiating dialogue between the country and the EaEU, for Free Trade Agreement, Russia has enabled India to participate in securing the political and economic development of the region. This Eurasian identity provides a platform for India to stretch its economic borders on the northern front. Energy-rich Central Asia is important for India to diversify its energy imports, which are heavily dependent on West Asian sources. The region provides a new destination of investments for private Indian entrepreneurs, as countries such as Uzbekistan and Kazakhstan redefine their investment policies.
- The GEP project opens new avenues for cooperation between the two countries. The economic subordination of Russia in the Eurasian region does not bode well for India as it may hinder its ability to invest in the region, especially given the backdrop of the region's economic dependence on China. Thus, both Russia and India must cooperate on investing in the region. India must convince Russia that the International North–South Transport Corridor (INSTC) project falls well within the purview of its GEP project and that the GEP can become the platform for such cooperation. The INSTC project has moved at snail's pace since its inception in the early 2000s. It was only in January 2019 that Russia and India signed a Memorandum of Understanding to fast-track the implementation of the project.
- An important aspect of Russia–China relations in Asia, which could pose a challenge for Indo-Russian relations, is their shared view on the security of the Asia Pacific. India's participation in the first "quadrilateral" dialogue on the Asia Pacific in 2017 with the US, Japan and Australia raised concerns in Moscow. Russia's foreign minister responded by stating that sustainable security architecture in the region cannot be achieved through "closed bloc" arrangements. Russia is thus against any exclusive multilateral grouping in the Asia Pacific. India must handle this issue by balancing its concerns regarding China's

unilateral actions in the South China Sea. It also has to walk a tightrope while participating in any such perceived exclusive arrangements to serve its geopolitical and economic interests.

- Heavy reliance on the political trust between Moscow and Delhi and the decades-long arms trade is increasingly coming under attack due to the changing nature of regional geopolitics. Concerned about a possible spill-over of the situation in Afghanistan to its borders, through Central Asia, Russia has reached out to Pakistan. This is an important component of Russia's Asia policy, through which it not only seeks gradual diversification of its defence exports to new markets but also hopes to gain an advantage in the negotiation process between the Taliban and the Afghanistan government. Russia extended an invitation to the group to participate in the recently held Moscow Format of consultations on Afghanistan. Moscow also hosted the Intra-Afghan dialogue, which saw the participation of Afghan leaders across the political spectrum along with the Taliban representatives, except the Afghan government. In the words of the Director of Carnegie Moscow Centre, Dmitri Trenin, "These new elements require strengthening of the foundation of Russo-Indian relations." While India and Russia may not find common ground when it comes to the peace process in Afghanistan and the role of Taliban, they must be open to dialogue. The two countries can cooperate on a non-military project in Afghanistan to allay their concerns.
- Russia's de-dollarisation process has serious implications for India. By ensuring payments in Roubles for the S-400 deal, Russia aims to reduce exposure to sanctions. In India's case, it also reflects frustrations over the stagnant bilateral trade that hovers around US$ 10 billion, with a deficit on India's side. This poor bilateral trade is an ironic feature of the Indo-Russia relationship, which, in political terms, has traditionally been one of trust and friendship. Russia would insist on receiving payments in its national currency for the duration of sanctions on its industries. This would likely be a message for India to step up its trade with Russia.

Conclusion

Russia's tilt towards Asia has been a gradual process and comes with limitations. Russia must avoid relying excessively on China in harnessing its Arctic energy. Currently, its relation with Japan is constrained due to Japan's strategic relations with the US. This US factor will continue to impede the growth and potential of Russia–Japan relations. Asia is not yet in a position to completely replace Europe in terms of the volume of energy imports from Russia, due to geographical and political constraints as well as competition from the Gulf countries and the US. However, while Russia's economic engagement with Europe will continue, political distrust may also be prevalent. This could influence Russia to further its engagement with Asia, leading to the establishment of new institutions and the redefining of the existing ones. The success or failure of Russia's tilt towards Asia thus depends on the extent to which it is able to align Asian institutions to its interests.

Russia is poised to play an increasingly active role in Asian politics in the coming decades, since Asia plays a vital role in Russia's domestic development and technological modernisation. Moreover, Asia's geopolitical significance allows Russia to re-emerge as an active global player. As India diversifies its defence imports by importing from countries such as France, Israel and the US, Russia will also pursue its national interests and extend its cooperation with Pakistan and China. As traditional partners, both India and Russia must maintain a favourable balance of power in Asia. Russia's renewed outlook towards Asia provides this necessary opportunity, to not only redefine the bilateral relations but also provide a basis for cooperation on regional and global levels.

INDO-SOVIET RELATIONS IN THE NEHRU YEARS

On 7 September 1946, India's first prime minister, Jawaharlal Nehru, set out the template of independent India's foreign policy in his broadcast to the nation as head of a new interim government anticipating the transfer of power. Nehru's speech, entitled "Free India's Role in World Affairs", was made before the British government had decided to partition India and create Pakistan, before India's formal independence on 15 August 1947, and before the emerging rivalry between the two main victors of the Second World War had hardened into the Cold War. Because Nehru and successive prime ministers of India believed that the attitudes and objectives outlined in this broadcast grew naturally from India's geostrategic location, its culture, history, and national movement, they continued to assert them despite changing international circumstances and skepticism in world capitals such as Washington and Moscow, which were grounded in realist considerations. Some of these initial statements on Indian foreign policy, which were very different from those of the former British government of India, and which were repeated and amplified by Nehru himself and Indian envoys over the years, require quotation here.

India's policy of nonalignment throughout the Cold War was presaged thus: "We propose, as far as possible, to keep away from the power politics of groups, aligned against one another, which have led in the past to world wars and which may again lead to disasters on an even vaster scale." India's anti-colonial activism in the United Nations was predicted: "We are particularly interested in the emancipation of colonial and dependent countries and peoples and in the recognition in theory and practice of equal opportunities for all peoples. We repudiate utterly [...] racialism, wheresoever and in whatever form it may be practiced." India's attempts to establish good relations with both superpowers were heralded by the following statement: "We send our greetings to the people of the United States of America to whom destiny has given a major role in international affairs. We trust that this tremendous responsibility will be utilized for the furtherance of peace and human freedom everywhere. To that other great nation of the modern world, the Soviet Union, which also carrics a vast responsibility for shaping world events, we send greetings. They are our neighbors in Asia and inevitably we shall have to undertake many common tasks and have much to do with each other."

New Delhi had the difficult task of persuading its own functionaries, as well as foreign governments, of its independence in international affairs while at the same time coping with the immense human costs and administrative burdens caused by Partition. Because of widespread skepticism, Foreign Secretary K.P.S. Menon (the Civil Service chief of the Ministry of External Affairs headed by Nehru) started his address to officers at the Defense Services Staff College in mid-1949 by asking: "Has India a foreign policy at all? If so, what is it?" He quoted US and Soviet officials as both being puzzled by India's equation of the two power blocs and its tendency to side with the Anglo-Americans on various issues, and pointed out that popular opinion about India, as reflected in the media of the respective superpowers, was hostile or unenthusiastic.

Menon went on to deal with three issues that had profound effects on the evolution of India's foreign relations: Kashmir, the UN, and Korea. Recently opened British archives reveal Britain's motives in creating Pakistan as a bastion of Western security and the colossal effort it made in 1948–9 to persuade the US and other members of the UN to support Pakistan's case on and invasion of Kashmir by ignoring the legal accession of the State of Jammu and Kashmir to India. At the time, as Menon commented in his speech, "it was an eye opener to us." Indian mistrust of Anglo-American pronouncements on Kashmir persists to the present day, more than 60 years later. Menon explained the unsatisfactory deliberations of the UN Security Council as an example of regarding a matter "not according to its intrinsic merits, but in its relation to power politics", from which point of view India had no standing. The exceptions were China, which tried to appreciate the Indian case, and "taciturn Russia, who did not utter one word throughout the Kashmir dispute" (Moscow's silence ended in 1952, when it became very critical of Anglo-American "interference" in Kashmir and then openly supportive of India's case).

Menon explained how the original conception of the UN as establishing a world order encompassing rival ideologies had suffered from Washington's effort to create an anti-Soviet alliance and Moscow's obsession with obtaining security through a widening belt of Communist control, resulting in a world divided into two blocs. "Between these two blocs," said Menon, "stands, alone, unfriended, melancholy, slow, India belonging to neither bloc and somewhat disliked by both." He explained why India could not join either bloc, articulating the theme of India's national interest lying in world peace, independence, and respect, which would be frequently reiterated. Furthermore, he cited India's acceptance of the chairmanship of the United Nations Commission on Korea as an example of a policy that was criticized as "neutral, passive, weak-kneed [...but] no more passive than non-violence" in Mahatma Gandhi's hands. Menon's speech on foreign policy was important not only because officers of the defense services needed to understand the policies they would be called upon to defend, but because K.P.S. Menon served as India's ambassador to the Soviet Union from 1953 to 1961. During these eight years, Indo-Soviet relations first flowered and began to bear fruit as Soviet support for India's nonalignment grew.

Nehru's admiration for the self-transformation of the Soviet Union into a world power was qualified by his distaste for the coercive methods used for the purpose; his attraction toward Socialism (as espoused by the Fabian Society) was matched by a repulsion from ideological Communism, especially as articulated then by the Communist Party of India (CPI), seen to be directed by Moscow. The "Zhdanov Doctrine" propounded at the 1947 meeting of the Communist Information Bureau (Cominform), and adopted by the CPI, divided the world into two hostile camps, espoused violent revolution, and excluded "bourgeois" nationalist movements – such as that led by Mahatma Gandhi in India – from the category of "national liberation" movements deserving of Soviet support. Nevertheless, Nehru made overtures to the Soviet Union by appointing his sister, Vijaylakshmi Pandit, who had been an active participant in the drafting of the United Nations Charter, as India's first envoy to Moscow. Stalin ignored her, depicting India as a mere tool of the "Anglo-American imperialists". Stalin's views on India changed in the last few years of his life, perhaps in consideration of United Front policies, perhaps because of an initial impetus for the loosening of Soviet cultural barriers that came after his death, and probably because India effectively demonstrated its independence of the Anglo-American bloc in its mediatory diplomacy at the UN on various facets of the Korean War, including the contentious issue of prisoner-of-war repatriation.

In 1950, acting on Moscow's instructions, the CPI began supporting Nehru's "progressive" foreign policy in parliament and abandoned its strategy of armed struggle, which had been unsuccessfully attempted in the Telengana and Tebhaga uprisings of the late 1940s. In 1951, an Indo-Soviet Cultural Society was formed to facilitate exchanges of artists, dance troupes, and intellectuals. In January 1952, the Soviet delegate to the UN broke his silence on Kashmir in support of India's case. In April 1952, Stalin received Pandit's successor, Dr. Radhakrishnan, and in February 1953, just two weeks before his death, Stalin held a wide-ranging conversation with the new Indian ambassador, K.P.S. Menon.

1953 was a pivotal year, and the annual report of the Indian embassy in Moscow explains why. A last spurt of Stalinist repression was followed by a "kind of springtime in the Kremlin" after Stalin's death, brought about by new policies and hopes of reduced international tensions after the war in Korea ended in July. Ambassador Menon mentioned his meeting with Stalin as a "memorable experience" and summed up his impressions of Stalin's "almost rustic simplicity, his spontaneous humor, his single-mindedness, his perspicacity, his vision of the world as divided into black and white – with a lonely grey, India, standing in between – his utter ruthlessness, and his cynical and thoroughly Marxist disregard of morals which he made no attempt to hide." Nehru made a tribute to Stalin in parliament as a gratuitously friendly gesture towards Russia that was reciprocated a few months later by Prime Minister Georgy Malenkov's open praise of India's contributions to peace, and subsequently by a complete rewriting of the entry on Mohandas K. Gandhi in the *Great Soviet Encyclopedia*.

The embassy's annual report included analyses of the removal of secret police head Lavrenty Beria, new economic policies, riots in East Germany, and conflicting views between the Soviet Union and the Western powers on the future of Germany that doomed the four-power conference held on the subject. The report noted incremental improvements in Soviet references to India as well as changes in Soviet attitudes towards Pakistan, from "lukewarmness" to "antipathy", saying: "This was due to the proposed defense pact between Pakistan and the U.S.A. The Soviet Union knew that such a pact was directed as much against her as against India. A formal note of protest was sent to the Pakistan Government. The generally unfavorable reactions in Asian countries to this pact were noticed in the press. In particular, our Prime Minister's statements on this subject and, indeed, on many international problems were quoted prominently in the Soviet newspapers." The report concluded with a detailed discussion of certain noticeable liberalizing tendencies in the arts, literature, and music.

The first trade agreement between India and the Soviet Union was signed in December 1953, ushering in a process of economic cooperation between the two countries that was to become the pillar of friendly Indo-Soviet relations over almost four decades. The Soviet government was eager to establish economic relations with countries outside its own Communist bloc on a practical basis of mutual advantage rather than on grounds of ideological conformity. The Indian government also wished to diversify its commercial relationships beyond the British Commonwealth and obtain industrial assistance from diverse sources, but did not accept Soviet offers without serious consideration. A note of April 1954 prepared by the Indian embassy in Moscow argued in favor of developing economic relations with the Soviet Union on a wider scale for the following reasons: First, the Soviet Union appreciated India's independent foreign policy and was anxious to obtain its goodwill in face of assertive US activity in Asia. Second, far from adversely affecting US economic assistance, "a little Soviet competition will only induce the U.S.A. to be less grudging in its proffers of technical and industrial assistance." Third, economic cooperation with the Soviet Union would pose no danger to India's internal security or democratic polity as the Soviet government was "now genuinely reconciled to [...] the need for the co-existence of rival systems of political economy." Fourth, there were limits to what the Soviet Union could offer and India could accept, but it was worth pursuing the possibility of the Soviet Union establishing a tractor factory in India first and perhaps a steel factory and oil refinery later on.

This tentativeness disappeared as India's Second Five Year Plan was drafted by Professor P.C. Mahalanobis and the powerful Planning Commission to further the social and economic goals outlined by Nehru: to increase the scope of the public sector; to develop heavy industries and strengthen the foundations of economic independence; to increase the domestic production of consumer goods; to eliminate unemployment gradually; to increase agricultural productivity and to improve the quality of social services. By the end of 1955, India was looking to the Soviet Union for technical advice and training in several specific industries and financial assistance in establishing some of them. The Indian government held high-level coordination committee meetings on the subject of economic cooperation with the Soviet Union in November 1955, leading to the preparation of an aide-memoire handed over by Nehru to Soviet leaders asking for "information or technical aid or equipment" in specific industries.

Due to Moscow's positive response, the Soviet bloc became the second-largest foreign contributor to Indian economic development by 1965. This arrangement was highly acceptable to India for many reasons.

It was a government-to-government programme for expansion of the public sector, a field that Western concerns were reluctant to enter. It opened and established an indigenous oil and petroleum exploring, distilling, and distributing industry in India, which had formerly been dependent on Anglo-American oil companies.

Soviet assistance appeared to come without the "strings" of Western criticisms of Indian foreign and economic policy and bolstered India's nonalignment. It was designed for long-term programmes of mutually supportive projects including training, design, use of products, and complementary plans rather than short-term projects.

Markets at both ends were assured. Furthermore, in 1959, after India had suffered a crisis of foreign exchange shortage, a new pattern of trade and payments in Indian rupees was established between India and the Soviet bloc countries. Some of the problems created by structuring economic cooperation outside the international market system, especially those related to pricing goods and keeping to delivery schedules, only surfaced after the collapse of the Soviet Union and India's turn to market economics in the early 1990s.

If 1953 was a pivotal year for the post-Stalin Soviet Union, 1955 was the first peak in Indo-Soviet relations. It was marked by the visit of Prime Minister Nehru in June and July 1955 to the Soviet Union – including some Central Asian Republics – as well as to Czechoslovakia, Poland, and the capitals of Austria, Yugoslavia, Italy, the UK, and Egypt. Nehru and two senior officials recorded their impressions, which were circulated as a confidential booklet to selected persons by the Ministry of External Affairs. Nehru's two notes were written in the informative, instructive, reflective style that had typified his letters to his daughter from prison in pre-independence days and was characteristic of his regular letters to chief ministers of Indian states. He shared his knowledge of history and world affairs so as to better explain his impressions and reactions to current events, people, and places; he was a natural teacher, and recognized as such by his contemporaries in government.

Thus, his remarks on the absence of "civil liberty as we know it or as the term implies" in the Soviet Union were accompanied by reflections on Russia's autocratic past, differences among the Communist states, the Soviet sense of "being surrounded by danger and by hostile forces", and descriptions of the tremendous economic and scientific advances being made there along with an emphasis on athletics, construction, and the education of children. He was very interested in learning the details of the Soviet planning process and its possible application to India. Nehru's meetings with the top echelons of Soviet leadership persuaded him "that the Russian outlook today is very definitely opposed to war" because they did not want to lose what they had built since World War II, that they were "eager for a settlement with the Western Powers and that they value India's friendship". Nehru conveyed these impressions to British Prime Minister Anthony Eden and other ministers, with whom he also discussed the two major Cold War problems of the day, Germany and East Asia.

Throughout his tour, Nehru stressed India's "special position" as an independent country that was not aligned with either side in the Cold War, speaking in a "soft, gentle voice" in the cause of peace; he found that Marshal Josip Broz Tito of Yugoslavia had "gradually come around to a policy very similar to ours". Nehru met a similar opposition to military pacts expressed by the new head of the Egyptian government in Cairo, Gamal Abdel Nasser. The following year, Nehru, Tito, and Nasser met on the Brijuni Islands. Their efforts to garner support for their positions of nonalignment led to the launching of a Non-Aligned Movement at the Belgrade Conference of September 1961. Canada was never a member of the non-aligned group of nations, being a founder member of the North Atlantic Treaty Organization (NATO), but enjoyed close relations with India at the time, and the two countries pursued similar approaches to the role of neutral mediators in keeping world peace in the nuclear age. In that context, a secret and detailed report by Canadian Prime Minister Lester Pearson of his conversation with Khrushchev in October 1955 is of special interest, as it was shared with India.

Soviet Prime Minister Nikolai Bulganin and Communist Party Secretary Nikita Khrushchev reciprocated Nehru's tour in the Soviet Union by making a well-publicized three-week visit to India in November-December, 1955. Nehru recorded a long note assessing the visit. He cited Soviet willingness to try and understand India and express confidence in it by asking for its inclusion in international conferences on Korea and Indochina. He contrasted Soviet behavior with Western reactions of "anger and resentment" at India's rising international prestige and the persistence of "over-bearing attitudes" based on past colonial relationships. Nehru made an exception for Canada, which he described as "sensible" and free of such "bias as well as from the extreme attitudes of the United States". He mentioned his own discomfort with the Soviet leaders' uninhibited public expressions of support for India and their denunciations of the West.

The Indian public and press, however, were delighted. Nehru explained the public reaction as a result, in part, of high-profile mutual accusations over the failure of recent Geneva conferences between the US and the Soviet Union.

More seriously, public support for the Soviet Union was attributed to reactions against the formation of the Baghdad Pact, which was directed against the Soviet Union and brought the area of conflict "right up to our borders" by including Pakistan, as the South East Asian Treaty Organization had also done, as well as US Secretary of State John Foster Dulles' joint declaration with the Portuguese foreign minister stating that Goa (an enclave on the west coast of India) was part of metropolitan Portugal.

During the visit, Nehru raised the matter of the CPI violently opposing the Indian government while receiving direction and support from Moscow, which Khrushchev denied. They discussed various aspects of Indian industrialization and economic development, in which the Soviet leaders were willing to assist.

The Ministry of External Affairs made summaries of the talks held between Nehru, Bulganin, and Khrushchev on 19 and 21 November and on 12 and 13 December. They discussed the four-power foreign ministers' conference in Geneva in some detail on 19 November, and US and Soviet policies on disarmament, nuclear energy, and the Middle East on 21 November. When the Soviet leaders returned from an official visit to Burma in December, Nehru met them in his house on 12 and 13 December and inquired about their impressions of India. Both admitted that the opinions they had held in Moscow had been changed because their earlier perceptions had been shaped by "colonizers of India" and "books not written by friends of India" and so advocated greater cultural exchanges to dispel mutual ignorance. Nehru again brought up the subject of the CPI being a negative factor in Indo-Soviet friendship and referred to the five principles of peaceful coexistence, including non-interference in domestic affairs. Khrushchev denied responsibility for the CPI and repeated assurances that he would "do everything to strengthen friendly relations with India". The following evening, with senior officials present, the leaders discussed agriculture (the Soviet Union donated equipment for a 30,000-acre new mechanized farm in Suratgarh, Rajasthan), China, the UN, and Kashmir, and finalized the precise wording of the joint statement to be issued on conclusion of a mutually satisfactory visit.

The annual political report of the Indian embassy in Moscow for 1955 briefly recapitulated Soviet and international events since 1953, the flow of visitors, and the efforts made by the Soviet government "to make the people here India-minded". The report also comments on Western speculation on the friendly relations between the Soviet Union and India and cites an opinion expressed in a British journal that "Russia is courting India as a counterpoise to China." Looking back, we recall that the mid-1950s was a time of very high Indian involvement in international issues manifest in high-level pronouncements on conflicts in the Middle East and Indochina, on the need for nuclear disarmament and cessation of nuclear testing, as well as activism in the UN for admission of new members, speeding up the process of decolonization, and trying to calm the shrill vituperation of Cold War rhetoric. The personal prestige of Prime Minister Nehru was high, and he felt that his exchange of visits with Chinese Premier Zhou Enlai had laid the basis for a strong and friendly relationship based on the five principles of peaceful coexistence, which was one of the prime goals of Nehru's foreign policy. Disillusionment came a few years later, when ties that had been forged in the meantime with the Soviet Union proved useful.

In the mid-1950s and later, India was most troubled by the formation of Western-sponsored military pacts in Asia that channeled military aid to Pakistan and so posed a direct threat to India's national security. Nehru expressed his objections vociferously in parliament and in talks with visiting British, French, and US foreign ministers in 1956, all of whom assured him that SEATO and the Baghdad Pact were defensive pacts against possible Soviet threats. Nehru also spoke to Anastas Mikoyan of the Soviet politburo. The note made of the latter conversationreports Nehru sharing the gist of his conversations with the Western officials and Mikoyan reporting on his talks with the president and prime minister of Pakistan, who had both told him that "these pacts were necessary for defense against India [...and] that Pakistan bases and Pakistan armed forces would never be used against the Soviet Union." But Mikoyan did not want this to be repeated in public, lest his Pakistan interlocutors denied their statements.

Mikoyan also gave Nehru a summary of proceedings at the 20th Party Congress held that year, which came to be known as the historic initiation of de-Stalinization in the Soviet Union. Nehru, for his part, reported on his friendly talks with the Shah of Iran and his intention to accept US President Dwight D. Eisenhower's invitation to visit the US; he did so in December 1956. Soviet opposition to Western military pacts in Asia as well as its support, without strings attached, of India's anti-colonial motions in the UN pleased New Delhi.

Many in India and abroad were disappointed, or even outraged, by India's dispassionate reactions when the Soviet Union used military force to suppress the Hungarian uprising of late 1956; the more so because the invasion of Egypt by forces of Israel, France, and Britain in September 1956 had evoked high anti-colonial rhetoric and active Indian involvement in UN actions to staunch that crisis, including contribution of the largest contingent to the United Nations Emergency Force to keep the peace. That episode posed no dilemmas for India, because its condemnation of colonialism and colonial-type actions was open and well known, and because there was no real danger of the Suez Crisis causing the Cold War to erupt into a hot war.

As far as Hungary was concerned, India had little knowledge of the country, no resident diplomatic representation there at the time, and no emotional involvement with it. Moreover, the militant rhetoric issuing from Radio Free Europe and US representatives at the UN seemed to pose a risk of war for some time in October-November 1956. India's nonalignment, as well as its relations with the Soviet Union, came under strain and obliged it to perform a delicate balancing act. On the one hand, Nehru in parliament praised and sympathized with the revolt of the Hungarian people, describing their actions as a "national uprising"; when Soviet troops re-occupied Budapest on 4 November and Imre Nagy was replaced, Ambassador Menon conveyed India's "deep concern and regret over the events in Hungary". On the other hand, Nehru appeared to give public credence to Moscow's explanations of the crisis, and India's representative at the UN opposed condemnatory or punitive resolutions against the Soviet Union, trying, without success, to secure permission for the UN secretary-general to visit Hungary.

As the danger of war passed, Nehru was more openly critical of the Soviet military presence in Hungary and advocated a mutual withdrawal of Warsaw Pact and NATO forces from Central Europe. He was deeply shocked when Imre Nagy was executed in June 1958 and, in a personal letter to Menon, expressed his feelings of dismay at this "cold blooded act" as well as general discouragement that a "succession of foolish actions" had spoiled some good positions and "almost put an end to the idea of real peace in our generation". It was not the first or the last time that the reproaches of an Indian prime minister were ignored by Soviet leaders.

Khrushchev stopped in India for talks with Nehru in February and March 1960. At the time, Khrushchev's confidence in his personal authority and in the economic, military, and scientific advances being made by the Soviet Union was high. In his conversation with Nehru, he held forth at some length about US failures and Soviet strengths, and did not fully answer questions on how the German problem could be resolved or disarmament achieved.

The two men agreed that disarmament negotiations should include the larger Asian countries and that the People's Republic of China should not be excluded by the US from the UN. Nehru then referred "to a matter that is of great interest and embarrassment to us": the relationship with China, which was deteriorating because of military incidents along the contested border. Nehru hoped that a personal meeting with Zhou would be helpful, but feared "that our respective positions are so different that at present there is no bridge between us."

The penultimate page of the record is missing, but Khrushchev does not appear to have confided the problems he himself was experiencing with China's supreme leader, or to have made any offer of support or mediation, because Nehru said he did not "expect a judgment", but was sending the Soviet leader material so that "Mr. Khrushchev and his friends may have familiarity with our position."

In Calcutta, on Khrushchev's return from Burma and Indonesia, the two leaders spoke about French nuclear tests, prospects for disarmament, Eisenhower's Atoms for Peace programme, and the progress of the Soviet and the Indian economic plans, with India now receiving more Western and Soviet assistance.

In the course of 1960, Cold War tensions and harsh rhetoric were ratcheted up as a result of what was known as the U-2 incident. A US surveillance airplane taking off from a secret military base in northwestern Pakistan was shot down over the Soviet Union, and Khrushchev effectively canceled a scheduled summit conference. Foreign Secretary Subimal Dutt provided Prime Minister Nehru with a summary of relevant developments. While Indian media criticized the US for the incident and for asserting the right to send its airplanes into the airspace of another country without permission, it also, with the exception of the Communist press, criticized Khrushchev's cancellation of the summit meeting. No action by the UN could be expected. Meanwhile, the Chinese government used the incident as a propaganda opportunity, accusing India of "supposed indifference" to the U-2 incident and continued publishing personal attacks on Nehru. Both China and India hoped for Soviet support or neutrality in their by now irreconcilable border dispute. Indian President Rajendra Prasad, accompanied by Foreign Secretary Subimal Dutt, made a two-week ceremonial visit to the Soviet Union in June and July 1960. They gained favorable impressions of general improvement in standards of living and loosening of restrictions. They saw that the Soviet experience could not be applied to India, "where we value freedoms enshrined in our constitution of thought, speech, and religion", but wanted to learn more about comprehensive planning and the leveling of social inequalities.

Indian Ambassador Menon and First Secretary A.S. Gonsalves kept New Delhi informed of developments inside the Soviet Union as well as relations with Poland and Finland in the later half of 1960. They reported Soviet and Polish concerns about trends in West Germany, as well as Moscow's dissatisfaction with the UN's handling of disruptions in the former Belgian Congo. New Delhi at the time was more concerned with its border problems with China and ways of financing the Second Five Year Plan, but subsequently became a mainstay of UN peacekeeping operations in the Congo and opposed

Soviet proposals to replace the UN secretary-general's office, then occupied by Dag Hammarskjöld, by a collective executive of three, a "troika", with each member representing the Western, Socialist, and Nonaligned group of states.

The annual report for 1960 remarked on Khrushchev's "extravagance" of language in approaching various issues of the day, but repeated the assessment that he wanted a relationship with the West based on peaceful coexistence. Khrushchev's visit to Southeast Asia had resulted in a decision to establish a "Friendship University" in Moscow for students from Asia, Africa, and Latin America and his visit to India evoked praise, expressions of friendship, increase in Soviet credits, and expansion of bilateral trade.

An important new item was the Soviet sale to the newly formed Border Roads Development branch of the Indian Army of eight An-12 aircraft, capable of carrying heavy equipment to high altitudes, on rupee payment and easy terms. During 1960, the ideological dispute between the Soviet and Chinese Communist Parties on the inevitability of war and the violent transition to Socialism surfaced at the Bucharest Congress of 81 Communist Parties. The resulting joint statement was seen as a "distinct triumph" for Khrushchev, and the Indian mission was particularly pleased at its creation of a new category of states deserving full cooperation.

The label "independent national democracy", which was used to describe this group, fit India. The following years brought increased friction between the Soviet Union and China as well as open conflict between India and China. Details and documentation of both conflicts are plentiful in the public domain, but junior officers in the Ministry of External Affairs produced an accurate analysis of differences between the Soviet and Chinese Communist Parties in 1963. Each of these analysts, A.P. Venkateshwaran, J.N. Dixit, and C.V. Ranganathan, subsequently became very influential in shaping and executing Indian policies abroad.

India invited several Soviet dignitaries for reciprocal visits, including then First Deputy Prime Minister and former head of Gosplan Alexsei Kosygin. Menon assessed him as "a rising, or risen, star" whose presence, "when we launch our Third Five Year Plan, will be particularly appropriate". Menon depicted Kosygin as one of the most outstanding and influential members of the Presidium who had risen through "sheer intellectual and administrative ability" and was being groomed as Khrushchev's successor.

Nehru and Kosygin exchanged views in New Delhi on 20 February 1961, and Kosygin also met India's vice president and had two meetings with members of the Planning Commission on 21 February and 3 March 1961. Kosygin gave Nehru a detailed letter from Khrushchev explaining Soviet views on questions of disarmament, the UN, and the situations in the Congo and Indochina. Nehru was ready to cooperate in his capacity as chairman of the International Commission for Supervision and Control in Laos (Canada and Poland were co-members) if the UK and the Soviet Union decided to reconvene it. A senior Indian diplomat, Rajeshwar Dayal, was the UN secretary general's special representative in the Congo, where Prime Minister Patrice Lumumba had been murdered. Kosygin visited some of the main projects assisted by the Soviet Union and held detailed talks with the Planning Commission.

He also suggested raising salaries in the public sector, giving executives more power, employing more technicians and training large numbers of specialists, and ensuring continuity and dovetailing of the planning process. In the late 1960s, Kosygin became more critical of the Indian economy. He is remembered in India chiefly for his successful mediation in January 1966 at Tashkhent after the Pakistan-India War of 1965, and his efforts to expand Soviet influence throughout South Asia.

One important era in Indo-Soviet relations came to an end when Nehru passed away in May 1964 and Khrushchev was ousted from power in October of that year. The two had constructed a mutually satisfactory relationship for their countries from unpromising beginnings. The Soviet Union was able to overcome Western trade boycotts prompted by the US policy of containment by establishing economic ties with India and other nonaligned states in Asia and the Middle East.

Moscow sought to enlarge its field of operation beyond its immediate periphery and its minority position in the UN by befriending newly independent countries in the age of decolonization. India, as the first and largest of these nations, and presumed to be the most influential among them under the leadership of Jawaharlal Nehru, was a natural object of Soviet courtship in the mid-1950s.

Moreover, support for Indian anti-colonial and anti-racism stances in the UN came without cost to Soviet policies; both countries found their security interests threatened by the US-sponsored creation of military alliances in their respective neighborhoods and voiced similar concerns for peace openly. In the polarized climate of the Cold War, the Soviet Union obviously gained from India's friendship.

India gained too, in both intangible and tangible ways. Nehru saw his foreign policy of nonalignment vindicated by the "non-exclusive" friendship of the Soviet Union based on peaceful coexistence and non-interference in internal affairs. The attention that US Presidents Eisenhower and Kennedy paid to Nehru, as well as their acceptance of India's nonalignment, was welcomed by Indians and sometimes ascribed to Soviet competition. Such enhancement of prestige, albeit intangible, was greatly valued by a nation that had no assets of hard power at the time and relied so heavily on moral influence.

India derived one tangible benefit of Soviet interest in the UN Security Council when the problem of Kashmir was raised in 1952 and 1957 and Anglo-American resolutions were countered by a Soviet veto. The other substantial contributions went to India's planned industrial development. Though US economic assistance to India during the 1950s and 1960s exceeded that of the Soviet Union, it was constrained by free-market ideology from bolstering India's public sector, which was so central to Nehru's economic policies of the time, in a way that Soviet assistance was not. Soviet military sales to India began in 1960, but were not yet as important as they became later. A third concrete gain was virtual Soviet neutrality in its border dispute with China, saving India from the nightmarish prospect of having both its giant Communist neighbors arrayed against it.

Nehru and Khrushchev had every reason to congratulate themselves on the state of Indo-Soviet relations. The next decades brought new issues and new leaders to the forefront of new narratives.

INDIA-RUSSIA TIES: 70 YEARS AND COUNTING...

In April 2018, the year-long calendar of events marking the 70th anniversary of India-Russia diplomatic relations came to an end. Looking back at the seven decades of close interaction between the two countries, some significant moments stand out. India and the Soviet Union established diplomatic relations on April 13, 1947, some months before India's formal Independence in August that year, through an exchange of diplomatic notes between their envoys in China. This method was resorted to because of the reluctance of the United Kingdom, which was still the colonial power in India, to endorse the decision of India's Interim Government to establish diplomatic relations between India and the Soviet Union.

The year 1955 was critical for India-Soviet Union relations, marking the first exchange of "summit" level interaction between the two countries. Prime Minister Jawaharlal Nehru visited Moscow as the leader of independent India in June that year. Intriguingly, this was several decades after his first visit to Moscow in 1927, and almost eight years after India's Independence. This was reciprocated by the visit of the top Soviet leadership of First Secretary Nikita Khrushchev of the Soviet Communist Party and Prime Minister Nikolai Bulganin to India in November. The visits laid the foundation for today's strategic partnership between India and Russia.

The political impact of these visits was evident internationally in the UN Security Council, where the Soviet Union used its veto power for the first time to block anti-India initiatives on Jammu & Kashmir (in February 1957 and June 1962) and Goa (December 1961). The economic impact of these visits was the creation of an infrastructural launch pad for India's aspirations to become a manufacturing and knowledge-based economy. Already in February 1955, bilateral agreement had been reached on constructing the Bhilai steel plant.

This was followed by the creation of major Indian public sector enterprises, which are household names today, such as Bharat Heavy Electricals Limited (BHEL) and Oil and Natural Gas Corporation (ONGC), among others. In 1958, the Indian Institute of Technology (IIT) Bombay was established with financing received from the Soviet Union through UNESCO. In 1963, the defence manufacturing sector was added to bilateral relations, with the first licensed production of MiG-21 aircraft in India. Aeronautics India Limited, set up specifically for this purpose, was merged in 1964 with Hindustan Aircraft Limited of Bangalore to become Hindustan Aeronautics Limited or HAL.

The third landmark is 1971. In August that year, India signed a Treaty of Peace, Friendship and Cooperation with the Soviet Union. During the December 1971 war with Pakistan, which resulted in the independence of Bangladesh, India was able to use the diplomatic space provided by this treaty to successfully implement its military and diplomatic objectives. The Soviet Union cast three vetoes in the UN Security Council on December 4, 5, and 13 to block attempts to stop India from its ongoing military campaign. (In an ironic twist, the first veto used in the UN Security Council by the newly admitted People's Republic of China as a permanent member on August 25, 1972, was to prevent the admission of Bangladesh as a member of the UN).

1991 was a watershed year for both India and Russia. In July that year, India's annual Budget presented to Parliament outlined its historic economic reforms. In December that year, one of the final decisions of the Soviet Parliament was that the Russian Federation would be the successor state of the dissolved Soviet Union.

Since 1991, India and Russia have taken different paths towards achieving their socio-economic objectives. India, building on the resilient structures of parliamentary democracy established in the country after Independence in 1947, followed the path of phased economic reforms for growth. This process has withstood the test of successive General Elections to catapult the country into its current position as the seventh biggest economy in the world, valued at $2.26 trillion. The socio-political impact of this has been reflected in India's aspirational policies. India's foreign policy objectives have been consciously directed towards integrating India more effectively into the complex matrix of bilateral and multilateral cooperation to ensure the peaceful external environment needed to sustain its growth.

Newly independent Russia embraced the path of radical economic reforms in 1992, based on the concept of "shock therapy". Russia opted for a presidential form of democracy, based on its Constitution adopted after a referendum in 1993. Unlike India, where there has been continuity in its political discourse while undergoing economic reforms, Russia experienced the unique phenomenon of breaking out of the political shackles of Communist ideology, rediscovering its rich civilisational heritage in the process.

Today, the World Bank lists Russia as the world's 12th biggest economy by the GDP, valued at $1.28 trillion. From its initial period of volatile socio-economic and political developments, including weathering the 2008 global financial crisis, Russia has stabilised into a strong nation-state. Russian foreign policy reflects the objective of securing peace and stability around its immediate periphery in order to sustain its socio-economic development.

In his historic address to India's Parliament during his first state visit in 2000, President Vladimir Putin had said that, "Russia and India are ancient civilisations, but at the same time, they are living democracies." During that visit, the then Prime Minister Atal Bihari Vajpayee had asserted that "as traditional friends, we wish to see Russia as a strong and confident state, an important constituent of a multi-polar world order". These two statements highlight the core values that lie at the heart of the formal India-Russia strategic partnership launched during that visit, which was elevated to a "special and privileged strategic partnership" in 2010. It is evident from the seven decades of bilateral relations that both India and Russia have consistently supported each other's aspirations to re-emerge as revitalised nation-states on the international stage.

Today, the India-Russia strategic partnership faces some daunting challenges. Some of these challenges emanate from within the relationship itself, especially in the acknowledged shortfalls in the areas of economic cooperation and people-to-people exchanges. Some of these challenges are linked with the disruptions being caused to the international order by the continuing threat of terrorism, which directly impacts multi-religious societies like India and Russia. The emergence of assertive unilateralism is the most recent of such challenges, which threatens the carefully built balance and structure of international cooperation where India and Russia have cooperated to mutual benefit.

Looked at from this perspective, it is possible to identify at least five specific steps which could steer India-Russia strategic relations towards their mutually agreed objective.

First is the annual summit mechanism. President Putin, as "the original architect of India-Russia strategic relations", created the annual summit mechanism in 2000, alternating between India and Russia, to drive the strategic partnership by ensuring the regular meeting of the executive heads of the two countries. The 18th such summit was held in St Petersburg in 2017 during Indian Prime Minister Narendra Modi's visit, demonstrating the viability and resilience of this idea.

The recently announced informal summit (called "working visit" by the Russian side) between Prime Minister Modi and President Putin to be held in Russia on May 21, 2018, is a harbinger of the kind of innovation that is needed to enable more frequent, and less structured, discussions between the executive heads of India and Russia.

Through such informal meetings, India and Russia would be better placed to pursue mutually agreed policy options to counter the disruption that directly or indirectly impinges on their strategic partnership. A good example of the kind of challenge that would require such informal meetings is the response of the India-Russia strategic partnership to the unilateral imposition of sanctions by third countries.

Second, India and Russia signed an agreement on principles of cooperation between the states and union territories of India and the constituent entities of the Russian Federation at their summit in 2000. Prime Minister Modi, when he was Chief Minister of Gujarat, and the then Governor Anatoly Guzhvin of Astrakhan implemented this agreement by entering into a cooperation agreement between their respective entities during the 2001 summit held in Moscow. Last June, Prime Minister Modi had interacted with Russia's Regional Governors. Discussions have been held on making this mechanism more effective and extending its coverage.

One proposal is to apply this mechanism to the Russian Far East. The natural resource-rich Russian Far East, bordering China, Japan, and the Korean Peninsula, comprises nine constituent entities of the Russian Federation, with a population of about seven million people. Bringing India's new focus on "cooperative federalism" into play, this mechanism could become a delivery vehicle for boosting economic and people-to-people exchanges, contributing to the substance of the strategic partnership in a sensitive region of Asia. For this, both sides would need to carefully identify those states and entities which have the capacity and interest to interact meaningfully in the Russian Far East. Sectors such as pharmaceuticals, gems and jewellery, agro-processing, tourism, and IT-enabled services could become the specific drivers of greater exchanges. The success of such a "pilot project" would have a major impact on this area of cooperation, and on the overall strategic partnership between

India and Russia. Third, steps could be taken to integrate the discussions and work of the three structured platforms servicing the annual summit with the objective of enabling the effective participation of India and Russia in each other's manufacturing sectors. These three platforms are the India-Russia Inter-Governmental Commission (IRIGC), mandated to look at economic cooperation; the India-Russia Military Technical Commission (MTC), mandated to look at defence cooperation; and the newly created High Level Science and Technology Commission for scientific and technological cooperation.

The successful synergy of using strategic relations and objectives to bring together technology (including research and development), manufacturing, employment generation, and marketing is evident in the bilateral cooperation between India and Russia in the defence production arena under the MTC and can be used as a template in a wider context to boost economic relations.

The manufacture and supply of tanks and missiles (T-90 and BrahMos), ships and submarines (the Talwar-class stealth frigates, the aircraft-carrier Vikramaditya and the nuclear submarine (Arihant), fighter and early airborne warning aircraft (Sukhoi 30MKI and IL-76) are all examples of such cooperation. Each of these contracts significantly supported the Russian manufacturing sector, including in the development and application of innovative technologies, and generated employment in Russia during a time of great tribulations within the Russian economy and society. Each of the products that were acquired by India through this cooperation has significantly enhanced India's defence and security capacities. In some cases, Russian technologies and platforms have been inducted into the Indian armed forces before they were inducted into the Russian armed forces. This dimension has added the vital element of trust, which anchors the strategic partnership between India and Russia.

Integrating the work and output of the three structures would help identify and achieve specific steps to give substance to India-Russia economic cooperation. Such a step would implement Russia's declared objective of increased participation in the Make in India programme, and open similar opportunities for Indian entities, including small and medium enterprises, to enter corresponding sectors in Russia. Eventually, the emergence of an integrated platform of policy-makers and entities actually engaged on the ground would drive the India-Russia strategic partnership in the future, implementing the core vision.

Fourth, steps should be taken to create a sustainable structure to take India-Russia energy partnership into the Eurasian region. This cooperation has been remarkable since 2000. The ONGC's external arm, OVL-Videsh, has invested 20 per cent in Russia's $12 billion Sakhalin-I project, in which the other shareholders are Exxon of the United States, Sodeco of Japan, and Rosneft of Russia. In 2015, the OVL invested $1.5 billion for a 15 per cent stake in Rosneft's Vangkor oilfield, one of the largest continental oilfields in Russia. In turn, Rosneft has invested $13 billion in Essar Oil, which owns Gujarat's Vadinar Oil Refinery, the second largest in India. Gazprom of Russia has a 20-year supply agreement with GAIL to supply 2.5 million tonnes of LNG annually to India, beginning this year.

As analysts have pointed out, the contracted volumes are sufficient to cover 10 per cent of gas and 5 per cent of oil imported by India at present. In non-fossil energy, Rusatom of Russia is currently the only foreign investor in India's civilian nuclear energy sector, with the first two 1,000W units of the Kudankulam power plant already commissioned. India and Russia presently plan to construct up to 20 nuclear power plants in India. Clearly, the foundation exists for creating a Eurasian energy grid of producers and consumers, which can become economically viable and sustainable, and one of the drivers of India-Russia strategic cooperation.

Fifth, to become more vibrant, steps need to be taken to connect the younger generations of India and Russia as future stakeholders in the partnership. Historically, the role played by individuals in generating greater awareness and understanding about India and Russia cannot be underestimated. India has played an important role in the Russian imagination for centuries. A Russian trader, Afanasy Nikitin, compiled the first Russian travelogue on India during his journey between 1466 and 1472 (before Vasco da Gama "discovered" India in 1498 for the Western world). The first major Russian Indologist, Gerasim Lebedev, lived and worked in Kolkata at the close of the 18th century. His grammar of East Indian languages was published in 1801. The famous Russian 19th Century artist, Vasily Vereshchagin, (with his wife Elizabeth Kondratievna) first visited India in 1874, spending two years painting hundreds of portraits and landscapes of India, many of which can be seen today in Moscow's famous Tretyakov Gallery. The impact of Indian films on Russian society is acknowledged by both sides at all levels of interaction.

Russia's influence on India over the centuries is being gradually put into the public domain. Connectivity for transport of goods, services and ideas enriched the interaction between India and Russia through the Silk Road, the precursor of today's ambitious North-South Transport Corridor project between the two countries. The Caspian port city of Astrakhan was a major confluence of India-Russia contact, and even had its "Indian Quarter" as noted in a book published in 1716. In the 20th Century, Russia's role in the evolution of Indian thought was symbolised by the correspondence between Mahatma Gandhi and Leo Tolstoy dating back to 1899. Russia was carried into the popular imagination by the writings of Rabindranath Tagore, who visited Russia in September 1930. Rukmini Devi Arundale, India's famous Bharatanatyam dancer, who founded the cultural and educational centre Kalakshetra in 1938, acknowledged the influence of Russia's legendary ballerina Anna Pavlova on her as a "spiritual teacher" and inspiration. The life and work of Nikolai Roerich, the philosopher-artist, who was born in Tsarist Russia in 1874 and died in independent India in December 1947, is symbolic of the spiritual dimension of India-Russia relations.

The strength of India-Russia strategic relations will be enhanced by supporting the work of talented individuals from both countries in all aspects of human endeavour to give direction to the future development of bilateral relations in the 21st Century. In this context, the third International Conference of Indologists held in St Petersburg in April 2018 showcased the need to broaden and deepen people-to-people interaction to cover the entire gamut of social sciences between the two countries as a top priority. This will generate "knowledge leaders" in different areas, who can transform and sustain this relationship as a popular relationship. In the process, the values that imbue the India-Russia ties today can be better appreciated, including the impact of the civilisational dimension.

The international ecosystem in which the India-Russia strategic partnership functions is undergoing a period of great churn, especially in Asia. The common membership of India and Russia in Eurasian bodies, like the Shanghai Cooperation Organization and the Conference on Interaction and Confidence-Building in Asia, provide a broader framework for the partnership. Imaginatively used, these platforms can help India and Russia contribute to stability in international relations, based on the principles of the UN Charter and a mutual interest in focusing on national development with a supportive external structure of peace and security.

70 YEARS OF INDIA-RUSSIA RELATIONS: A HISTORIC MILESTONE

Relations between India and Russia are rooted in history, mutual trust and mutually beneficial cooperation. This is a strategic partnership that has withstood the test of time, and which enjoys the support of the people of both countries.

Diplomatic relations between India and Russia began even before India achieved independence, on 13 April 1947. In the period immediately following independence the goal for India was attaining economic self-sufficiency through investment in heavy industry. The Soviet Union invested in several new enterprises in the areas of heavy machine-building, mining, energy production and steel plants. During India's second Five Year Plan, of the sixteen heavy industry projects set up, eight were initiated with the help of the Soviet Union. This included the establishment of the world famous IIT Bombay.

A watershed moment in relations between India and the Soviet Union was the signing of the Treaty of Peace and Friendship in August 1971. The Treaty was the manifestation of shared goals of the two nations as well as a blueprint for the strengthening of regional and global peace and security.

The nineties were a tumultuous period for both countries. In 1990, India extended loans to the USSR in the form of technical credit and in 1991, India extended food credit and gift of 20,000 tonnes of rice. After the dissolution of the Soviet Union, India and Russia entered into a new Treaty of Friendship and Cooperation in January 1993 and a bilateral Military-Technical Cooperation agreement in 1994.

In 2000, during the visit of President Putin to India, the partnership acquired a new qualitative character, that of a Strategic Partnership. The strategic partnership institutionalized annual meetings between the Prime Minister of India and the President of Russia and meetings have been held regularly since then. During the 2010 visit of President Dmitry Medvedev the relationship was elevated to the status of a Special and Privileged Strategic Partnership. So far, eighteen Annual India-Russia Summits have been held since 2000. These have led to personal contacts and close understanding at the highest level between our leaders.

Both the countries have institutionalized dialogue mechanisms that report to two leaderships. These are the Inter-Governmental Commission on Trade, Economic, Scientific, Technological and Cultural Cooperation (IRIGC-TEC), co-chaired by the External Affairs Minister of India and the Deputy Prime Minister of Russia and the Inter-Governmental Commission on Military and Military Technical Cooperation (IRIGC-MTC) co-chaired by the Defense Ministers of both countries. These meetings identify priorities and review cooperation on a regular basis and are key platforms to take our cooperation forward.

This year, in the 70th anniversary of establishment of diplomatic relations, India participated as Guest Country in the St. Petersburg International Economic Forum-2017. The Prime Minister of India Shri Narendra Modi was the Guest of Honour. During this time the 18th Annual Bilateral Summit was also held, which saw the adoption of the historic St. Petersburg Declaration: Vision for the 21st Century, and signing of 12 Agreements in economic and political areas.

Both countries are celebrating the 70th anniversary by organizing events across the length and breadth of the countries reflecting the deep and multifaceted relationship. In addition to the Annual Summit, 2017 has seen visits to Russia by the senior most leadership of India, such as External Affairs Minister, Defence Minister, Finance Minister and National Security Adviser. From the Russian side, two Deputy Prime Ministers have visited India, and more high level visits are planned till December 2017.

India has participated in all major economic forums in Russia including SPIEF, Eastern Economic Forum, Innoprom, Technoprom, IT Forum, Arctic Forum and others.

Defence

The defence facet of the relationship is one of the strongest pillars of the India-Russia relationship and has withstood the test of time. India, with Russia's cooperation, has achieved capacity building in strategic areas through acquisitions and development of weapons. The relationship is evolving from the traditional buyer-seller one to that of joint production and development, with emphasis on technology sharing. Russia is committed to becoming a partner in the 'Make in India' programme

This year two rounds of the India-Russia Military-Industry Conference were held in March and August in which a large number of companies from Russia and India participated. India is the largest buyer of Russian military equipment and, at the same time, Russia is India's principal defence partner. This year India participated in Army 2017, the Army Games and the spectacular Spasskaya Bashnya Band Festival. The first-ever TriServices Exercise, Indra 2017, that India has ever held with any country was held with Russia on 21-29 October 2017 in Vladivostok, in keeping with the close cooperation between our two countries in the defence sector. Several steps are being taken to increase training of officers in each other's Institutions and more military exchanges.

Economic

Trade between the two countries is an area which has been identified for special focus by both countries. Bilateral trade in 2015 amounted to US$ 7.83 billion. In 2017 there has been an upward trend in the trade figures. In terms of volume, the present figures do not reflect the strength of the relationship or the potential of our economies, which is immense. Realising this, our leadership has set a target of total trade in goods and services of US$ 30 billion each way by 2025. In 2016, the top three items of import into India from Russia were precious metals, mineral products and chemicals. The largest exports from India to Russia were chemical products, engineering goods and agricultural products. India ranks fourth in the world in terms of production of generic pharmaceutical products. Both sides are working to expand the trade basket and identify new areas of trade.

Both sides are making progress towards achieving the target of mutual investment of US$ 15 billion each way by the year 2025. In 2016, Indian oil companies bought stakes in Russian companies and oilfields worth US$ 5.5 billion, and Rosneft has acquired an Indian company, ESSAR, in a deal worth US$ 13 billion. This is not only Russia's largest investment in India, but also India's single largest FDI. India and Russia have set up a US$ 1 billion Fund to promote mutual investment in infrastructure and technology projects.

India is also significantly increasing cooperation between the States of India and Regions of Russia. We have nine sister State and sister city agreements, and more are under consideration. A new stage in India's interaction with Russian regions was reached during Prime Minister Shri Narendra Modi's meeting with Regional Governors in June 2017, and between External Affairs Minister Sushma Swaraj's meeting with Governors of the Far East. The Russian Far East is a new focus of our policy.

India, Russia and other neighbouring countries are engaged in efforts to operationalise the International North-South Transport Corridor which promises to propel connectivity and trade relations between the two countries. We are also working on a 'Green Corridor' to ease trade and customs formalities. The two countries have signed a Protocol on 24 December 2015 to simplify visa procedures for businessmen.

In an important new step to integrate our economies, India and the Eurasian Economic Union have agreed to begin negotiations on a Free Trade Agreement. The two countries have agreed to cooperate in projects in third countries. Already, we are discussing cooperation in the Roopur Nuclear Power Project in Bangladesh. Indian and Russian companies have been cooperating in oil and gas exploration in Vietnam.

Nuclear

Russia is an indispensable partner in the sphere of nuclear energy and recognizes India as a responsible country with advanced nuclear technology with an impeccable non-proliferation record. After the Paris Agreement on Climate Change India considers nuclear energy as an important source of energy to meet its energy and climate change obligations. This has brought both countries together into a mutually beneficial relationship.

Rosatom is building six units of nuclear reactors at the Kudankulam site in Tamil Nadu. Two units are already operational and the next four are in different stages of implementation. This is in line with the "Strategic Vision" document signed in 2014 between President Putin and Prime Minister Narendra Modi. India attaches very high importance to local manufacturing in India of equipment and components for upcoming and future Russian-designed nuclear power projects.

Science and Technology

India and Russia have several ongoing cooperation activities in the areas of space, science and technology, education and research. A new High Level Science and Technology Commission was established in 2017. The Indian Department of Science and Technology and Russian Foundation forBasic Research have celebrated ten years of fruitful scientific joint projects. We have set up a Russia-India Network of Universities, and cooperation is underway in different aspects of space technology. The most recent area of cooperation which is emerging is the Arctic which has a lot of multi-disciplinary potential.

Culture

India and Russia have strong cultural ties, which are an important contribution to the strong and robust relations between the countries. Historical linkages have contributed to creating goodwill between the nations. As the Prime Minister of India Shri Narendra Modiremarked, in India, every child knows that Russia is our country's greatest friend and has always stood with us during the toughest moments.

The linkages that started with Afanasy Nikitin reaching India even before Vasco-da-Gama revealed India to the West, Gujarati traders settling in Astrakhan and the establishment of the Russian theatre in Kolkata have all brought peoples of our countries closer. Russian scholars like Gerasim Lebedev and Nicholas Roerich have travelled to India and studied Indian culture and philosophy. The grand epic of India, Mahabharata, has been translated into Russian. Similarly, Russian literature and thinkers like Leo Tolstoy, Alexander Pushkin and others have had a profound influence and contribution to Indian literature and thought. Several generations of Russians have grown up watching Indian films. Yoga in Russia has been growing and becoming increasingly popular since the 1980s, particularly in majors cities and urban centres.

India sponsors the Mahatma Gandhi Chair on Indian Philosophy at the Institute of Philosophy, Moscow. Russian Institutions, including leading universities and schools, regularly teach Hindi to Russian students. Apart from Hindi, languages such as Tamil, Marathi, Gujarati, Bengali, Urdu, Sanskrit and Pali are taught in Russian Institutions. Chairs on Ayurveda and Contemporary Indian studies have also been set up in different Russian Universities.

The number of Indian tourists to Russia and Russian tourists to India has shown significant increase in the last two years. The two countries are taking steps to facilitate easier access to each other's citizens. The two countries have agreed to renew their Cultural Exchange Programme for the period 2017-2019. It has been decided to celebrate 2018 as 'Year of Tourism' between India and Russia.

Regional and International Cooperation

In the international arena both countries have similar positions and coordinate their actions. We cooperate closely within the United Nations, BRICS and G-20 groupings, as well as in the various structures in the Asia Pacific region such as ASEAN and East Asia Summit Forum. Russia supported India's membership to the SCO and India was admitted as a full member of SCO in 2017.

The unique political proximity between the nations is reflected in congruence in global priorities. Both the countries share similar views on fighting terrorism without double standards, a more representative multi-polar world order based on international law with UN playing a central role, and resolving threats to international peace and security.

Russia supports India's permanent membership of the United Nations Security Council. On Syria and Afghanistan, both countries have called for resolute action to bring about a lasting and peaceful solution, and defeating the forces of terrorism. We cooperate on other global challenges such as cyber security, preventing weaponisation of outer space and prevention of weapons of mass destruction.

Looking Ahead

India and Russia have identified several new areas of cooperation. These range from deep sea exploration to building knowledge based economies based on science and technology, innovation, robotics and artificial intelligence, focussing on infrastructure, skill development, agriculture, shipbuilding, railways, aviation and greater connectivity, especially people-to-people contacts. Special focus will be given to cooperation between the younger generation and cultural sphere.

As stated in the St. Petersburg Declaration of June 2017 between India and Russia, "advancing the comprehensive development of the Indian-Russian relations is an absolute priority of the foreign policy of both States. We will continue to widen our scope of cooperation by launching large-scale initiatives in different spheres and enhance and enrich our bilateral agenda so as to make it more result-oriented." India and Russia will continue to remain a role model for harmonious and mutually beneficial partnership and strong friendship between States. This will be to the benefit of our States and international community as a whole.

INDIA-RUSSIA RELATIONS SET TO GROW IN 2015

It may be difficult to expect a spectacle in India-Russia relations in 2015, but it is certain that the relations will not deteriorate; rather it will gain substance. Both the countries will have stable regimes, unlike in 2014 when New Delhi witnessed change in regime, and more importantly both the countries have strong leaders in Narendra Modi and Vladimir Putin, who share camaraderie and a sense of pragmatism, which will likely permeate the bilateral engagements in 2015.

Mark the words of Modi when he welcomed Putin in December 2014: "Times have changed, our friendship has not." This spirit will pervade the relations in 2015. The 'continuity' element in bilateral relations is so strong, long and deep-rooted that the 'change' in national, regional and global politics and economics will likely unsettle the special relationship between the two countries.

The Russian Defence Minister, Sergei Shoigu will visit India in the new year. The visit will display the importance Russia gives to the defence relations between the two countries. Russia remains India's largest supplier of defence products, and this trend will likely continue in 2015. The response of Russian leadership to India's call for 'Make in India' is particularly noteworthy in this regard. Even before the declaration of this drive, both the countries have BrahMos as a testament of joint design and production. 2015 may witness further widening of joint efforts in designing and producing fifth generation fighter aircrafts and military transport aircrafts. It is possible that a concrete roadmap will develop in 2015 in relation to these two defence items.

Both the countries have myriad opportunities, and also myriad challenges. Some of the challenges are within the bilateral framework such as the one related Bilateral Investment Promotion and Protection Agreement (BIPPA), and some others emanating from outside the bilateral framework such as religious extremism and terrorism. The year will likely witness resolution of bilateral differences on trade and investment, and evolution of a consensual architecture on economic partnership. This is possible particularly as the leaders of both the countries realize the imperative of sorting out differences in a competitive global economy. It is also possible that both the countries will evolve a framework to trade in rupee and rouble as the economic sanctions have impacted the trade, and also goaded Russia to explore other alternatives away from a dollar dominated economy. Russia is also exploring a similar arrangement with China, and this drive may lead the RIC countries, and possibly BRICS countries, to have an economic arrangement to tame the economic crisis arising out of the conflict in Russia's east.

Will BRICS, in which India and Russia are key players, play a role of facilitator in the Ukraine crisis in 2015? This is a complicated question, but it may not be out of range that powerful BRICS players like India and China, who enjoy robust relationship with Russia, may use the framework to bring different parties to the conflict to the dialogue table. The sanctions might have affected the Russian economy, but this has not contributed to real peace and stability in Ukraine. Any role of India to end the crisis, keeping in mind Russian sensitivities, may be welcome by Russian leadership.

India and Russia have shown resilience and understanding to diversify their relations to match their interests. This trend will continue in 2015. India expressed understanding at Russia's recently concluded energy deal with Pakistan. At the same time, Russia expressed understanding in India inviting the US President to its Republic Day celebrations in January 2015.

The challenges also include removing obstacles in speedy implementation of policies. It is rightly held that red-tapism is a big problem in both the countries. Some of the bureaucrats are caught up in a time-wrap and suffer from a biased approach. It is expected that Modi and Putin will address this problem by galvanizing the administrative machinery in respective countries to implement the policies. It is also an urgent need that people to people contact, and institution to institution, exchanges are encouraged to bring people together. There are some steps in this regard such as easing visa rules. 2015 will likely witness more such steps. The cooperation not only at the country level but also at city level and province to province level will also likely to be encouraged.

2015 will certainly be busier than 2014 in India-Russia relations. India and Russia will give concrete shape or implement various deals signed in 2014. Russia will build 12 more nuclear reactors in India for production of energy. The number may go up. Similarly, the agreements between Alrosa, the Russian diamond company, and Indian companies will witness more trade regarding cutting and processing diamond in India. Both the countries will sign landmark deals on defence. In consumer goods sector, another area – the diary products (besides the buffalo meat) may be added to the list. The list is indeed long.

Good will and mutual trust notwithstanding, India and Russia need to revamp economic relations and clear bottlenecks. In the changing global order, economic diplomacy has trumped over political diplomacy. It is expected that both the countries will take steps to realize the goal of $30 billion trade by 2025. Not a tall order at all in comparison to their trade with China, and in keeping in view the potentials of cooperation. Russian expertise in defence equipments, space technology, building of smart cities, nuclear energy, and its natural resources of oil and gas are certainly elements of attraction for India. Add this to Indian consumer goods, pharmaceuticals, diamond processing, information and communication technology; the relations come in a complete package. Even if all the announcements, memorandums of understanding and agreements signed in 2014 are given concrete shape and implemented in 2015 – that itself will be a tall order.

Peace and stability in the vast Eurasia will be major challenge for India and Russia in 2015. Whether it is the crisis in Ukraine or the transition in Afghanistan, or defeat of the Islamic state, or the evolution of a multipolar world order – India and Russia can work together for a better world. The international forces, led by the US, have officially withdrawn from Afghanistan. The Taliban has proclaimed itself to be victorious, and already expressed its sympathy for the Islamic state in Iraq and Syria. The emerging vacuum is a big challenge to multiethnic and pluralistic states like India and Russia. Other issues like SCO expansion, climate change, Arctic exploration, drug trafficking and money laundering too need attention of both the countries. It may not be a surprise that in 2015 both the countries push for a comprehensive convention on international terrorism at the 70th anniversary of the United Nations, and strengthen bilateral mechanisms to counter the menace.

International relations in 2015, unlike in 2014, will be less compartmentalized and more cooperative. Isolation as a foreign policy tool will be less valued. India and Russia with their huge capital of good will and mutual understanding will contribute to this trend. Whether making international institutions fair and just, or infusing the spirit of friendship and cooperation into international politics, India and Russia will lead the trend. Both the countries will synergize their policy tools and make their 'institutional dialogue architecture more result-oriented and forward-looking' in 2015. It is quite in the range of possibility as the leaders of both the countries are dynamic and capable of taking quick decisions.

RUSSIA-INDIA RELATIONS: NEW AGENDA IN MILITARY-TECHNICAL COOPERATION

India is one of the world's largest national arms markets, behind the United States, Saudi Arabia, and (until recently) China. However, India's military-technical cooperation (MTC) with foreign countries pursues the exclusive aim of strengthening its own security, and therefore is unlikely to have a negative impact on regional security in South Asia. India's elites (supported by a significant proportion of the society) are keen to continue substantial "supplementary arming" of India, considering it a deterrent to the "geopolitical expansion" of China, a country that has experienced problematic relations with India following the border conflict in 1962, and as a means of implementing the military-political doctrine of India that aims to transform the "Elephant" into a leading force in the area from "Suez to Singapore."

India is diversifying the products supplied on the Indian market by a variety of foreign manufacturers, working towards saturating its defence-industrial complex with science and technology capacities, including broad based "naturalization" of foreign ideas and R&D. The main purpose of this is to stimulate the creation and development of domestic original ideas and solutions. The main feature of India's MTC is the trend aimed at purchasing weapons systems that are manufactured in accordance with individual requirements of Indian customers. Almost all newly-purchased air and sea platforms feature cockpit equipment and armaments from various manufacturers. As a result, India has enjoyed access to the maximum number of technologies that are available on the market.

Due to the stable trend in India's MTC towards focusing on the quality and technological prowess of purchased products the importance of price factors has declined. For several decades, India has been purchasing large consignments of armaments together with licenses allowing domestic production. However, the Indian industry is currently experiencing considerable difficulties as it tries to develop licensed production of high-end weapons systems. The country's defence industry does not seem able to substitute arms imports in the foreseeable future.

Since the early 1980s, India has been trying to implement its own national programs to manufacture major weapons systems. To date, most projects have not entered serial production, with the results India has demonstrated in creating an advanced national defence-industrial complex being far from encouraging. Limited success has been achieved only in ballistic missiles production.

Meanwhile, the practice of organizing tenders for arms and military equipment purchase as a means of internal political struggle has emerged in India. The domestic political opposition invariably declares that tender results do not serve the country's best interests and has accused the ruling party of corruption. This practice has now resulted in extreme delays around tender procedures: the bidding process can last a very long time due to fears it could trigger a political crisis or that tender results could be cancelled and the tender reopened.

STATUS, PROBLEMS AND PROSPECTS OF RUSSIA-INDIA MILITARY-TECHNICAL COOPERATION

Russia is a major exporter of arms and military equipment to India. Russia accounts for 55.3 percent of all purchases made by India in this area in 2008-2011. Overall the portfolio of orders contracted for March 2013 amounts to $10.3 billion.

For reference. The United Kingdom was the second-largest exporter of military equipment to India in 2008-2011 at $2.007 billion. Orders booked in 2003-2010 comprise $4.094 billion. Israel ranks third at $1.839 billion and has an order book of $3.452 billion. The United States ranks fourth with $1.144 billion (and $3.986 billion on order), while Italy comes fifth with $690 million (and an order book of $4.23 billion). Overall, India imported armaments from 14 countries in 2008-20116.

In 2012-2015, Russia's share in the Indian arms market will fall to 37.5 percent, whereas maintaining leadership in absolute figures. This is related to several factors:

- India's diversification policy;
- Russia's inability to compete with other countries on a full range of purchased arms and military equipment (while India increases the number of areas for MTC);
- Our main competitors' consent to supply licenses for military production and the most advanced weapons to India (which they often refused to do previously);
- Indian armed forces' efforts to acquire the most combat-effective systems with payment issues being moved to the background.

The Indian party has consistently raised issue of state control over the quality of products and after-sales services exported expressing dissatisfaction with the "superfluous" (intermediary) links in the Russia-India military-technical cooperation.

MTC with India may have a favourable effect on the industrial structure of the national economy due to the programs' long-term nature and consistently significant purchase volumes. There is a clear need to approach the Indian market with unique solutions and technologies on operations and sub-strategic levels (in the area of missile defence, missile warning systems, nuclear-powered submarines, and missile technology) along with the opportunity to link these deliveries with conventional arms procurement. Russia may also join the Indian program to build INS Arihant nuclear submarines (multiple flaws were identified after the first submarine was built).

It is necessary to find a breakthrough branch in military-technical cooperation with India. This could be a major project for a national missile warning system and air defence development (the Indian system is based on outdated Soviet technology). The Indian party is very interested in developing a modern AMD system. This is an area in which the Russian Federation is in a position to offer India new developments, particularly in long-range air defence systems demonstrating extensive anti-missile potential, such as the Antey-2500 military air defence system, the Tor-M2E-2 and Buk-M2E anti-aircraft missile systems, and new modifications such as the C-400 (C-500 for the future). The Russian party could facilitate the joint design and production of a fifth-generation light fighter, given the advanced aviation know-how that already exists in the national defence complex.

The two countries' participation in joint projects involving third countries (chiefly Israel) seems a promising and profitable avenue for both parties to explore. Criticism consistently levelled by the Indian side over delays in spare parts delivery for imported Russian military equipment is largely caused by the Russian side's cumbersome bureaucracy. Claims to Russian enterprises go through Rosoboronexport, resulting in delays that may last several months. Reputable companies should be selectively allowed to perform independent operational interventions.

The time schedules followed by Western competitors should be used as benchmarks (replacing a unit normally takes 3-4 days). There is also a clear need to align servicing operations and provide technical maintenance for Russian equipment through to the end of service life, as other vendors do when dealing with India.

It would also be advisable to establish and finance an adequate and aggressive information support strategy for military cooperation, neutralizing the negative propaganda funded by Russian companies' competitors. Particular attention should be paid to Indian professional defence and technology sector magazines, while special emphasis should be placed on working with them. These magazines play a crucial role in shaping the opinion of the national military elite and that of the individuals that make decisions on MTC.

INDIA-RUSSIA TIES: STRATEGIC COOPERATION TO TRANSACTIONAL ALLIANCE

The attention of the nation is focussed on President Obama's visit as the chief guest for this year's Republic Day parade since the announcement was made. In the bargain, the recent visit by President Vladimir Putin of Russia has not been given the important it merits.

President Putin met with Prime Minister Narendra Modi in December 2014 for the 15th India-Russia annual summit, a relationship that has been described as a "special and privileged" strategic partnership since it was signed in 2000. India's new policy to diversify its sources of defence procurement, especially its reliance on Western weapons platforms, has not been appreciated by Russia and the relationship has deteriorated into a transactional rather than a strategic one.

The erstwhile Soviet Union and its successor state Russia had stood by India on Jammu and Kashmir over several difficult decades. One-sided UN Security Council resolutions on J&K were vetoed by the Russians many times.

The Indo-Soviet treaty of "peace, friendship and cooperation", signed before the 1971 War with Pakistan, stood India in good stead. Though the agreement was not a military alliance, India was perceived by the US and its Western allies to have joined the Soviet camp.

In its foreign policy, India has not lagged behind in supporting Soviet or Russian positions. The Soviet Union invaded Afghanistan in December 1979. India was privately opposed to the ill-conceived intervention as it brought the Cold War to India's neighbourhood, but opted not to condemn the invasion publicly. Similarly, India is closer to the Russian position on Iran's violation of its NPT commitments than to the US approach of imposing sanctions and holding out military threats.

The collapse of the Soviet Union in December 1991 and the consequent end of the Cold War led to the emergence of a unipolar world order with the US as the sole super power. In the mid-1990s, Boris Yeltsin's Russia and Jiang Zemin's China repeatedly made joint statements favouring a "multipolar world," while denouncing "unipolar domination.

" In the prevailing era of strategic uncertainty, Russian Prime Minister Yevgeny Primakov floated idea of China-India-Russia "strategic triangle" in December 1998. China was disinterested and India's stand was one of ambivalence.

China had opened up to the US and was building a strong business relationship. It was following Deng Xiao Ping's doctrine of "strategic patience", expressed in the "22-character" strategy: Hide your capacity, bide your time..." China gradually began to integrate itself with the global economy under the cloak of its self-proclaimed "peaceful rise".

However, China simultaneously launched a large-scale drive for military modernisation and, combined with its recent assertiveness, this made its Asian neighbours wary of its growing power and influence. Some of them see the US as a declining power and have begun to hedge their bets.

Russia has been apprehensive of NATO's creep forward policy, moves towards an enlarged European Union, the planned forward deployment of ballistic missiles defence – ostensibly aimed at Iran but of equal effectiveness against Russian nuclear-tipped missiles, and the pro-active wooing of erstwhile Soviet states like Ukraine.

The era of "Cold Peace" has dawned over Eastern Europe and Putin's Russia has begun to gradually drift towards China. However, it is a relationship on the rebound and remains unrequited. Due to Russia's apprehension about China's military assertiveness, the China-Russia strategic partnership is unlikely to gather momentum despite the US "pivot" or strategy of re-balancing to the Indo-Pacific.

Defence technology cooperation

India's acquisition of weapons and defence equipment from Russia has been the most enduring part of the India-Russia strategic partnership. Almost 60 to 70 per cent of India's defence imports are still sourced from Russia. Russia offered strategic technologies to India when India was being subjected to technology denial regimes. Civil nuclear cooperation between the two countries has a long history. Russia gave India nuclear submarines on lease and provided assistance for the development of the cryogenic rocket engine.

State-of-the-art fighter-bombers, including the MiG-25 strategic reconnaissance aircraft, were sold to India. The two countries cooperated on the Russian GPS satellite system GLONASS. The Russians had offered India the 300/S-300V BMD system way back in the mid-1990s. During the December 2014 summit meeting, it was agreed that Russia will supply 12 nuclear power reactors over the next 20 years. Russia also supports India's quest for membership of the Nuclear Suppliers Group (NSG)and the other related groups.

The Soviet Union sold hi-tech weapons and defence equipment to India at "friendship prices" and on the basis of barter trade as India did not have sufficient foreign exchange reserves. However, it remained a buyer-seller, patron-client relationship. While fighter aircraft and tanks were manufactured under licence in India, no transfer of technology (ToT) ever took place and India's defence technology base remained low. The coproduction of the BrahMos supersonic cruise missile is the only example of a successful joint venture.

The decline of Russia's defence industry after the collapse of the Soviet Union had an adverse impact on India's defence procurement. Defence production from Russia declined by almost 90 per cent in five years. India found it difficult to obtain spare parts, get its equipment overhauled and seek upgrades. There were unacceptable time and cost overruns in executing pending orders. The five-year delay and the three-fold cost escalation of INS Vikramaditya (Admiral Gorshkov) aircraft carrier is a typical example.

Though these challenges are gradually being overcome, the Russian defence industry has fallen behind the West in the development of cutting-edge weapons technologies. Future defence technology cooperation will be undertaken in keeping with Prime Minister Modi's push to "make in India" with Russian help will need to demonstrate their competitiveness and enter into JVs with Indian public and private sector companies to bid for future contracts.

INDIA-RUSSIA DEFENCE COOPERATION

Defence cooperation is an important pillar of the India-Russia strategic partnership. It is guided by the Programme for Military Technical Cooperation signed between the two countries which is valid, at present till 2020. It enshrines the interest of the two governments to further develop and strengthen the military and technical cooperation in the sphere of research and development, production and after sales support of armament systems and various military equipment. The two sides also have periodic exchanges of armed forces personnel and military exercises.

India and Russia have an institutionalized structure to oversee the complete range of issues of military technical cooperation. The India-Russia Inter-Governmental Commission on Military Technical Cooperation (IRIGC-MTC), set up in 2000, is at the apex of this structure. The two Defence Ministers meet annually, alternately in Russia and India, to discuss and review the status of ongoing projects and other issues of military technical cooperation. There are two Working Groups and seven Sub-Groups under the IRIGC-MTC, which review and discuss an array of military technical issues. In 2008, a high level committee called the High Level Monitoring Committee (HLMC) was set up with Defence Secretary from the Ministry of Defence of the Republic of India and Director of Federal Service for Military Technical Cooperation (FSMTC) from the Russian Federation as its co-chairs.

Bilateral projects currently underway include indigenous production of T-90 tanks and Su-30-MKI aircraft, supply of MiG-29-K aircraft and Kamov-31 and Mi-17 helicopters, upgrade of MiG-29 aircraft and supply of Multi-Barrel Rocket Launcher Smerch.

Over the years, cooperation in the military technical sphere has evolved from a purely buyer-seller relationship to joint research, design development and production of state of the art military platforms. Production of the Brahmos cruise missile is an example of this trend. The two countries are also engaged in joint design and development of the Fifth Generation Fighter Aircraft and Multi-Role Transport Aircraft.

Joint exercises between the two Armed Forces are held under the title "INDRA". In the year 2014, Joint exercises of Army, Navy and the Air force were conducted. Joint exercises for the year 2015 for all the three services are under consideration.

RUSSIA'S CURRENT PERCEPTIONS OF ITS RELATIONSHIP WITH INDIA

This analysis would be incomplete if current Russian perceptions of its relationship with India are not taken into account before reaching conclusions. Leaving aside political statements of Russian leaders, a sampling of views by Russian political analysts are quoted below to highlight the emerging trends:

Vladimir Baranovosky

"In an era of massive realignment, Russia appreciates India's continuing insistence with non-aligned status and its caution and restraint in development of ties with the United States of America, especially in the area of arms transfers."

"India's ascendance to the status of a declared nuclear weapon power has produced mixed feelings in Russia... However, the very fact of India going 'nuclear may be seen by Russia as devaluing its own nuclear arsenal which is almost the sole remaining symbol of its great power status and an important bargaining chip in the international arena."

"It seems clear, however, that both powers assign each other considerable roles in their respective foreign policy calculations. In particular, the rapprochement is generated by India's search for higher international status and Russia's desire to prevent further erosion of its global role."

Vladimir Moskalenko & Tatiana Shaunna

"The appearance of two new possessors of nuclear arms in South Asia is a serious challenge to Russia's National Security."

At the same time an improvement of Russia's relations with Pakistan as the second party in the South Asia confrontation seems possible and must run in parallel to further expansion and strengthening of relations with India."

Felix N Yurolov

"With the emergence of a new President of the Russian Federation, it has to strengthen its eastern policy by making it more concrete, more substantial, and more dynamic. Russian-Indian bi-lateral relations and international cooperation between the two countries must be a very important part of this policy." The signing of the 'Declaration of Strategic Partnership' between Russia and India should not be further delayed."

"It is also in Russia's interests to call for support of India's entry to UN Security Council as a permanent member.

"In any case we have to admit that the fundamental changes in the world balance of forces have had a direct bearing on Russia-India relations.

While formulating their strategy of national interests and security, Russia and India should fully take into account the radical changes that have taken place in the international system. They cannot ignore the new realities."

These are very interesting Russian thoughts, but somehow they seem to compartmentalise Russia. India focus to South Asia only. The Russian analysts are also silent on the strategic coalition that has emerged between Russia and China and how it impacts on the India-Russia relations. Felix Yurolov (the last named Russian analyst) seems to be conceding that by implied analysis, namely, each country to take into account its own national interests and security.

Concluding Analysis

In state craft and foreign policy formulations, as Lord Salisbury once stated that there are no permanent friends or foes, only permanent interests. The same dictum applies to India-Russia relations also. The changed parameters of Russia's foreign policy according an overriding priority to its China relationship and building up a Russia-China coalition aimed at the United States unipolarity, imperatively demands that India too carries out a re-appraisal of what was once a strategic relationship between India and Russia.

When Russia made a conscious decision to enter into a strategic coalition with China, it could surely not have been oblivious to India's threat perceptions about China. It could have been foreseen that Gorbachev's concessions to China would release her from her Pacific preoccupations and permit additional Chinese military formations for deployment on its Southern Peripheries complicating India's security problems. Russian upgradation of Chinese offensive capabilities cannot be exclusively confined for use against USA; they could be used elsewhere. However, Russia in its defence could argue, that these determinations were made in Russia's national interests. Similar India prerogatives need to be conceded by Russia, without rancour.

While Russia in pursuance of its national interests and security has cast its lot with China, India's national interests and security needs demand that:

* India moves away from its erstwhile strategic relationship with Russia and exercise alternative options.
* India drastically reduces its military dependency on Russian weapon systems and spares. Immediate diversification is the answer.

* India unambiguously declares that it is not interested in creation of any multi-polar structures and especially not the kind being advocated of a Russia-China-India triangle. There are many other 'poles' which will emerge in the natural evolution of the global structure.
* Many years ago, USA gave an assurance that American arms given to Pakistan in aid will not be used against India. Pakistan did use the same. There is no guarantee that Russian arms given to China will not be used against India in any future India- China conflict. India must take into account enhanced Chinese offensive capabilities arising from Russian arms supplies.

India and Russia can surely continue to have good friendly relations based on their proximity of the past. India and Russia can surely look for convergence of interests in the international field. However, seeking convergence with Russia cannot be at the expense of India's quest for newer strategic cooperative link with countries like USA, France, Israel, Vietnam, Japan and South Africa. More realistically, and in tune with the emerging international system, it is Russia which would need to be more accommodative in seeking strategic convergence with India. India needs to be aware of the many alternative strategic options open to her, other than Russia, which the emerging international security environment provides her. India should be ready and have the will to play the 'India card'.

SOUTH ASIA AS A PLACE FOR PRIMAKOV INTELLIGENCE

India's position on Russian foreign policy sounds different from China's. India is far from Russia and has no shared border. Russia and India are rarely antagonistic toward each other, and are able to cooperate when there is a strong need to do so. In this sense, India seems to offer a perfect opportunity for Russia's "balance" foreign policy. Reviewing post-Cold War Russian foreign policy toward India, close attention should be paid to the two Soviet periods of "balance" policy before and after the Russo-Chinese military conflict of 1969.

The first period began with India achieving independence from British rule in 1946. Combatting US influence was Russia's top priority at the time. Russia never supported India unilaterally and balanced its position between India and Pakistan to maintain its interests against the US. In the 1950s when Pakistan joined the SEATO and the Baghdad Pact under the auspices of the US, The Soviet Union sought to weaken US influence in South Asia. Nikita Khrushchev supported India's position on Kashmir (that it belonged to India), which brought India closer to the Soviet Union, and then proposed to offer Pakistan economic aid and atomic technology for peaceful use in order to make a rapprochement with Pakistan.

In the 1960s, the Soviet Union revised its complete support for India on the Kashmir issue (Russia now believing that it should be negotiated between the parties concerned, while still backing India's position) and signed a barter trade agreement with Pakistan. In 1965, Pakistan's president visited Moscow and Premier Aleksei Kosygin, as a show of goodwill, organized the "Tashkent meeting" to mediate between the belligerents India and Pakistan. China's active influence was growing in the region.

China's geopolitical position toward South Asia is different from Russia's. China has a shared border with Afghanistan, Pakistan and India. China and India had serious disputes over the border and the status of Tibet. In the mid-1950s, China and India sought a policy of "good neighborliness" over the border to achieve a "balance" against the US, but it did not last long. War erupted on the border. The Soviet Union did not fully side with China, and this later proved to be one of the reasons that Soviet-Chinese relations deteriorated. Why did the Soviet Union not fully support China? It is true that the Soviet Union was tired of Chinese aggression against the US, exemplified by Mao Tsedong's assertion about a possible nuclear war against the US. The underlying reason was that South Asia was, for the Soviet Union, a space for "balancing" vis-à-vis the US. The Soviet Union seemed not to realize that Sino-Indian border antagonism could exceed the centripetal force between India and China against the US. The dissymmetry of India's positioning between Russia and China should have been considered.

After the border clash between the Soviet Union and China in 1969, the meaning of a South Asian space for the Soviet Union shifted to another dimension of the "balance" policy: "deterrence of a neighbouring power." The Soviet Union was inclined to rely on India to deter China, while China and Pakistan strengthened the axis in reaction. After the Soviet invasion of Afghanistan in 1979, the US strongly assisted Pakistan while India went out of its way not to criticize Soviet action. In South Asia, Soviet-Indian relations functioned as a balance against the China-Pakistan axis backed by the US. South Asia was the perfect place to test Primakov's maxim.

Back from Inertia to Balance

In the late Gorbachev era, Perestroika foreign policy, which assigned higher priority to the US, Europe and China, did not pay much attention to India. However, Mikhail Gorbachev visited India twice in 1986 and 1988 and played up their "traditional friendship" to others. In particular, the former was famous for the "Delhi Declaration." However, the declaration, entitled "For Principles of Non-Nuclear and Non-Violence in the World," obviously followed a Gorbachev initiative on the "disarmament of nuclear weapons" and a "new world order" on the basis of the "New Thinking." The declaration was provocative to the US and was closely related to the unsuccessful Reykjavik summit with US President Ronald Regan in October 1986. On the other hand, India had concerns over Gorbachev's Vladivostok speech in which he urged Russia to "reconcile" with China and put forth his idea of building a comprehensive security regime in Asia.

At the time, the Soviet priority in Asia was with China and the war in Afghanistan. After 1989, when Gorbachev withdrew the Soviet army from Afghanistan and paid a historic visit to Beijing, India was low on the Soviet Union's foreign policy priority list. In this context, its relations with Pakistan had a chance of improving, but Pakistan overestimated the "Delhi Declaration" as a sign of close partnership between the Soviet Union and India. Foreign Minister Eduard Shevardnadze's visit to Islamabad did little to improve Soviet-Pakistan relations. Gorbachev next turned his attention to improving its ties with Japan. India officially kept its position as best partner in South Asia for the Soviet Union, but economic relations were downsized. In fact, bilateral trade had waned to somewhere between the $3 billion and $4 billion level, similar to its bilateral trade with China, but below that with Japan. Soviet-India relations were nominal at best and a de facto vacuum at worst. Neither the Soviet Union nor India showed much interest in improving their relations.

Following the birth of the new Russia, the early foreign policy of Russia was more pro-Western than Gorbachev's, but it did not necessarily ignore its Asian "far neighbours": Gennady Burbulis visited in May and Ruslan Khasbulatov visited in August 1992. At the end of 1992, Foreign Minister Kozyrev, departing from Russia's pro-Western policy, naturally reminded his fellow Russians of India's importance. He tried to redefine Russo-Indian relations in the post-Cold War period. President Yeltsin visited Delhi and signed a friendship and cooperation treaty, as well as certain agreements such as rescheduling of Indian debt and military cooperation, including rocket technology transfer.

It is, however, apparent that the new treaty was a step back from the previous one: the new treaty omitted the word "peace" and the clause "mutual consultant in crisis." Military cooperation was also suspended. President Yeltsin suspended the transfer of technology to India, accepting US concerns regarding the situation.

Their economic relations faltered as well: less than one billion dollars from 1992 to 1994, and not exceeding more than $2 billion since 1995. In contrast, India's new open economic policy was given a warm welcome by the US, and India enjoyed a sort of honeymoon with the US because of the keen attention paid to Asia by the Clinton administration, which came to a halt following the exposure of India's nuclear capabilities in May 1998. Russo-Indian relations are the only variable subordinate to US-Indian relations or to US-Russian relations. The better the latter becomes, the worse the former becomes, and vice versa.

Following the deterioration of US-Russian relations in 1994, Russia began to urgently retreat from the prolonged inertia of Russo-Indian relations. Russia did not hesitate to sell its most sophisticated weapons to India; big deals concerning the sale of MIG–29, Su30–MKI, S–300 and submarines were quickly and satisfactory arranged. Energy cooperation including the construction of an atomic station and space exploitation facility was advanced.

India's traditional dependence on Soviet weapons in the Cold War and Indian tactics of maintaining its distance from the US caused India to move toward accepting a Russian proposal. After the US imposed an economic embargo on India after India's nuclear experiment in 1998, Russia only verbally criticized India and did not participate in the embargo. With Russia seeming to be a good "card" for Indian interests, Primakov visited Delhi and disclosed the idea of a "strategic triangle." India considered its relations with the US extremely important and vital to its interests, and much to Russia's dismay, maintained a cool attitude toward Russia.

Here, it is important to note the new dynamics of Russo-Indian relations that emerged in the mid-1990s. An independent Central Asia became a contributing factor to the dynamics in their relations.

Although India and Russia have no shared border, the area between the two countries had begun to transform, which had an effect on Russo-Indian relations. Since the early 1990s, India has been concerned about the stability of Central Asia because of the ruling Taliban regime in Afghanistan and the civil war in Tajikistan that had the potential to adversely affect the Kashmir issue. The disputed region of Kashmir controlled by Pakistan shares a border with both China and Afghanistan. Border politics in this context are analysed with the presence of Pakistan in the region.

Pakistan in Border Politics

While the differences between the Russian approach to India and the Indian approach to Russia were apparent, Pakistan kept a close eye on Russia. To insure its own security against India, Pakistan sought to "balance" the great powers in the region. Undoubtedly, the major actors are the US, China and Russia. Although the US has been Pakistan's most important partner, US support of Pakistan has been contingent on Pakistan's ability to contain or conduct war against such "big enemies" as the Soviet Union in the Cold War era or the Taliban and al Qaeda in the "post-9/11" era. US concerns about Pakistan's Islamic statehood and political instability, e.g., repeated military coups, also need to be factored in. In contrast to the political regime of Pakistan, which leaves little to be desired or emulated, the US admires Indian democracy. The better US-Indian relations, the worse US-Pakistan relations.

Concerning the Soviet Union, Pak-Soviet relations were relatively good in the 1960s, but after Russo-Chinese military conflicts and the third Pak-Indian war, they deteriorated (although it should be noted that Premier Zulfikar Ali Bhutto did visit Moscow in 1974, so relations were not completely frozen). The decisive halt to relations happened after the Soviet invasion of Afghanistan in 1979. Pakistan was now a de facto "enemy" of the Soviet Union.

After the Soviet withdrawal from Afghanistan, the Soviet-Chinese reconciliation changed the basis of Soviet-Pak relations. But Gorbachev's "indifference" (particularly on Pakistan) to South Asia and the collapse of the Soviet Union lessened the chances of drastic improvement.

RUSSIA-INDIA PARTNERSHIP LIFTED TO NEW HEIGHTS

This visit reinforced interests of both states in maintaining their traditionally close and friendly relationship and in strengthening a multipolar world order. In recent times, both India and Russia have been pursuing a multi-vector approach in their foreign policies. This visit was Indian Prime Minister Modi's second visit to Russia within a year's time; his first visit was in July 2015 to Ufa (Russian Federation) to participate in the BRICS (Brazil-Russia-India-China-South Africa) and SCO (Shanghai Cooperation Organisation) Summits.

The bilateral relationship between India and Russia was revived with the declaration of a Strategic Partnership between the two countries during the visit of President Putin to India in the year 2000. Since then the Indo-Russian relationship has diversified enormously and today it is uniquely strong and also expanding in the areas of defence, nuclear energy, hydrocarbons, space research, science & technology. Prime Minister Modi's recent visit re-activated the ties between two countries. During this visit India and Russia signed number of significant agreements, including the agreement for manufacturing of Kamov 226 helicopters in India. This is going to be the first project for a major defence platform under Modi's 'Make in India' policy, and also to enhance the defence partnership between Russia and India. Cooperation on number of other significant defence projects would also boost defence cooperation.

Bilateral cooperation in nuclear energy is increasing over the years. India and Russia made progress regarding twelve Russian nuclear reactors at different sites. The agreement on nuclear cooperation will increase Indian manufacturing content for these reactors. This also supports Prime Minister Modi's 'Make in India' mission. Other benefits from this agreement would include research and development, construction of nuclear plants and reprocessing of spent fuel. The signing of this landmark inter-governmental agreement on the peaceful use of atomic energy between the two countries has the potential to expand the horizon of nuclear relationship between the two Nations.

Prime Minister Modi mentioned that Russia being world's largest reserves of hydrocarbons can be a critical source of energy security for India; hence, the agreements signed for Indian investments in Russian hydrocarbon sector will enhance energy cooperation between two countries. Agreement for cooperation for geologic survey, exploration and production of on-shore hydrocarbons between Rosneft Oil Company, Oil India Limited and Indian Oil Corporation Limited has been signed during this visit.

India and Russia are also moving towards expanding the economic relationships which is the weakest link in the bilateral cooperation. It has been observed that in spite of accelerated growth and immense opportunities in each other's economy, statistics show business transaction is much less than the real potential.

Promises had been made by the leaders of both countries earlier, but not much has happened. However, to put these words into practice and strengthen the economic relationship, India has created a special notified zone to facilitate direct trade between the world's largest uncut diamond exporters (Russia and India process 90% of the world's uncut diamonds and will now cooperate in this sector successfully).

Also the work on logistics is going on to make trade and economic cooperation faster.

The Green Corridor project took off and the International North South Transit Corridor (INSTC) through Iran is expected to significantly reduce transportation time and cost. Now India and Russia are also moving forward to fulfil the India-Eurasian Economic Union (EEU) Free Trade Agreement. This will also benefit to connect Central Asia easily. The agreements and the announcements made during this visit gave confidence that now India and Russia will see huge increase in investments and trade from both directions.

Prime Minister Modi and President Putin assured strong commitment to deepen the cooperation in the international arena too. Prime Minister The leaders agreed that early political settlement through dialogue in West Asia is essential for restoring stability and containing extremism in the region. There is a close synergy in Indo-Russia perspectives. The joint declaration reinforced the warmth that exists between the two countries. Although differences arise over certain issues on certain occasions, the overall parallelism in the India-Russia relationship definitely symbolizes the trust that still exists between the two nations.

RUSSIA-INDIA STRATEGIC PARTNERSHIP: HAVE WE HIT A PLATEAU?

The President of the Russian Federation achieved yet another success while treading the "three seas" at the BRICS Summit in Goa, especially for large Russian companies that are growing their businesses in India. However, despite the fact that Moscow and New Delhi were able to reach new agreements on military and technical cooperation and energy, both countries will have to take a serious look at their approach to building relations if they want to take their partnership to the next level.

The BRICS Summit took place in Goa on October 15–16 and reaffirmed yet again the close partner ties enjoyed by Russia and India. In keeping with tradition, the BRICS platform was chosen as the venue for preliminary agreements and contracts on military and technical cooperation and energy to be signed. However, despite the impressive set of documents signed in Goa, it would seem that cooperation between Moscow and New Delhi has lost its former dynamism and, in terms of size and import, is far from the declared "Strategic Partnership" that has characterized Russia–India relations since 2000. The latest summit can serve as a convincing reason to try and discover exactly what it is that could threaten the partnership between Russia and India in the future and what is preventing this relationship from moving to the next level.

A Farewell to Arms

As always, the recent BRICS Summit was fruitful for the Russian defence industry. Military and technical cooperation traditionally serves as a driver of the Russia–India partnership. Moscow is the largest supplier of military equipment to India, with contracts worth more than $5 billion signed since 2012. At the same time, India is the world's biggest importer of military equipment, and it is little surprise that Russian suppliers are facing increasing competition on the Indian market. An intergovernmental agreement was signed in Goa on the supply of modern Russian S-400 missile systems to India. A contract worth somewhere in the region of $4.5 billion is expected to be signed in early 2016. The sides also signed an agreement on the purchase by India of Russian naval ships. In addition, an agreement has been reached between Russia's Rosoboronexport and the Indian company HAL on the creation of a joint venture to localize production of Kamov Ka-226 helicopters in India.

Although India has been the leading purchaser of Russian weapons since 2007, Russia's share in the Indian arms market has been shrinking gradually in recent years. The trend is unmistakable. The first hints appeared in 2012, when the Russian MiG-35 lost out in a tender for the purchase and localization of production of 126 fighter jets for the Indian Air Force to the French *Rafale*. By the end of 2014, Russia had relinquished its position as India's leading arms supplier to United States

The most recent tenders have demonstrated that tactical and technical products may not be enough in the long term to secure the custom of the Indian side.

Russian companies have failed primarily because India considers developing its own defence industry to be a priority, while the Russian side is not prepared to accept all of the conditions connected with localizing arms production, including as part of the *Make in India* programme to stimulate industrial production. The Indian Armed Forces are also unhappy with the fact that delivery deadlines have been missed. One of the most high-profile examples of this was the late delivery of the *Vikramaditya* (formerly the *Admiral Gorshkov*) aircraft carrier. It is against this background that the Indian political establishment is keeping a close, and rather exasperated, eye on the supplies of advanced weapon systems to China and the burgeoning military and technical cooperation between Russia and Pakistan.

Considering the amount of weaponry sold to India throughout the 2000s, it could be argued that Russia does not need to worry about losing the Indian market in the foreseeable future, as the Armed Forces are heavily dependent on supplies of Russian components. However, the most recent tenders have demonstrated that tactical and technical products may not be enough in the long term to secure the custom of the Indian side. New Delhi will expect foreign suppliers to make lucrative offers that involve the transfer of technologies so that it can create its own production base and develop the Indian defence industry.

Oil in Exchange for Investments

Energy is another source of pride in the Russia–India strategic partnership. In the long term, this could be of even greater benefit that the arms trade. And nuclear energy has been on the agenda of bilateral relations for a long time now. The official ceremony to mark the commissioning of the Kudankulam Nuclear Power Plant was held during the Summit in Goa, and the ground of units 3 and 4 was broken. In addition to nuclear energy, the oil and gas sector is also showing increasing promise in terms of bilateral cooperation. India has always shown great interest in purchasing Russian oil and gas, but the logistical difficulties, coupled with the fact that India could satisfy its energy needs by purchasing oil and gas in Europe, meant that Russian suppliers saw no benefit in developing such projects. However, it would be short-sighted to ignore the Indian market at a time like this: energy prices are low, and the Indian economy is stepping up oil imports faster than any other country, including China.

It would be short-sighted to ignore the Indian market at a time like this: energy prices are low, and the Indian economy is stepping up oil imports faster than any other country, including China.

Rosneft announced at the BRICS Summit that it has signed a deal, alongside its partner, the major independent oil trader *Trafigura,* to purchase the Indian company *Essar Oil* for around $13 billion. As part of deal, Rosneft will receive a 49-per cent stake in the Vadinar Refinery, the second largest refinery in India in terms of volume, as well as a chain of 2700 *Essar* gas stations. The oil will most likely be delivered from Venezuela, where Rosneft has production and exploration operations, and sold primarily on the Indian market, or exported from there to South Asia and South East Asia. The deal has strategic importance for the Russian company: the acquisition of *Essar* will give it a presence on the world's fastest growing oil market, with 70 per cent of its requirements coming from imports. Moving forward, it may be able to apply pressure on suppliers from the Gulf, which have rushed to fill the void left by Russia after it was forced to withdraw from the European markets following the sanctions.

While Russian oil companies, faced with falling prices and international sanctions, are interested in foreign processing companies, the Indian side is doing the exact opposite, seeking to gain access to the sources of raw materials. In May 2016, the Indian company *ÎNGC Videsh* bought a 15-per cent stake in the Vankor Field from Rosneft, and in September it signed an agreement to purchase another 11 per cent. At the same time, Rosneft is discussing the possibility of selling a further 23.9 per cent of the field with a consortium of Indian investors that includes *Oil India, Indian Oil Corporation* and *Bharat Petro Resources*. Vankor Field will account for the largest amount of Indian investment in oil production in Russia since Indian companies purchased shares in Sakhalin-1.

The role of India as a potential investor in the Russian oil and gas industry is growing. This much is clear from information coming out of India (but which has yet to be confirmed in Russia) suggesting that Moscow is considering India as a possible participant in the upcoming partial privatization of Rosneft.

Getting Russian gas onto the Indian market appears to be a much more difficult proposition. The contract between Gazprom and GAIL for the supply of 2.5 million tonnes of liquefied natural gas starting in 2018/2019 for a period of 25 years was signed back in 2012. However, development of the Shtokman field, which was to supply the raw materials, has been frozen, and Gazprom does not currently have the output capacity to fulfil its obligations. It is expected that the gas will be delivered to India from the Yamal LNG plant, the first train of which is planned to be commissioned in late 2017. In addition to the technical difficulties, it seems that Gazprom will also be faced with commercial risks: the fall in gas prices has caused India to re-examine the delivery prices in its long-term contracts.

Have We Hit a Plateau?

Unfortunately, the isolated successes of Russian arms dealers and energy companies in India that were covered in glorious detail during the Goa Summit do not alter the fact that the strategic partnership between Russia and India has seemingly hit a plateau. And without serious political will, this plateau will not be overcome in the near future.

When the Declaration on Strategic Partnership between the Republic of India and the Russian Federation was signed in 2000, the trade turnover between Russia and India was a modest $1.5 billion. The foreign trade departments of the two countries decided then to increase this rather embarrassing figure to $10 billion (which is far more fitting of a strategic partnership) by 2010. That goal was reached only in 2012, however, which turned out to be the peak year in terms of trade turnover between Russia and India. Trade dropped to $7.83 billion in 2015, which falls well below Moscow's expectations of its cooperation with New Delhi.

Unfortunately, the isolated successes of Russian arms dealers and energy companies in India that were covered in glorious detail during the Goa Summit do not alter the fact that the strategic partnership between Russia and India has seemingly hit a plateau.

The devaluation of the rouble obviously had an impact on this drop in 2015. But this should not divert our attention from the systemic problems. the old model of partnership based on cooperation in strategic industries (or, in simpler terms, in industries where the government has a big presence), has exhausted its growth potential. India has been paying special attention to its relations with developed countries ever since the current government under the leadership of Narendra Modi came to power – the United States, Japan, Australia, France, Germany and the United Kingdom. As far as the Indian leadership is concerned, these countries are sources of investments, investments that India sorely needs in order to modernize its infrastructure and speed up economic growth. With this in mind, relations with Russia are no longer a major priority in India's foreign policy objectives. And there may not be enough administrative leverage to further stimulate the development of an economic partnership on orders from above.

The old model of partnership based on cooperation in strategic industries has exhausted its growth potential.

In order to bring economic ties to a new level, it is necessary to expand the product range. This will allow private companies and ordinary citizens, and not only state corporations, to contribute to the trade turnover between the two countries. Relations between Russia and the other Asian giant, China, are developing according to this model. To compare: trade turnover between Russia and China totalled roughly $68 billion in 2014. And we are not just talking about arms and raw materials here. Russians spent around $3.5 billion in Chinese online stores in 2014, which is around the same price as the contract for the supply of the S-400 missile systems to India. And customers spend an average of less than $20 on these online orders.

If the partnership between Russia and India does not go beyond the "strategic" sectors in the near future and does not expand to include goods and services, then relations between Moscow and Delhi risk being reduced to an investment and economic partnership of little note.

4

Russia, China, and India Overcome Friction in their Relations

The Russia-China partnership has clearly helped to foster bilateral relations after more than two decades of tension and hostility. This partnership has also enhanced the international standing of both countries. At the same time, however, political trust is still rather weak. Moscow and particularly the Russian Far East are clearly worried that the further economic decline of that region will lead to its abandoning by Russians and even Chinese occupation.

China is not perceived by the majority of Russian experts as an immediate military threat, because it is not expected to close the gap with Russia in nuclear and conventional weapons anytime soon. However, more and more Russian commentators, including in the military, are worried about the consequences for Russia of arming China with sophisticated Russian weapons while the Russian army itself cannot afford to have them.

Russia's growing political, economic, and military dependence on China has provoked a certain alarm and anxiety in Russia's academic and political circles. Alexei Bogaturov believes that in spite of impressive rapprochement, Russia and China remain countries that have historically been in conflict and that the geopolitical source of the conflict has not been removed or reduced. Hence, he argues against attempts to pick China as an ally or key partner in the region. Such views are not rare in Russia, even among government officials, in spite of a general official euphoria and an informal taboo on anti-Chinese comments. Common views toward US politics and close military cooperation may not be enough to sustain and enhance the "strategic partnership" between Russia and China. To make it complete, the two countries will have to get rid of their traditional suspicion of each other and engage in a stable and long-term economic cooperation. The relationship between India and China also has an important influence on the character of regional order and significant geopolitical implications. Friction in this bilateral relationship could have direct effects on China's relations with other neighbours. Stable and cooperative relations between India and China build trust and contribute to Beijing's own sense of security and confidence, providing a counterbalance should other important relationships deteriorate.

The near-rapprochement of relations (driven by the mutual consensus that economic development should have priority) between India and China diffuses, but does not dispel, three decades of friction. Four of the five primary causes of disquiet in India-China relations have been addressed by both powers: India's values-driven Tibet policy has ceased;

Chinese support for secessionist insurgents in Assam and the North East has been withdrawn; the collapse of the Soviet Union reduces Chinese fears of a containment-driven strategic nexus; and, most important, tensions stemming from border disputes between India and China are addressed, though not resolved, through the negotiation of confidence-building measures and agreements. The principal friction in contemporary relations between New Delhi and Beijing is India's belief (apparently well-founded) that China provides nuclear-related military technology and hardware to Pakistan. This abrasion is compartmentalized from India's overall bilateral relationship with Beijing. (New Delhi may be reassured by China's decision to join, and work constructively with, the Non-Proliferation Treaty Exporters Committee [or Zangger Committee].) New Delhi's preference for longer-term prudence in its relationship with China is one consequence of China's military nuclear exports to Pakistan.

India's approach to the management of tensions with China offers important lessons for other regional actors in how to manage relations (especially on sensitive issues) with China. New Delhi has handled Beijing more successfully than Washington has during the corresponding period. India and China have established and maintained regular reciprocal high-level personal visits between political leaders. Both states have improved trade relations and take care to compartmentalize intractable issues that continue to irritate long-standing tensions. Such a policy has perhaps returned dividends of its own with China in turn assuming a "position of `careful neutrality' on Kashmir." In contrast to recent US policy on China, India takes care to respect the principle of noninterference in the internal affairs of another state and eschews a values-driven foreign policy. These developments are especially significant given the depth of India's embedded longer-term strategic concerns with China and the record of mutual tension that has only eased in recent years. India's democratic status also may make it an attractive partner to those East Asian states condemned by the United States for abusing human rights or for falling short of democratic standards. The renewed Russian-Indian strategic partnership, fuelled by common concern regarding Islamic revivalism, has thwarted Moscow's initial intention to follow a more balanced policy in South Asia, improving in particular its relations with Pakistan. Instead, Moscow-Islamabad links have further deteriorated, especially because of the latter's pro-Taliban role in Afghanistan prior to recent events. Moscow's strategic interest in India motivates Moscow to promote India's inclusion into the leading forums and institutions of the Asia-Pacific. Having become a member of the Asia-Pacific Economic Cooperation (APEC) organization, Moscow is now backing New Delhi's bid for membership in this regional body. During consultations with the Indian Foreign Ministry in November 1998, Russian Deputy Foreign Minister Grigory Karasin noted that "Russia will try its best to help India develop ties with APEC and eventually to join the organization."

Although Russia and India have renounced an openly anti-Chinese policy, both countries continue to share suspicion and fear toward China. In spite of Moscow's public denunciation of India's nuclear tests in 1998, Russia appreciates India's concern about adequate military preparation in case of Chinese aggression. Moscow supports India not only morally, but also through the resumption of arms supplies, which, after a brief pause in the early 1990s, have been steadily increasing.

INDO-RUSSIAN RELATIONS IN COLD WAR ERA

The end of the Second World War in summer of 1945 was followed by a new type of war known as Cold War in which Soviet Union and the USA were hostile rivals. In this war each side barked at other but could not dare to bite for the fear that the next war would be fought with the nuclear weapons which would cause irreparable loss of men and material on the both sides.

Relations in pre-independence period during cold war era

On October 29, 1946, addressing the United Nations General Assembly, the Soviet Foreign Minister said, "It is high time that the just demands of India were recognized...... And yet, have we not heard here in the General Assembly India's appeal for support or assistance?

We cannot turn a deaf ear to all this". As India was a member of the United Nations, under the UN Charter, mentioned this, the Soviet Foreign Minister declared that "India's relationship with Britain should be based on sovereign equality." On the next day, in an interview to Reuter, Mrs. Vijaya Lakshmi Pandit, leader of the Indian delegation to United Nations Organisation, welcoming Soviet Foreign Minister's speech said that it was "a sign of understanding and friendship between our two countries".

On March 14, 1947 in a speech in the Central Assembly Jawaharlal Nehru stated that the question of sending an economic mission to the Soviet Union to study the results of successive Russian (Soviet) economic plans and other similar proposals would be taken up after the establishment of diplomatic relations. Simultaneous announcements were made both in Moscow and New Delhi that the USSR and India "Being desirous of maintaining and further strengthening the friendly relations existing between India and USSR, the Government of India and the Government of the USSR have decided to exchange diplomatic missions at Embassy level."

It is to be mentioned here that the Soviet Government send E.P. Yerzin to New Delhi for talks with the Indian Government for establishing diplomatic relation with India. Mr. Yerzin met Jawaharlal Nehru a number of times. Finally the decision of establishing diplomatic relations were taken by the two governments. As a result on June 25, Mrs. Vijaya Lakshmi Pandit was appointed as the first Indian Ambassador to the Soviet Union and on August 13, 1947 she presented her credentials to the Soviet President Shvernik at the Kremlin just two days before India's independence.

Indo-USSR Relations in Nehru Era

India got independence on 15th of August, 1947. In Post-independence period on same day, Soviet Foreign Minister M. Molotov sent a congratulatory message to the Prime Minister of India, Jawaharlal Nehru, saying: *"I request you, Mr. Minister, to accept the congratulations of the Soviet Government and my personal ones together with very best wishes to you and the Indian people on the occasion of the national celebration in India of Independence Day."*

On October 23, 1947, the Government of the *Union of Soviet Socialist Republics (USSR)* announced the appointment of Kyrill V. Novikov as the first Soviet Envoy to India and on December 21, he, the Ambassador designate arrived in New Delhi and on January 1, 1948, he presented his credentials to Lord Mountbatten, the Governor General of India, as Soviet Ambassador to India. On September 9, 1949, Dr. Sarvepalli Radhakrishnan presented his credentials as Indian Ambassador to the Soviet Union.

In 1951, though not directly involved, India played a major role in bringing about a peaceful settlement of Korean War. She refused to support the US resolution calling China an aggressor in Korean war and supported the Soviet proposal for a cease-fire along the 38th parallel. Nehru's appeal for ending hostilities in Korea was very well received in the Soviet Union. This was the Soviet Union, alone among Great Powers, who from very beginning since the accession of Kashmir to India in 1947, categorically *asserted that this State is an integral part of India.* The Soviet Union supported India in 1948 and 1952, whenever Kashmir question was raised in the Union Nations. On October 18, 1952, Mr. K.P.S. Menon took the charge of Indian Ambassador to the Soviet Union. On December 23, 1952, Soviet representative at the Security Council *reiterated his country's firm opposition to the introduction of foreign troops by the United Nations into Kashmir*. On July 4, 1953, I.A. Benediktov, the new Soviet Ambassador to India, presented his credentials to the President of India. Presenting his credentials to the Indian President, Dr. Rajendra Prasad, he declared: *"The Government of the Soviet Union is convinced that India is also interested in strengthening peace and extension of international cooperation, and this undoubtedly will favourably influence the development of international relations."*

On behalf of the Soviet Red Cross Society, the USSR Ambassador designate Menshikov presented Prime Minister Nehru a cheque of Rs. 296,560/- for the Prime Minister's Relief Fund as a token aid to the flood victims of the country on October 26, 1953. On the occasion of the 36th Anniversary of the Great October Socialist Revolution, Indian Prime Minister Jawaharlal Nehru sent his "most cordial greetings" as well as "sincerest good wishes" to the Soviet

Prime Minister. In this message Nehru also hoped that *"the existing friendship and goodwill between our two countries will be strengthened further to serve the cause of peace in the world."* The Soviet Union highly valued India's contribution in strengthening world peace. In April, 1954, Soviet Union proposed that the UN Disarmament Sub-Commission be enlarged and the Republic of India be included as member of the Sub-Commission. When the British representative, Sir Pierson Dixon, opposed India's inclusion, the Soviet representative, Andrei Vishinsky, strongly demanded India's inclusion. Here it is to be mentioned that India's role at the General Conference was highly appreciated by the Soviet Union. Later India's name was proposed by the Soviet Union as Chairman of three Control Commissions set up to supervise cease fire in Vietnam, Laos and Cambodia as Neutral Nation's Commission.

Nehru's role at the Bandung Conference of non-aligned nations in April, 1955 was highly appreciated in the Soviet Union. On his arrival in Moscow on June 7, 1955, a rousing reception was given to Jawaharlal Nehru, the first Prime Minister of Independent India. Nehru in reply to rousing reception declared that he had come to the Soviet Union "as a pilgrim with a message of goodwill and peace" from India. During his visit, Jawaharlal Nehru addressed a public meeting at the Dynamo Stadium in Moscow of an audience of 100,000 people. But it is worth recalling that originally the meeting had been scheduled to be held in a hall which could accommodate only 12,000 people, but so massive was the enthusiasm generated in the Soviet capital by the visit of the Indian Prime Minister that the venue had to be changed at the last moment. In a Joint Indo-Soviet Statement, issued after Jawaharlal Nehru's visit to the USSR, it was stated that "..... *States of different social structures can exist side by side in peace and concord and work for the common good.*" This visit has clearly given strength to the strategic relations between the two during the Nehru era.

On November 18, 1955 The General Secretary of the Communist Party of the Soviet Union (CPSU) N.S. Khruschev and the Prime Minister of the USSR, N.A. Bulganin arrived at New Delhi for a friendly official visit to the Republic of India for three weeks. The Soviet Prime Minister N.A. Bulganin addressed the joint session of both houses of the Indian Parliament. A Joint Soviet-Indian Statement published in New Delhi. On December 29, Soviet Prime Minister N.A. Bulganin delivered his report to the Supreme Soviet of the USSR on their recent visit to India and other countries of Asia stated that *"there is still a small Portuguese colony on an integral part of Indian territory – Goa. The Indians are rightly demanding that this intolerable state of affairs should be ended and Goa liberated. We have only to glance at the map of India and at these "possessions" of the Portuguese intruders to see how justified and lawful is the claim of the Indian Government that this Indian Territory should be reunited with the motherland. The Soviet Government supports this just demand....".* With reference to the Kashmir question, the Soviet Prime Minister, in his above report, said, "As regards the Kashmir problem, it has been generated by countries pursuing definite military and political aims in this area. On the pretext of supporting Pakistan on the Kashmir question certain countries are trying to entrench themselves in this part of India in order to threaten and exert pressure on areas in the vicinity of Kashmir. The attempt was made to sever (cut) Kashmir from India artificially and convert it into a foreign military base."

In February, 1956, in the report of the Central Committee of the Communist Party of the Soviet Union to the Twentieth Congress of the Party stressed the desire of the USSR "to consolidate untiringly bonds of friendship and cooperation" with India. Both the USSR and India opposed the Anglo-French intervention in Egypt and described it as a "flagrant violation of UN Charter" and a case of "clear, snaked aggression". The Soviet Prime Minister, in a letter to the Prime Minister of India, expressed the belief that the voice of India in support of measures against aggression "could play an outstanding part" in bringing about a negotiated settlement of the Suez crisis. On January 24, 1957, The Soviet Defence Minister, Marshal Zhukov, arrived New Delhi in a friendly official visit to India.

The Soviet delegate at the meeting of UN Security Council strongly supported the Indian stand that the people of Kashmir had already decided their future in a democratic way. He opposed the efforts of Western powers to utilize the Security Council of the United Nations to increase the trouble in the Indian sub-continent. On February 18, 1957, when the Western powers brought forward a resolution providing for the induction of "a temporary UN force" into Kashmir to facilitate the holding of a plebiscite, the Soviet delegate in a hard-hitting speech termed the move as not designed to strengthen the forces of peace in the Indian sub-continent, but "no excite local conflicts and to complicate the international situation in the area." He offered *a series of amendments to the Western draft resolution to make it less harmful to the interests of peace. When these amendments were not accepted, the Soviet delegate vetoed the resolution*. Again on November 5, during the discussion on Kashmir question in the Security Council of the United Nations the Soviet delegate *fully supported India's stand.* The Soviet delegate voiced strong opposition to proposals involving induction of foreign troops into Kashmir or reference of the problem of demilitarization to arbitration or mediation.

On December 10,1957, the Soviet Prime Minister in his reply to the Indian Prime Minister in response to his appeal to the governments of the USSR and the USA dated November 28 appreciated India's efforts and stated, "As for the Soviet Government, it has paid utmost attention to your appeal to stop and nuclear test explosions and is ready to declare solemnly that the Soviet Union will not stage any explosions of nuclear weapons as from January 1, 1958, if the United States and the United Kingdom possessing such weapons also declare their agreement to stop as from January 1, 1958, the tests they are preparing."

On July 19, 1958, in connection with the situation which has arisen in the Middle East due to Anglo-American aggression against Jordan and Lebanon the Soviet Prime Minister N.S. Khruschev proposed the convening of summit conference of the governments of the USSR, the USA, Great Britain, France and India with the participation of the UN Secretary General. In his message to the Indian Prime Minister the Soviet Prime Minister said, "By supporting the proposal for an immediate conference and by her own active participation in it, India would make an inestimable contribution to the cause of preserving peace." On the next day in reply to the message of the Soviet Prime Minister, Jawaharlal Nehru, Prime Minister of India stated, "We shall gladly offer our services to it in the cause of peace if they are needed."

On February 5, 1959. in the concluding speech at the 21st Congress of the CPSU, the First Secretary of the CPSU Central Committee, referring to the warm friendship between Soviet Union and India, declared that he was confident that "all the intrigues of the imperialists, who are striving to prevent the future development of Indo-Soviet friendship and obstruct our joint struggle for peace and for the triumph of the principles of peaceful co-existence" would be scotched. In October, The Third Session of the Supreme Soviet commented on the Sino-Indian conflict and regretted the incidents which had occurred on the frontier between two state friendly to the Soviet Union and called for friendly negotiations for solving the disputed frontier question.

On January 20, 1960, Chairman of the Presidium of the USSR Supreme Soviet, Marshal K.E. Voroshilov arrived in New Delhi on a goodwill visit to India, at the invitation of the President of the Republic of India & Indo-Soviet Joint Statement was issued. In next month February, Chairman of the Council of Ministers of the USSR N.S. Khruschev and other top officials arrived in New Delhi at the invitation of the Government of India for an official visit from February 11 to 16.

The Chairman of the USSR Council of Minister (Prime Minister) addressed the members of the Indian Parliament. At the end of the visit of Soviet Prime Minister to India a Indo-Soviet Joint Statement was issued. On June 20, Dr. Rajendra Prasad, President of India, arrived in Moscow on a goodwill visit to the USSR. President Rajendra Prasad called on the Soviet President L.I. Brezhnev.

He said "*Soviet people are firmly convinced that in as much as our friendly relations rest on the granite foundation of the immutable principle of peaceful co-existence and good neighbourliness, there is great scope for the further development of political, economic and cultural. Co-operation between the Soviet Union and India to the benefit of our peoples. Unquestionably the friendship between our great peoples will continue to develop and gain in strength successfully, heartening all friends of peace and progress.*" Dr. Rajendra Prasad, President of India, replying to the reception said : "...... *the USSR and India have shown that two great countries, following different traditions and holding different philosophies, can freely and happily co-operate, not only in promoting peace. May this friendship between India and the Soviet Union, which is as immovable as the Himalayas,* ..... *remain for ever as a beacon to the policy of not merely peaceful but fruitful co-existence.*"

In 1961, A.N. Kosygin, First Vice-Chairman of the USSR. Council of Ministers, arrived in New Delhi on an official visit. On April 12, Yuri Gagarin became the first man to enter space. Prime Minister of India hailing this triumph of mankind as a "wonderful achievement" said in New Delhi that "this triumph should be considered as a victory for peace...." On September 6, Prime Minister Jawaharlal Nehru arrived in Moscow from Belgrade for an official visit to the USSR. A joint Indo-Soviet Statement was issued. On December 15, President of the Presidium of the USSR Supreme Soviet, L. I. Brezhnev, arrived New Delhi, on a 15th day visit to India.

Liberation of Goa and Soviet role at UN

On December 18, 1961 India liberated Goa from Portuguese colonialists. The USA through a resolution in the UN Security Council accused India as an aggressor and demanded the withdrawal of Indian forces from Goa.

On the other hand, the Soviet delegate in the Security Council of the United Nations declared : "*.... We openly declare that we side with the people of India, with the people of Goa who are fighting to free themselves from Portugal's colonial domination. This position may not be to the liking of some, but we consider it necessary to state it openly before the whole world.*" The US resolution was negatived. President L. I. Brezhnev who had already been in India on a state visit, also warmly welcomed Indian action in Goa. He declared in one of his speeches, "*The Indian people have got now the opportunity to see clearly who are their really friends and supporters of national liberation of the peoples,....*"

On June 21, 1962, when the US delegate kept on referring to the earlier resolutions of the Security Council on Kashmir, with the obvious intention of resurrecting the idea of a plebiscite to decide the future of Kashmir, the Soviet delegate strongly dissented and remarked in course of his speech : "*It is now quite unrealistic to demand a plebiscite, just as, in the words of the representative of India, obviously no one would now demand a plebiscite in Texas, Ohio or any other state in the United States of America.*"

Sino-Indian war and USSR

When the Sino-Indian war broke out in 1962, USSR get confused that either it should support the nation, which had same spirit of communism or should support the country that was among the list of her friends. The situation was complicated for USSR's think tank. There USSR showed maturity and obliged her responsibility as a world power. On one side, she made pressure on China to some strategic help stop the war and on other hand, she provided India also. The Soviet favor to India, put the thought confirm that the relations between India and USSR was stood on a solid base. But it was clear that USSR was not happy with Indian attachment with other powers of Europe and America as well.

On November 5, referring the Sino-Indian border conflict the Soviet Communist Party newspaper Pravda in its editorial strongly pleaded for immediate ceasefire and opening of negotiations for the peaceful settlement of the border conflict. On November 12, The Soviet Prime Minister expressed the ardent desire of the Soviet Union that "the great powers, People's China and India, fully restore and strengthen their ancient traditional friendship."

Moscow's attitude, which apparently had not until then crystallized, became critical of the supply of western arms to India. In a broadcast on

December 2, 1962, Moscow Radio attacked British and American plans to give military aid to India, and said that the "senseless fighting along the Sino-Indian border has stopped, but imperialist dealings have in no way ended." The radio said that Britain and the United States had "even sent envoys to Pakistan to persuade that country not to raise the question, at least for the moment, of Kashmir." This was to enable India to withdraw her troops from the Indo-Pakistani border and throw them on to the Sino-Indian frontier.

In view of this critical statement, misgivings were expressed in India about Soviet sincerity in supplying India with MIG-21 planes and in setting up a factory for their manufacture.

Nehru told the Lok Sabha, two days after the Moscow, broadcast, that the Russians would fulfill their promise to establish the factory and that MlG-21 planes due for delivery that month would arrive, although there might be some delay. More than two months later, the Russian freighter, Dobrush, arrived in Bombay with four MIG-21 planes in crates, comprising the first installment of 12 promised by the Soviet Union. Two Soviet technicians also arrived in connection with the MIG factory.

On February 24, 1964, a ten-member delegation of Soviet Parliamentarians, led by Spiridonov, Chairman of the Soviet of the Union of the USSR Supreme Soviet and Chairman of the Parliamentary Group of the USSR, arrived in New Delhi at the Invitation of the Speaker of the Lok Sabha.

The 4th meeting of the Indo-Soviet Joint Committee on Cultural and Scientific Exchange Programme opens in New Delhi. Inaugurating the meeting Mr. M.C. Chagla said that the cultural and scientific exchange programme between India and the USSR for 1963-64 was very comprehensive and had been implemented successfully.

S. Romonovsky, Chairman of the USSR state Committee for Cultural Relations with Foreign Countries and leader of the Soviet delegation said that scientific and cultural cooperation between the USSR and India is developing successfully and becoming ever more fruitful from year to year. On March 2, a programme of cultural and scientific exchange between Soviet Union and India for the year 1964-65 is signed in New Delhi.

On May 27, 1964 Soviet leaders send messages of Condolence on the demise of Jawaharlal Nehru, the Prime Minister of India. On the next day, USSR Government delegation, headed by A.N. Kosygin, arrived in New Delhi by a special plane to take part in the funeral of the late Prime Minister Jawaharlal Nehru and place wreaths by the body of late Prime Minister of India on behalf of the Soviet Government. On May 29, at a mammoth public meeting held at Ramlila grounds to pay tributes to the Late Prime Minister of India, A.N. Kosygin, leader of the Soviet Government delegation said, *"The*

Soviet people take this irreparable loss to their hearts with particular feeling of sorrow as every body in our country knows what invaluable contribution has been made by the departed Prime Minister to the Cause of development of Indo- Soviet relations and of strengthening friendship between our peoples, in order that our two countries, which earlier did not know each other, could become now not only good neighbours but sincere friends."

Indo-Soviet Strategic Relations (1964 to 1966) during Shastri era

On August 16, 1964, a special programme, *"India – Our Friend"*, was televised in Moscow on the occasion of the 17th anniversary of India's Independence Day. On August 26, a special postal stamp was issued, in memory of Jawaharlal Nehru, by the Ministry of the Communications of the USSR. On August 28, an Indian delegation, led by Y.B. Chavan, Defence Minister of India, arrived in Moscow at the invitation of the Soviet Defence Minister, Marshal R. Malinovsky. On September 11, Dr. S. Radhakrishan President of the Republic of India arrived in Moscow on a 9 day state visit to the USSR. Speaking at an Indo- Soviet Friendship meeting in Moscow at the Grand Kremlin Palace, Dr. S. RadhaKrishnan, President of the Republic of India, said that *"We have arrived at the conclusion that disputes must be settled at the conference table."*21 On October 12, in an interview to the Moscow Radio Correspondent in New Delhi, President Dr. S. Radhakrishnan congratulated the USSR on the remarkable achievement on the launching of spaceship "Voskhod".

On October 29, 1964, Mrs. Indira Gandhi, India's Minister for information and Broadcasting who was in the Soviet Union on her way back from France to India, called on the Chairman of the Presidium of the USSR Supreme Soviet, A. Mikoyan and had a friendly talk with him. A.N. Kosygin, Chairman of the USSR council of Ministers received Mrs. Indira Gandhi, Union Minister for Information and Broadcasting and had a cordial talk with her. In November, The Indian Embassy in Moscow issued the first issue of illustrated quarterly journal India in Russian language. First issue devoted in memory of Jawaharlal Nehru, the architect of the Indo-Soviet friendship.

On November 17, First Deputy Minister of Foreign Affairs of the USSR, S.G. Lapin, arrived in New Delhi on the invitation of the Indian Government. On November 27, India's Minister of External Affairs, Sardar Swaran Singh, arrived in Moscow on his way to New York for the 19th session of the U.N. General Assembly. On May 12, 1965, Mr. Lal Bahadur Shastri, the Prime Minister of India, arrived in Moscow on an eight-day official visit to the Soviet Union. He was received by the Chairman of the USSR Council of Ministers, A.N. Kosygin and other Soviet Ministers and high-ranking officials.

THE FIRST STAGE: THE RUSSO-CHINESE ENCOUNTER IN THE POST-COLD WAR PERIOD

The collapse of the Soviet Union

The rapprochement between the Soviet Union and China began with Perestroika's foreign initiatives presented in Gorbachev's Vladivostok speech in July 1986 and his Krasnoyarsk speech in September 1988. The former speech became famous for its new proposal for resolving the three problems that China stated as: the withdrawal of the Soviet Army from Chinese border areas, the peaceful settlement of the Cambodian war, and the withdrawal of the Soviet Army from the Afganistan.

In 1989, after settling these issues, the General Secretary of the CPSU, Gorbachev, visited China in the midst of the Tiananmen students' movement for liberty and democracy against the Socialist regime.

Russia and China officially reconciled for the first time in 30 years and declared a "peaceful co-existence" between the two states. The problems on the eastern border, which resulted in the Russo-Chinese conflict of the 1960's, were resolved in the 1991 territorial agreement, when Zhang Zhemin visited Moscow.

But Russo-Chinese relations still had not improved greatly at that point. Both sides wanted peaceful relations but no more. The backlash of the Tiananmen incident made China more cautious of radical reforms in the market economy, while the West strongly protested China's repressive attitude towards political freedom. Conversely, Russia expected a pro-western Perestroika policy to develop even further. Rumours suggested that Gorbachev opposed China's actions to suppress the students' movement, although he did not comment on it officially because of the generally accepted non-interference principle mandated by "peaceful co-existence".

The unsuccessful coup'd by Russian conservatives in August of 1991 worsened the Russo-Chinese relationship, because Chinese officials anticipated a victory by Russian conservatives, who felt anxious about the future of the Socialist regime. However, Yeltin's new Russia arose with much more help from Western countries. In 1992, after the Soviet Union collapsed, the new Russia was born as a much more pro-western state than Gorbachev's. Russian President Yeltsin considered the West, including Japan, as a "natural ally". In his declaration, the new Russia was positioned as a "democratic country in the market economy", whose closest partner was the West. This was the first Russian strategy of the "post-Socialist" era. There was little opportunity for improving Russo-Chinese relations at this time.

The "Post-Socialist" transition

The collapse of the Soviet Union, the most powerful Socialist state, shocked the Chinese Communists. They were afraid of crisis in their own Socialist regime. But the collapse of the Soviet Union did not only give China a sense of crisis, fueled by fears that it might suffer the same fate, or be obliged to confront the United States. It also gave China a sense of relief from the threat from the North, and a feeling that China had now become the front runner among the world's socialist states. The Chinese considered this appealing situation as an opportunity for change.

In February 1992, Deng Xiaoping made the "Southern Speech" in Shinchen and Jiuxai, in which he stated that China needed to speed up reforms towards a market economy and never go back to past stagnation. This was a new Chinese "survival plan" for the post-Cold War period. In October 1992, the 14th Congress of the Chinese Communist Party declared that the market economy must play a key role under the Socialist regime. From that point, China officially adopted the doctrine of a "socialist market economy" which gradually has gained greater importance for the market economy than for the Socialist regime.

Although Russia is officially "democratic" and China "socialist" (that is, they have different ideologies), both sides share the common doctrine of a "market economy." Indeed, both social systems were more or less different; Russia was a centralized state, in which political reforms preceded economic ones; China seemed less centralized, and had started economic reforms decades before.

However, they have much the same manner of a centrally-controlled "command" principle as opposed to a free market one. We can identify the two states as in (or on the way to) the "post-Socialist" period, though China officially adheres to the name of Socialism. The official difference of the doctrines play no important role, as long as they observe the non-interference principle. Rather, the two countries have a common base to cooperate in transition to the same goal of a "market economy."

International circumstances helped the two states to become more intimate. In the latter half of the 1992, Russia became cool towards the West for several reasons: Russia was receiving less financal assistance than the West had promised on paper, there was no improvement of the Russian national economy, and the Russian people's feelings of inferiority had increased with the flood of western goods into Russia.

The Russian people felt that Russia needed to revive its national prestige vis-a-vis the West. Even the famous "pro-western" foreign minister, Kozyrev, discarded the "pro-western" foreign policy, which was fiercely attacked by "Eurasian" proponents in the parliament, and switched to a "balanced" one, that considered other great powers (China, India, etc.) as important as the West. However, the Russian government did not dare to confront the West because its ultimate goal was to develop Russia into a "civilized" great power with a market economy which would play a great role in the world community .

Some Russian officials began to pay close attention to the Chinese transition to a market economy as the model "post-Socialist" state. They said that the Chinese transition had proceeded very well without inner disorder, allowing China to retain its foreign prestige throughout the world.

Considering the Chinese side, it is true that its ultimate goal is also to develop China into a great power with a market economy, which would play a great role in the world community. In the same manner as Russia, China is in a position in which it can not confront the West because a lack of western assistance and investment would damage the development of the Chinese economy.

Russia may not be the optimal partner for China, but China has to be friends with its northern neighbor in order to securepeaceful existance.

China understands the technical and infrastructural gap between China and Russia. After the Russo-Chinese rapprochement, China was pleased that Russia finally accepted the equality of the two nations. The 1991 territorial agreement and other documents were characterized as a legal basis of equality in Russio-Chinese relations.

The Chinese side also needs Russian assistance, especially in the areas of atomic technology, equipment and weapons. While trade battles against the US and Taiwan issues sharpen, the ties with Russia will count for China.

This is the first stage of Russo-Chinese relations in the post-Cold War period. We conclude in this stage that: regardless of ideology, Russo-Chinese relations found a common purpose in the post-Socialist transition: becoming a developed country with a market economy which would play a key role in the world community.

THE SECOND STAGE: ANOTHER COMPLEX STORY OF RUSSO-CHINESE RELATIONS

The "China syndrome" in the Russian Far East

In 1993, Russo-Chinese relations developed dramatically in a manner which the two states had never experienced during the Cold War period. The trade value between the two states increased to almost eight billion dollars.

China suddenly became a second partnerto Russia. Local trade along border areas in the Russian Far East also increased to an estimated one forth of the total volume. In addition, the comings and goings of citizens of both countries was over one and half million, a first for both states. However, these figures did not indicate a close relationship between the two nations.

In the Cold War period, both Socialist regimes tightly controlled the transportation of peoples and goods within the states and from abroad. But after both states adopted an open policy towards the outside under Gorvachev's and Deng Xiaoping's initiatives, dynamic changes took place on both sides. The transition to a market economy meant that each government would exert less control over the economy and society than before. The unexpected disappearance of the Soviet Union accelerated the uncontrolled situation in the border areas of the Far East. The Russian side did not have enough time for its transition to a market economy as compared with the Chinese side's prudent preparation for over a decade.

As one measure of Perestroika's open policy, the Russian government permitted Chinese citizens to enter Russia without a visa. After the collapse of the Soviet Union and the Chinese acceleration of economic reform in 1992, Chinese businessmen eyed trading chances with the suddenly opened Russian market. Heilongjian province, the biggest Chinese border region facing the Russian Far East, also adopted a new plan of "open the north, linkage to the south" that provided Heilongjiang with opportunities to profit by moving goods from richer Southern China to the Russian Far East, where the market was short of supplies from Central Russia due to the economic disorder in Russia.

Against this background, many Chinese "shuttles" rushed to the Far East to carry daily necessities through the common border and sell them in the Russian market. This massive transfer of peoples and goods from China to Russia characterized Russo-Chinese relations in 1993.

Russia and China have a 4300 kilometer common border. The border areas are unequal in population; Chinese Northeast provinces have a hundred million people, while the Russian Far East has only seven million. In addition, there are great differences in culture and standards of living. An uncontrolled situation could result in serious clashes between the two nations in the border areas.

In 1994, the Russian side demanded that the Chinese obtain visas before entry into Russia, in response to requests by the local authorities in the Far East. But the comings of Chinese into Russia did not halt immediately. Some used "group tours," which were permitted to enter Russia without visas. Once they entered Russia, they traveled freely for business. Others tried to pass over "green borders," which border guards did not control very strictly. The number of unregulated Chinese residents in the Martime province was estimated at over 7000 in 1994.

At that time, Russian uneasiness towards China had peaked. The most famous Martime paper "Vladivostok" reported that three fourths of Chinese residents in the Martime krai were not registered.

In April 1994, the authorities of Khabarovsk krai challenged the the Upper Parliament delegation, which inspected the Russo-Chinese borders to prepare a report for its international committee. The vice governer, chief of the security office, and commander of the Far East Military District appealed to the delegation regarding to the Chinese threat to Russia, referring to fears of increasing Chinese "immigrants" and their "cunning" in business. The Khabarovsk governor, Ishaev also commented on this issue.

The local authorities in the Far East began to conduct a series of operations, named the "foreiger (inostranec)," which aimed to sweep illegal Chinese residents out of the Far East. We can find many episodes regarding these operations. A newspaper reported that in Blagoveschensk, the capital of the Amur oblast, when the local inspectors conducted this operation in a special hotel for Chinese, some Chinese jumped out of the window like "cockroaches" to avoid arrest, and a Chinese woman entrenched herself in a toilet for three hours. The Chinese government fiercely reacted to these operations, condemning the Russians for ignoring Chinese "human rights."

As Prof. Larin pointed out, Russian newspapers had begun to organize the campaign against China at the end of 1993. We can find many anti-Chinese articles in the local newspapers in the Far East, regardless of where they were issued. Generally speaking, by the end of 1994, the "China syndrome" had spread not only throughout the border areas but nationwide. We can read why many Russians feared the "Chinese threat" and what actions they were taking both in national and in local papers. The most shocking article, The Chinese republic in the Russian Far East? was written by the famous writer, J. Medvedev, in the begining of 1995.

In short, the Russian Far East was afraid of an uncontrolled situation vis-a-vis China, caused by the their own sudden transition in the "post-Socialist" era. The "China syndrome" seemed common in all the border areas in the Russian Far East.

The divergence of Far East views on China

In the beginning of 1995, a new event added to the difficulties in Russo-Chinese relations. The Martime governer, Nazdrachenko, began to campaign aginst the Russian central government to reconsider the 1991 Russo-Chinese territorial agreement, which favored the transfer to China of about 1500 hectors of Martime border lands. Although he did not directly challenge President Yeltsin, he used the local press to attack some of the foreign ministry's experts and the central press, which supported the 1991 agreement.

The Chinese government reacted to his announcement quickly and the top of the Russian Foreign Ministry warned that Nazdrachenko's action could worsen Russo-Chinese relations, putting them back to the 1960's when there were disputes concerning the border islands. On February 16, a special correspondent of Tokyo Shinbun in Vladivostok sent the sensational news to Japan that the Chinese People's Army had begun to conduct a large exercise in the border area to oppose Nazdrachenko's actions. The reporter estimated the numbers of the Army at a half million. Just after this sensational news, local papers in Vladivostok discussed whether or not this news was true.

My conclusion is that the Chinese did excercise in the border area, though the number of men mobilized was overestimated. However, much more important than this sensational exercise itself was the Martime's attitude towards China at that time. It was true that tensions between Russo-Chinese border ran high. A Russian border guard captain, Dashuk, was shot by Chinese invaders in April. A prophet, Tamara Globa, spread the word that a "war against China" would break out in 1996. Some residents rushed to question the military office about the Russo-Chinese "war". The rumor of an outbreaking of "war" spread in the Far East though the local military authorities continued to reject it.

Comparing these events in the Far East to the relative calm of the central government ties between two states, we find a deep gap in the concept of Russo-Chinese relations.

In 1995, central government relations went smoothly. It was said that they were stabilized. Many top leaders of both states developed friendly relationships. In the first half of 1995, Kozyrev visited China in March, Yabulinskii in April, Zhuganov and Grachev, the defense minister, in May, and Lipeng, the Chinese Prime Minister, visited Moscow in July. Yeltsin's visit to China was also planned for the end of 1995, though it was eventually cancelled due to health problems. A Russian official of the foreign ministry stated that China was a "natural ally." Some believed that China hoped to make an alliance with Russia.

While Russo-Chinese relations may be a "union" at the central government level, on the regional level, "war" was threatening. What was the true state of Russo-Chinese relations at this time?

To answer this question, we must give additional attention to the deterioration of Russo-Chinese relations caused by the remarkable Martime challenges. From 1994, the position towards China in the three Far East regions had begun to diverge. In reference to this divergence, the differences in trade balances should be considered.

Economic ties between Russia and China suddenly weakened in 1994. The amount of trade in this area seemed to drop to a third of that of the previous year. This can be explained in many ways: both sides' avoidance of barter trade and hoping for increased trade based on the foreign currency ; China's economic regulatory policy, inflation, the unification of foreign Yuan to domestic Yuan, and the bad quality of Chinese goods; Russia's economic stagnation, delayed procedures of trade, increased tax on imported goods, and the presidential mandate to limit deals with natural resources.

But we can not ignore the negative effect of the Russian visa control policy towards the Chinese and the Far East campaign against China. It seems undoubtable that such legal and psychological barriers had a detrimental affect on the two nations' flux of goods and people.

The sharp deterioration of Russo-Chinese economic relations was illustrated by the divergence of trade balances in the three Far East regions. In the Martime, the drop in Chinese imports in 1994 was replaced by an increase of goods from Japan and South Korea. While this tendency was also seen in Khabarovsk to some extent, there was a sharp contrast between the former two and Amur oblast. Amur was unable to substitute another country's goods for Chinese goods, thus the sharp drop of Chinese goods meant a sharp decrease in the amount of imports in this region.

The differences between the Khabarovsk and the Martime regions are also significant if we focus on import figures. In Khabarovsk, 1993's sudden increase in the importation of Chinese goods was exceptional, and China continues to play an important role in imports in comparison with Japan and South Korea. That is why Khabarovsk is considered to be holding a middle position between the Martime province, which might not be so greatly influenced by Chinese goods, and Amur, whose well-being would be jeapordized without them.

It isn't possible to illustrate all the differences among the three regions looking only at this trade balance data. It is just one of the many aspects of divergence. But local governments have quoted this data at times in order to legitimize their own policy towards China, thus we cannot ignore the divergence of their policies towards China and the fact that it is caused mainly by the differentation of economic ties.

Another reason for the divergence is due to the Martime's remarkable challenge. The common borders along Amur oblast and Khabarovsk krai are basically along a river (the Amur or the Ussuri), while the Martime's border mainly consists of land area. The border most often crossed illegally by Chinese hoping to poach is the Martime's. The tragic death of Dashuk, who was shot by the Chinese, happened along this border.

This strained news concerning Russo-Chinese conflicts was mainly limited to the Martime krai and its borders. In March 1995, it was reported that the Khabarovsk governor, Ishaev, criticized the 1991 Russo-Chinese agreement, placing himself on Nazdrachenko's side. But this news was not precise. He merely expressed his belief that the 1991 agreement was inadequate as it did not clarify the status of the two islands near Khavarosk, Bolshoi Ussuriskii and Tarabarov, as a part of Russia, but he did not demand the renouncement of this agreement as Nazdrachenko did.

The different positions of the two governors is clear. Khabarovsk's two islands are de facto under Russian control, regardless of the fulfillment the 1991 agreement in which the issue of the two islands remained unresolved. What Ishaev demanded was district control of the Chinese in and near Khabarovsk city.

The change in the area is obvious when one compares local opinions in Khabarovsk krai in 1995 with ones in 1994. The "China syndrome" cooled down. Khabarovsk has already accepted the presence of "China," without which Khavarovsk's ecomony could not function, especially in the agriculture and construction industries. Chinese laborers were seriously counted as a necessary supply of inexpensive and efficient labor.

The local papers in Khabarovsk krai adopted a pragmatic attitude towards China and attached great importance to local relations between Khabarovsk and Heilongjiang. They began to report warm relations with China in many articles: the Chinese consul general was given a heartful reception in the regional parliament, both region's delegations warmly welcomed each other, the chair of the Khabarovsk parliament appealed for giving Heilongjiang province observer status at the Far East - Trans Bikal Parliament Conference in May, the Khabarovsk krai began a friendly relationship with Heilongjiang when Heilongjiang's governer Tian Fushan met with Ishaev in Khabarovsk.

The Amur oblast is much more active towards partnership with China. In this area, there are no territorial issues. The local paper, "Amurskaia pravda," promptly rejected the possibility of a Russo-Chinese "war" in 1996 which had been foretold by Tamara Globa. Diachenko, the former pro-Chinese governor, criticized the foreign ministry's policy towards China as affected by the "China syndrome." He declared the colonization by Chinese to be unreal and fantastic, and demanded an open policy towards China, which consisted of simplification of visa controls. The Russo-Chinese contract to build a bridge over the Amur River in June 1995 was the most obvious event in the development of this region's friendship relationship.

Such divergence between the areas of the Russian Far East is not limited to its local governments. We need to pay careful attention to the different attitudes towards China between the military commanders of the Far East District in Khabarovsk and of the Pacific District in Vladivostok. The former, who have met with Chinese colleagues much more than the latter, changed their previously strict attitude against China into a more flexible and warm one in 1995. We do not have any more details concerning the Russian military, but we can not ignore such a change in opinion about China.

Conclusion: towards a third stage?

In reviewing the Russo-Chinese relations from 1992 to 1996 from the typical central government framework, most Russo-Chinese watchdogs concluded that Russo-Chinese relations have developed successfully, although troubling and complicated issues between two states have arisen.

In this context, a debate has arisen about whether Russo-Chinese relations will be "allied" or not. When Russian President Yeltsin visited Beijing on 25 April 1996, the two governments declared Russo-Chinese relations to be in a new stage of "strategic partnership." Does this mean a quasi-Union ? Of course, we can answer either "yes" or "no"!

Many think "no". One Chinese official said the concept of a "strategic partnership" has no important contents and that it was suddenly requested by President Yeltsin on the plane to Beijing. The Chinese side did not seem to hope for a "strategic" relationship, a concept which could be understood as an "alliance." Both governments rejected the concept of an "alliance" and many watchers also confirmed this. It may be persuable in the current situation, when the priority of both states is no longer to confront the West but to change themselves into developed states with Western assistance.

But we can also provide evidence pointing to the other answer, "yes." We have to pay attention to the timing of this joint declaration. Yeltsin finally visited China just after President Clinton's visit to Japan. The Russo-Chinese declaration might be a counterbalance to the "redefined" US-Japan security alliance. In Northeast Asia, tensions mounted over the Taiwan straits and North Korean border. Russo-Chinese relations may not be a "union" now, but in future, what could develop?

It is not enough to look at the situation only from the typical central government framework and to evaluate whether this relation is a "union" or not. My conclusion demands a different analysis of the forming Russo-Chinese relations. In the post-Cold War period, both Russia and China were merely in a transit stage as "post-Socialist" states. Russians sometimes say that a "powerful and unified" China will be a credible partner, not a threat. This may be true of Russia for the Chinese side also. The most dangerous threat for both sides will be uncontrolled Russo-Chinese relations. In the Russian Far East, just after the collapse of the Soviet Union this kind of disorder along the border area arose.

Of course, as we know, both of the central governments have striven for stable relations. And, for the time being, it is successful. But all of its success can not be attributed to the central government. We know the "China syndrome" spread in the Far East in 1993 and 1994. We also know of the confident building of Russo-Chinese relations on a regional level, especially Khabarovsk and Amur's initiatives, in spite of the artificial crisis created by the Martime authorities in 1995. We can not ignore the existence of autonomic and differentiated regions as a factor which has begun to influence the new Russo-Chinese relations in the Post-Cold War period.

My perspective of Russo-Chinese relations depends on the transition process of both states. Now these relations seem stable and the Russian government dominates in the Far East. But differentiation in this area has just started. What will be the third stage in the future?

WHAT'S NEXT FOR THE INDIA-RUSSIA STRATEGIC PARTNERSHIP?

When Indian Prime Minister Narendra Modi and Russian President Vladimir Putin had an "informal" meeting in Sochi in late May, the two leaders discussed a number of bilateral issues such as military and defense cooperation and international issues relevant to both India and Russia. The meeting once again put the attention on the strategic partnership between New Delhi and Moscow, which continues to be significant, but also faces a number of challenges.

Many of the areas of convergence were unsurprisingly on display during the meeting at Sochi. In terms of outlook, the two leaders endorsed and emphasized the importance of their Special and Privileged Strategic Partnership for global peace and stability and the role of the two in shaping "an open and equitable world order." Both Modi and Putin underlined the need to develop "a multipolar world order" while increasing consultations and coordination including on the Indo-Pacific, even though the two sides differ in their characterization. Foreign Minister Lavrov, while speaking to the media on the informal summit, talked about it as the Asia-Pacific region, a formulation preferred by China, whereas the Indian Ministry of External Affairs referred to it as the Indo-Pacific region. Putin and Modi also reiterated the importance of continuing their work together in platforms such as the United Nations, Shanghai Cooperation Organization (SCO), Brazil, Russia, India, China, South Africa (BRICS), and G-20.

Issue-wise, cooperation in the energy and economic sectors dominated the two leaders' discussions. The progress seen in the bilateral trade – about 20 percent in 2017 and about 40 percent in the first few months of 2018 – was highlighted by both sides. In an effort to keep up the momentum, the NITI AAYOG and the Russian Ministry of Economic Development will be engaged in an annual strategic economic dialogue.

More fundamentally, while the two leaders highlighted the tried and tested nature of their partnership, in truth India-Russia ties have been lately going through a rough patch. For more than a decade now, the bilateral relationship has been characterized by increasing strains.

Several factors have contributed to it. For one, in the wake of the Ukraine crisis in 2013, it is clear that Russia wanted China's support because China's opinion carries greater weight globally than India's. This is evident in the continued strategic outreach efforts made by Russia towards China, further reflected in a number of strategic agreements between Moscow and Beijing. The manner in which Putin in 2013 rapidly wrapped up an agreement on natural gas sale to China for 30 years – negotiations that had been dragging on for a decade – was a reflection of Moscow's eagerness to work with China. This was over and above the earlier deals in 2009 and 2013 for the sale of oil on a long-term basis.

But far more consequential is the Russian sale of weapons systems to China that have direct security implications for India. Moscow's sale of Su-30 30MKK/MK2 fighters and especially the Su-35 are likely to have an immediate and tangible impact on the Sino-Indian military balance and India's security. Then there is the sale of S-400 long-range anti-aircraft missiles, which China is reportedly already deploying, though it seems like India may get the same system too.

Second, India's efforts at diversifying its defense procurement and thus bringing in other partners such as the United States, Israel, and France has also impacted the relations. In the absence of a strong bilateral economic and trade relationship, India-Russia relations must have a robust defense ties and any downgrading of those ties could have adverse impact on the overall state of India-Russia ties. Till a few years ago, India's largest defense trade partner was Russia, but Israel and the United States have overtaken Russia in the last few years.

Even so, India's defense inventory continues to be dominated by Soviet/ Russian systems, to the tune of close to 70 percent. Also, when it comes to certain critical platforms such as nuclear submarines, Russia's importance cannot be understated. Therefore, as India engages in the process of diversifying its defense trade partners, perception management and explaining the rationale and imperative to Russia will go a long way in assuaging Moscow's concerns about India's leanings.

Third and possibly the most significant has been India's growing proximity to the United States. Driven by fear of China, India has grown strategically closer to Washington in recent years, though lately New Delhi's foreign policy leaning may appear a lot more confused. Prime Minister Modi's Shangri-La Dialogue speech earlier this month in Singapore was a good reflection of this.

These three developments have dampened bilateral relations between India and Russia. For India, the critical question is whether Russia will stand by India in any dispute with China. Moscow's stand during last year's Doklam crisis did not inspire much confidence in New Delhi. On the other hand, New Delhi understands that it cannot afford to drive Moscow into Beijing's hands. Any strategic partnership between Russia and China does not augur well for India. Whether India can do much about this is unclear, but New Delhi is definitely trying.

INDIA, RUSSIA RELATIONSHIP TAKES A GREAT LEAP FORWARD

India and Russia signed 16 agreements on defence, nuclear energy and other key areas during Prime Minister Narendra Modi's visit to Moscow, with the two sides announcing that Russia plans to build at least six new nuclear power units in India, in addition to inking key deals like the production of BrahMos missiles and the attack chopper Kamov-226 in India.

Prime Minister Narendra Modi, on Day 2 of his visit to Moscow, conveyed to Russian President Vladimir Putin that their summit talks would give a fresh impetus to the bilateral relations between India and Russia, referring to Moscow as New Delhi's "strong and reliable" friend.

As part of the annual India-Russia summit, Modi and Putin held a one-on-one meeting before they were joined by their respective delegations. The two sides continued their deliberations over lunch at the Kremlin before they signed the agreements.

"India and Russia have a long history of cultural relations. And now we have a strong and reliable friend on the political and international arena — Russia. Russia has always been with us in hard times. We have a strategic partnership, a true strategic partnership," Modi said at the summit.

Modi invited Russian CEOs to invest in Indian infrastructure and aerospace sectors, among others, stating that his government had created a favourable environment to boost economic growth.

Hailing the "strong collaboration" between India and Russia in the United Nations, Modi also recognised the understanding shared by New Delhi and Moscow in the BRICS, the East Asia Summit, the G20 and the Shanghai Cooperation Organisation.

The PM also discussed global terror, calling for the world to unite against the scourge without distinction or discrimination between terrorist groups and target countries. Expressing his condolences over the death of over 200 Russian citizens in a plane crash in Egypt in October, Modi also mentioned the recent downing of a Russian military jet on the Syria-Turkey border.

Putin, in his opening remarks during the meeting with Modi, said, "I am pleased to note, and I am happy to do that, that we are consistently and confidently developing the privileged strategic partnership between India and Russia." He expressed happiness over the two countries going ahead "consistently and confidently" in developing the privileged strategic partnership.

Putin announced that Russia planned to build at least six new nuclear power units in India over 20 years. The Russian President said Moscow and New Delhi were successfully cooperating in the production of Brahmos missiles and planned to jointly produce the Kamov 226 military helicopter, a major boost to the Make in India initiative.

The Russian President conveyed his country's "strong support" to New Delhi's bid for permanent membership of the UN security council, calling India a "deserving and strong candidate" that could bring an "independent and responsible approach" within the global body.

A joint statement said the two sides confirmed their interest in intensifying cultural cooperation, announcing the organisation of a festival of Russian culture in India in 2016. The two countries affirmed the need for enhancing cooperation in the information sphere, welcoming a memorandum of understanding signed between Russian state-owned broadcaster VGTRK and Prasar Bharti for exchange of news and other content.

Modi started his second day in Moscow with a tour of EMERCOM, the Russian national crisis management centre, where he interacted with officials at their state-of-the-art office.

Later, the Prime Minister laid a wreath at the Tomb of the Unknown Soldier at Alexandrovski Cad, a war memorial dedicated to Soviet soldiers who died in World War 2. Putin, while hosting Modi for a tete-a-tete at the Kremlin, presented the visiting dignitary with a page from Mahatma Gandhi's diary and an 18th century sword from Bengal. Modi later took to Twitter to share his appreciation for the gifts. "President Putin gifted me a page from

Gandhiji's diary containing Bapu's handwritten notes," Modi posted. "President Putin also gifted an 18th century sword from Bengal, featuring intricate silver artwork. I thank him for the gifts," he added. Modi arrived in Moscow on Wednesday night and was accorded a red carpet welcome. After the welcome, Putin hosted a dinner for the visiting dignitary, where both leaders touched upon issues of mutual interest for both countries.

MODI IN RUSSIA: TRADE, DEFENCE, ENERGY TAKE CENTRESTAGE

Visiting Moscow at a time of trouble, when international sanctions over Ukraine are compounding the blow to Russia's economy from plummeting oil prices, Prime Minister Narendra Modi signalled clearly that, notwithstanding India's warming relations with the United States, Russia remains a privileged partner.

"We have stood together in bad times and good," Modi reminded businessmen and officials at the CEOs' Forum.

Defence, space and nuclear and hydrocarbon energy remain the four key pillars of the Indo-Russian partnership, but Modi placed an unusual focus on business and commerce. He talked up India as an investment destination, stating that its 7.4 per cent GDP growth is the highest amongst large countries.

"I have come to invite Russia to be a partner in India's economic development," said Modi. "We want to make India into a global manufacturing hub." Modi specially mentioned Russia's interest in participating in the Delhi-Mumbai infrastructure corridor. "I see Russia as a partner in India's economic transformation," said the Prime Minister. While bilateral annual trade languishes at $10 billion, the two countries have set an ambitious target of tripling that over the coming decade. The body language between the two leaders lacked the effusiveness of Modi's earlier engagements with the leaders of the US, Japan, UK and France. However, Modi personally credited Putin for resurrecting the Indo-Russian strategic dialogue.

"You are the architect of the India-Russia Strategic Partnership... I have always had great respect and appreciation for it," said Modi. Defence was expected to be the highlight of the dialogue, but the joint statement only mentioned the signing of an Inter-Governmental Agreement for manufacturing the Kamov-226 light helicopter in India.

"The agreement on manufacture of the Kamov 226 helicopter is the first big project under the Make In India initiative. It is rightly with our most important defence partner," said Modi. There was no indication whether the Indian partner for this project would be Hindustan Aeronautics Ltd, or Reliance Defence, both of which are keen on this project.

It is noteworthy that there was no official mention of the S-400 air defence missile system, or the Fifth Generation Fighter Aircraft, all projects that were discussed during the visit.

The joint statement after the talks has only a cursory mention of defence. Energy cooperation was an expected highlight, with the two sides talking about building 12 Russian nuclear reactors, in two different locations. While four reactors already have the green light in Kudankulam, Tamil Nadu, and another two are being discussed; the next six reactors will come up at another location, probably Andhra Pradesh. "Cooperation in nuclear energy will eventually involve 12 Russian nuclear reactors in two sites. The Indian manufacturing content has been increased in these. I thank President Putin for his support," said Modi. The Indian Prime Minister also talked up Indo-Russian cooperation in hydrocarbons, stating: "Russia can be a critical source of energy security for India. We are enlarging investment in Russia hydrocarbon sector."

In September, ONGC Videsh Ltd (OVL), the overseas arm of Oil and Natural Gas Corporation (ONGC), had signed an agreement to buy a 15 per cent stake in Russia's second-largest oil and gas field, Vankor. The joint statement put out by New Delhi and Moscow "welcomed the signing of agreement between Rosneft and ONGC Videsh Limited for acquiring 15 per cent stake by OVL in Rosneft's Vankorneft oilfields and discussions for further stakes in future."

The joint statement also "welcomed the first meeting of the joint study group for studying the possibility of hydrocarbon pipeline system connecting Russia and India held in Moscow on November 6, 2015 as part of the programme on enhanced cooperation in the oil and gas sphere signed in New Delhi in December 2014."

Modi flagged cooperation between India and Russia on Afghanistan and Central Asia, specifically mentioning the road-cum-rail transportation corridor being built, with Indian support, through Iran's Chabahar Port to those regions.

Significantly, the Indian Prime Minister backed Russia's role in Syria, which has been sharply criticised by western powers for being supportive of Bashar al-Assad's regime. The joint statement notes: "Russia and India voiced their strong support to sovereignty, unity and territorial integrity of Syria. Both sides expressed a common understanding that the internal armed conflict in Syria cannot be solved by the use of force, but rather through political and diplomatic means - through a substantive intra-Syrian dialogue without preconditions or external interference..."

This constitutes vital diplomatic support for Moscow. Putin told the media after the bilateral dialogue: "It is important Russia and India make similar approaches to key international problems. Our countries are for a political settlement of the conflict in Syria and promotion of national reconciliation in Afghanistan."

He also lauded the "high degree of (Indo-Russian) convergence on global issues," terming Indo-Russian cooperation on the United Nations, BRICS, East Asia Summit, G-20 and Shanghai Cooperation Organisation as "a partnership of global character."

INDIA-RUSSIA STRATEGIC COOPERATION IN THE PAST: THE CONTEXTUAL IMPERATIVES

The historical background of events that led to the emergence of the India-Russia strategic cooperation are well known. An analytical review of the historical background would indicate that in the main, the following contextual imperatives helped or spurred the forging of the India-Russia strategic relationship:

* United States military aid to Pakistan
* Sino-Russian confrontation
* Indo-US estrangement
* Sino-US quasi-strategic Alliance
* Sino-Pak strategic Nexus
* US – Pak military alliances
* Russia's need to reach out to the Third World through India, as a leading nation.

In terms of detailed examination of Soviet foreign relations, their policies and processes in relation to South Asia, the following observations stand made by an American Professor are relevant .

* "The Soviet-Indian relationship rests on two pillars of mutual interest: the containment of China and the reduction of Western influence in the region."
* "Additionally, the USSR "uses" India's status as a leader of the non-aligned movement to bolster Soviet policy in the Third World".
* "India uses Soviet economic and military aid to pursue its own regional goals, the most important of which are containment of Pakistan and Bangladesh."
* "In other words, the Soviet Union and India have the basis for an ideal relationship: India's needs are a match for Soviet capabilities, and Soviet needs are a match for India's strengths."
* "The Soviet-Indian relationship works best when both perceive a link between China and Pakistan."

A little realised facet which also facilitated a proximate India-Soviet relationship was that: "Over the years the monolithic structure of the defunct Communist Party of the Soviet Union (CPSU) established harmonious relationships with an equally monolithic Congress Party in India."

India-Russia Strategic Relationship : Time to Move Away?

In relation to the contextual imperatives that forged the India-Russia strategic relationship, a contemporaneous review of the regional and international scene reveals the following changes that have taken place:

* The Cold War ended a decade back, resulting in the emergence of the United States as a unipolar power.
* The disintegration of the Soviet Union, the collapse of the economy and the economic upheaval have diluted Russia's countervailing power both regionally and globally.
* Sino-Russian confrontation stands replaced by a growing strategic nexus between Russia and China. Their strategic aim is to dilute America's unipolar status.
* Post-Afghanisation withdrawal, Russia has embarked on repairing relations with Pakistan.
* The Sino-Pak strategic nexus in South Asia has gone to alarming lengths where China has not only provided nuclear weapons blueprints but also provided ballistic missiles and missile production plants to Pakistan.
* In March 2000, the United States drew the curtains on its special relationship with Pakistan. Concurrently it has embarked on building and repairing its relations with India.
* Islamic fundamentalism and Islami Jehad have raised their ugly heads in India, Central Asian Republics, China, Russia and targetted USA too.
* China has embarked on building its military power and force projection capabilities as pre-requisites for its aspirations for super-power status.

That the contextual imperatives which shaped the India-Russia strategic partnership have either been swept away or stand significantly diluted. Further "In the Cold War years, superpower rivalry tended to aggravate or even perpetuate conflict in South Asia in the form of contending alliances. The end of the Cold War and break-up of the Soviet Union, have however transformed that rivalry into Washington/ Moscow policy coordination and have in its wake brought about a grand shift from alliance to realignment in South Asia."

More significantly, in relation to what was the cornerstone of the India-Russia strategic relationship, the 1971 Peace and Friendship Treaty, itself was questioned by the Russians themselves as early as 1992. It has been observed that: "The breakup of the Soviet union has put an end to the Indo-Soviet special relationship. Both the Russian Federation and India have decided to sign a new political treaty to replace the 1971 Indo-Soviet Treaty of Peace and Friendship, which was extended for another twenty years in 1991. But according to Indian press reports, the Russian side has asked for deletion of security related articles from the original treaty."

After the disintegration of the Soviet Union, successive Russian Foreign Ministry spokesmen have consistently stressed that Russia will honour all past agreements and treaties, "But this rhetoric could not hide the fact that the Indo-Soviet treaty was no longer relevant to a situation in which India would be in a confrontation with both China and Pakistan, which conceivably was India's chief rationale in the first place ......" and further that "Article 9 of the Indo-Soviet Treaty, which provided for military cooperation in the event of a military threat to either party had, therefore, now become a benefit of dubious value for India."

Circumstantially, therefore, it is time that India moves away from the strategic relationship of a proximate nature that it enjoyed with Russia until Gorbachev came into power and disintegration of USSR took place. Gorbachev had given notice of change of priorities in Russia's foreign policies in favour of China at his famous Vladivostok speech – the border settlement, Kampuchea and Afghanistan. Somehow India missed noticing Russia's switch in priorities i.e. a China predominant policy as early as 1986.

RUSSIA'S STRATEGIC SWITCH: CHINA FAVOURED OVER INDIA

The mainstay of India-Russia strategic partnership and the Indo-Soviet Peace and Friendship Treaty of 1971 was to make India secure against threats from China and Pakistan. Russia in acceding to the 1971 Treaty had made a conscious strategic choice between India and China. Gorbachev set in motion the paradigm switch towards China. It is unclear whether the Indian authorities sensed it. His successor Yeltsin followed this switch more vigorously. Following Yeltsin, President Putin seems to be continuing the policies set by his two predecessors in giving China overriding priority in Russia's foreign policy relationship.

"By the middle of 1989, Indo-Soviet relations drifted into a situation, presaging the need for their complete re-casting which had to come about with Gorbachev's removal ....." so writes an eminent Indian Foreign Secretary. In fact it can be maintained that India's Russia policy needed rehashing soon after Gorbachev's Vladivostok speech in 1986 when he initiated the Russian switch towards China. It was Gorbachev who "called for a new China Policy" and it was he "who called for an end to a China encirclement policy" and it was Gorbachev who conceded China's "basic demands for normalisation of relations: Soviet withdrawal from Afghanistan, Soviet pressure to get Vietnamese withdrawal from Cambodia and the reduction of Soviet military presence along its borders with China."

The decade of the 1990s witnessed a rapidly galloping Russia-China relationship especially in strategic spheres. Concurrent with this was the growing cold-shouldering of India especially between 1989 and 1996 when some corrections were applied, Primakov became the Prime Minister.

Yeltsin while adopting a policy of building up a strategic relationship of coalition with China, "emphasised a need for de-ideologisation of its (Russia's) foreign policy" which "resulted in Russia adopting a 'wait and see' policy towards India " led to" in the new Russia placing the Indo-Russia relations in a precarious position." President Putin's Government documents 'Foreign Policy of the Russian Federation issued on July 10, 2000 continues to reflect the Russian switch to China. This document states the following objectives on China and India:

China

"The concurrence of the fundamental approaches of Russia and People's Republic of China to the key issues of world problems is one of the mainstays of regional and global stability. Russia seeks to develop mutually advantageous cooperation with China in all areas."

India

"Russia intends to strengthen its traditional friendship with India, including in the international affairs and to aid overcome problems persisting in South Asia and strengthen stability in the region."

An analytical observer would be able to grasp the subtle Russian nuances in terms of Russian priorities vis-à-vis China and India. This would indicate that what remains of the Russia-India strategic cooperation now is only 'traditional friendship'. Russia's switch towards China, and which is likely to grow further into an intensified 'strategic coalition' (they may both shy away from terming it a 'strategic alliance') necessitates examination of two other topics, namely:

India's military dependence on Russia

Russia's advocacy of establishment of a Russia-China-India triangle (Political and Security overtones).

5

The Russia-China-India Triangle Moves Forward

Soon after Russian Prime Minister Yevgeni Primakov arrived in New Delhi on Dec. 21 for a two-day official visit, a sensational piece of news sounded across the globe: Primakov had publicly called for the formation of a "strategic triangle" among the three giant nations of Russia, India, and China.

Encouraging India to see itself more as a world power, and calling for closer relations not only between India and Russia, but also between India and China, Primakov reportedly stated, "A lot in the region depends on the policies pursued by India, Russia, and China.... If we succeed in establishing a triangle, it will be very good."

As the Indian newspaper The Hindu commented, "The concept of a 'strategic triangle' covering India, China, and Russia, spelt out by the visiting Russian Prime Minister, Mr. Yevgeny Primakov, is of immense significance since this is perhaps the first time that a senior leader from Moscow has made such a statement."

Wasting no time to research the real background of Primakov's remarks, Western and other media were quick to impose their own distorted, mechanistic interpretation. The new "strategic triangle"—they intimated—was Russia's reply to the U.S.-British bombardment of Iraq, the attempt of the weakened and frustrated former superpower to put together a new, anti-Western bloc. When a spokesman of the Chinese Foreign Ministry, reacting to such press reports, emphasized China's strictly independent foreign policy and China's policy not to participate in any sort of blocs or alliances, the headlines of the British press proclaimed triumphally: "You see! China rebuffed Primakov"! In reality, the Russia-China-India triangle is no new invention made under the pressure of the Iraq crisis, but a crucially necessary feature of the entire Eurasian Land-Bridge development strategy, as repeatedly emphasized by Lyndon LaRouche and others in the pages of EIR. For competently informed persons, the actual emergence of the "strategic triangle" Russia-China-India, became virtually inevitable no later than Chinese President Jiang Zemin's historic speech at the Russian Science City Akademgorodok in Novosibirsk on Nov. 24, 1998.

There, Jiang Zemin put forward the basic principles of a policy to harness Russia's enormous scientific and technological potential, as typified by the "closed cities" of the military-scientific-industrial complex, for the economic development of the entire region. This policy, as Jiang emphasized, is integral to creating a "new, just, and rational world economic order," guaranteeing the sovereign economic rights of the world's developing countries. That same concept was affirmed in the official declarations of both the Chinese-Russian and Russian-Indian summit meetings.

The most appropriate comment to these developments, interestingly enough, came in the pages of China's official foreign press review, Reference News (Can kao xiaoxi) on Dec. 24. Reference News published on its front page a detailed summary of a speech given by Helga Zepp-LaRouche in early December at a conference in Mexico City.

Her speech laid out the background and implications of Jiang Zemin's Novosibirsk speech, and predicted that Primakov would push for the inclusion of India in the new China-Russia development partnership during his (then forthcoming) visit to New Delhi.

What was most significant in the Reference News coverage of Mrs. LaRouche's remarks, however, was her emphasis on the difference in attitude between the Chinese government—which paid attention to LaRouche's analysis and warnings on the financial crisis—and the attitude of most other governments. That fact, indeed, uniquely coheres with China's role as a centre-point of a growing circle of nations devoted to real development around the Land-Bridge policy, at a time when the United States and western Europe are plunging toward a self-imposed "dark age" of financial and socio-economic collapse.

Collision ahead?

It is only in this context, and not from some mechanistic geopolitical standpoint, that can one speak of the Russian-Chinese-Indian triangle as an "answer" to what is increasingly perceived in Asia and elsewhere as a dangerous pattern of insanity coming from the West. The turning-point in that perception was doubtless the outrageous, disgusting performance of Vice President Al Gore at the Kuala Lumpur meeting of the Asian Pacific Economic

Cooperation (APEC) forum on Nov. 17. Gore's "globalist" ravings and his brazen attack on Malaysia for asserting its sovereignty against international speculators, are increasingly viewed in Asia as a signal for the same insane, destructive policy and mind-frame, which characterize the Anglo-American attack on Iraq and the closely related escalation of the fraudulent "legal coup" against U.S. President Clinton. All add up to an unprecedented assault against the very institution of the sovereign nationstate—including, emphatically, against the constitutional system of the United States itself. Going handin-hand with a major escalation of British geopolitical destabilizations in the Near East and elsewhere, and a coming, new global financial earthquake of unprecedented dimensions, that assault has already brought the world closer to nuclear war, than anyone could have imagined a mere 12 months ago.

One should not forget, that it was China and India's stubborn insistence on maintaining their sovereignty in the face of "financial globalization," that has so far permitted those two countries to weather the so-called Asian financial crisis, while less prudent nations went under. The striving to restore to Russia a modicum of national sovereignty, is key to the constellation of forces behind the Primakov government. It is above all this issue of national sovereignty and economic development that is placing China, Russia, India, and other Asian nations—despite the repeated, and doubtless sincere affirmations that their growing partnership is not directed against any third party—on a collision course with the "globalist" policy championed by Gore.

The sharp reaction to the Iraq bombing, by Russia and China particularly, is a mild foretaste of what may come. Unequivocal condemnation of the Iraqi bombing was a major point of the Russian-Indian joint declaration signed during Primakov's visit. In an unprecedented action, Russia recalled its ambassadors from the United States and Great Britain, while at the same time calling a limited military alert.

Soon afterward, Russia gave the world a pointed reminder of its continued existence as a nuclear superpower, by deploying the first of its new generation of mobile, high-precision ICBMs. China's representative at the United Nations did not mince words in ripping apart the fraudulent basis for the whole operation, naming UNSCOM director Richard Butler in public. And after the Dec. 28 incident in which U.S. planes enforcing the so-called "no-fly zone" fired on an Iraqi anti-aircraft position, the speaker of the Chinese Foreign Ministry, Zhu Bangzao, declared: "The Chinese side has many times declared that the sovereignty, territory, and independence of Iraq must be fully respected.

China regards the action of creation of a 'no-fly zone' in Iraq as contrary to the United Nations Charter and to standards of international relations."

Another, increasingly angry message is implicit in the sharp statements and actions of the Chinese government, in dealing with the Western-supported political opposition movement in China itself.

A growing community of interest

Russia, India, and China make up 22% of the world's land area and over 40% of its population. As the world's largest and most populous developing nations, whose very maintenance requires enormous inputs of science and technology, India and China have a strong common interest in stabilizing and developing Russia. Russia, for its part, can only survive by bringing its scientific and technological potentials into full economic play, which in turn requires large and stable markets for the kinds of industrial goods it can best produce. All three nations have a vital joint interest in Central Asia, and so forth.

They also share, in different ways, the experience of significant joint development in the 1950s. At that time, both India and China profitted greatly from close scientific and technological cooperation with the former Soviet Union—a partnership which was also key, in its direct and indirect effects, to the relatively rapid rates of industrial growth in the Soviet Union in that period. In a limited, but significant way, the transfer of industrial technology and know-how from the Soviet Union to China and India, in that period, helped shape the Non-Aligned Movement's later striving for a "new, just world economic order."

For all these and other reasons, a profound community of interest now exists among the three giant nations. That community of interest is by no means limited to the three alone, but explicitly includes the concept of joint cooperation in other developing countries. It should be noted, for example, that the Russian-Indian agreements signed during Prime Minister Primakov's visit, provide for joint exploration and exploitation of oil and gas resources not only on each other's territories, but also in Kazakstan, Central Asia, and Iraq. Iraq has already been an important oil supplier to India, and India and Russia both have considerable interest in developing petroleum resources there.

But the pathway to consolidation of the Russia-China-India triangle is by no means an easy one. It will be necessary to overcome a long heritage of British geopolitical manipulation in Eurasia. That heritage is lodged above all in false axioms and habits of thinking among the elites, which have permitted the nations of the region again and again to be manipulated against each other in the name of falsely defined, so-called "competitive national interests." The earlier triangle was effectively smashed in the late 1950s and early 1960s, by geopolitical manipulations whose fruits included the Sino-Soviet split, the Sino-Indian war, the apparently "insoluble" Indo-Pakistan conflict, and so on.

One of the notable tools in those British-directed manipulations, incidentally, was none other than the late Armand Hammer, sponsor of the Gore family and supposed "great friend" of the Soviet Union. Some painful rethinking of old mistakes will be needed on all sides, if Russia and its partners want the "Great Triangle" to succeed today. That means above all gaining a more competent under-standing of the historical conflict between the United States and Britain—or in other words, why Lyndon LaRouche has the friends and foes he has.

LaRouche's ideas circulate in Russia by Rachel Douglas

One new publication and one reprint, issued in Moscow at the end of 1998, have put key strategic writings of Lyndon LaRouche into circulation among Russian-speakers.

Bulletin No. 8 of the Schiller Institute for Science and Culture (Moscow) is headlined "Russia's Relation to Universal History," and features LaRouche's "Letter to a Russian Friend," which was published under that title in EIR of Nov. 29, 1996. The subject-matter resonates with Chinese President Jiang Zemin's recent address to Russian scientists at the Novosibirsk centre of the Russian Academy of Sciences, as LaRouche develops why the greatest strength of Russia, defining its potential to make a decisive contribution to saving mankind, is the quality of bold, "dissident" thinking by the Russian scientific intelligentsia. The preservation of Russian science and collaboration with Russia on "such great projects of reconstruction and progress as are urgently wanted for the benefit of both Russia itself and Eurasia more generally," LaRouche writes, is in the vital interests of every nation, especially the United States.

Pictured here is the other justissued publication, a reprint of the proceedings of the April 24, 1996 round table held at the Free Economic Society in Moscow, at which LaRouche was hosted by Academicians Leonid Abalkin and Gennadi Osipov, to speak on "Russia, the U.S.A., and the Global Financial Crisis." The 92-page booklet is published by the Institute of Social and Political Research (ISPI) of the Russian Academy of Sciences, with an introduction by ISPI's director, Academician Osipov. In his keynote at the round table, LaRouche developed the need to revive Franklin Delano Roosevelt's design of collaboration among the United States, Russia, and China for genuinely post-colonial development of nations after World War II.

RUSSIA AND INDIA: TOWARDS ECONOMIC MODERNIZATION

Although the resource base and the socio-economic structures in Russia and India are different, the problems of maintaining development and modernization of the economy are common. Planning is key in managing the modernization of the Indian economy. Indian planning is based on a close relationship with the academia. First, this is determined by the composition of the Planning Committee, which incorporates both experts and officials. Second, various experts from research institutes, universities, government institutions and organizations, business communities, etc., take part in developing and preparing the plans, although they are not members of the Planning Committee.

All Planning Committee summary documents (group lists, their members, set objectives, and submitted reports) are openly accessible. This increases the responsibility of the working group members and allows a wide range of academicians and experts to review the reports and offer their assessments and suggestions. Where there is limited scientific and technological potential, it is not "innovations in general" that are regarded as a cornerstone, but those directions that have priority significance for the solution of problems at a given stage of economic modernization. The Planning Committee has therefore established the Committee for Scientific and Technological Research Orientation that is to draft its own report. Planning is the main mechanism ensuring that science is engaged in modernization and in the solution of the related problems, while the state's high demand for science stimulates its development.

Fiscal policy in India is based on the understanding that economic modernization and the overall acceleration of socio-economic development require an increase in capital investment, even if this results in budget deficit. Controlled deficit financing aimed at increase value-added investment is one way of accelerating economic growth in transition economies where structural modernization of the economy is the main priority. India uses zero base budget planning in order to optimize budget expenditures. Therefore the current year's budget is not extrapolated as a base estimate for that of the following year's. Even current expenditure items are scrutinized so as to determine whether they should be kept. Thus, zero base budgeting serves as an alternative to optional cutting of budget items.

India recognizes that foreign capital cannot form the basis of investment in a large country; only the increase of domestic savings may be the main source of growth. India is expanding the network of bank branches, particularly in the countryside where the majority of population lives, in a bid to mobilize the population's personal savings.

Foreign capital regulation policy in India pursues two main objectives. On the one hand, the government seeks to raise foreign capital to develop modern equipment and technologies and to finance development programs, particularly in the most capital-intensive industrial facilities, and in cases where construction involves foreign currency outlays. On the other hand, the government also strives to limit the foreign risk to capital influx that could destabilize the financial situation in the country, limit the competition of foreign capital preventing the growth of national capital, and establish Indian control over companies with foreign interest. Foreign private companies are not usually allowed to buy securities in Indian enterprises on the secondary stock market. Foreign investment in India is usually associated with creating new capacity rather than the transition of operating enterprises under their control. Therefore, raising foreign direct and portfolio investment is a tool to deter the attraction of loan capital, especially regarding short-term loans, and reduce foreign investment related to India's external debt increase. Industry-oriented foreign capital inflow corresponds mainly to the general priorities of the state's social and economic policy-the primary development of capital-intensive and technologically sophisticated scientific and engineering concerns, especially in the electronics sector, as well as the services industry (primarily information support, the software industry, business and consulting, data processing, etc.). As a result, the Indian government was able to channel most foreign direct investment to the strategic sectors determining the country's scientific and technical progress.

INDIA'S RELATIONS WITH RUSSIA

During the March 2010 visit of the Russian Prime Minister Vladimir Putin to New Delhi, the Indian Prime Minister Manmohan Singh described Russia in fulsome terms:

Relations with Russia are a key pillar of our foreign policy, and we regard Russia as a trusted and reliable strategic partner. Ours is a relationship that not only stands independent of any other, but whose significance has grown over time. Our partnership covers areas such as defence, civil nuclear energy, space, science and technology, hydrocarbons and trade and investment.

During discussions, bilateral economic as well as regional security issues were top of the agenda. Putin's India visit was also watched very carefully in many Western capitals as this was happening immediately after the London Conference, where the Western alliance had been working on exit strategies in Afghanistan. The Putin visit was seen by many in India as a precursor to any hedging strategy involving Russia, India, Iran and the Central Asian republics against the possibility of a Taliban return in Afghanistan. Since the signing of their Declaration on Strategic Partnership in October 2000, this had been the subsequent 11th summit meeting. Similar to earlier meetings, five more agreements were signed in March 2010. Apart from multi-billion dollar arms deals, an inter-governmental agreement on broad-based co-operation in atomic energy and a 'road map' for future co-operation were also signed. Similar to the last few summits, strategic congruence, defence purchases, hydrocarbons and nuclear power dominated the agenda. The visit obviously gained more significance because of a changing strategic scenario in India's neighbourhood. This chapter aims to analyse how and if, to use Manmohan Singh's phrase, its 'significance has grown over time', in a relationship that first took shape in the days of the old USSR.

HISTORICAL BACKGROUND

Historically, the USSR under Stalin (Iosif Dzhugashvili), was suspicious of the genuineness of India's independence and non-alignment. However, Indo-Soviet bonhomie started with Jawaharlal Nehru's visit to the USSR in June 1955 and the Nikita Khrushchev/Nikolai Bulganin visit to India in December 1955. This was also the time when the Congress party in India was afirming its belief in state planning and a 'socialistic pattern of society', and Nehru was playing a leading role in the Bandung Conference (1955) of 29 Afro-Asian nations. During the same period, the USSR began to use the instruments of aid, trade and diplomacy in developing countries, to limit Western influence. Subsequently, Indo-Soviet relations flourished over the decades in the metallurgy, defence, energy and trade sectors. During the India–China war in 1962, the USSR tried to be neutral between what it called 'brother China' and 'friend India', with the People's Republic of China seeing this as a betrayal of international communist solidarity on the part of the USSR, and a factor that reflected and further exacerbated the growing Sino–Soviet split. In the early 1970s both Indian and Soviet leaders looked on the emerging US-Chinese rapprochement as a serious threat to their security. Their response had been in 1971 with the Indo-Soviet Treaty of Peace, Friendship and Cooperation, which provided immediate consultation in case of military action against parties to the Treaty. During the India–Pakistan war in 1971, the USSR took a firm position in favour of India and sent ships to the Indian Ocean to counter any move by the USA, which had already sent its 7th Fleet ships into the Bay of Bengal. The results of the 1971 Indo–Pakistani war and emergence of Bangladesh established a trusted partnership between India and the USSR. During the 1980s both Rajiv Gandhi and Mikhail Gorbachev advocated a nuclear-free world. However, after the Soviet invasion of Afghanistan in 1979, India was also confronted with a dilemma of how to preserve its non-aligned credibility without jeopardizing its relations with the USSR.

In the initial post-Soviet period, bilateral relations in the 1990s went through a period of uncertainty when Russia was preoccupied with domestic economic and political issues, and with its relations with the USA and Europe. Now India had to deal with a new Russia which was Eurocentric, economically dependent on the West, and neither had the interest nor the resources for Third

World regimes. President Boris Yeltsin, during his visit to Delhi in 1993, tried to recreate the spirit of old friendship with a new Treaty of Friendship to replace the old India-Soviet 1971 treaty. However, the fundamental character of the Treaty was transformed and in case of any threat to peace, the new Treaty vaguely called for regular consultations and co-ordination. Although Yeltsin described India and Russia as 'natural partners', he was careful not to give the impression of a 'special relationship'. Although relations were restored to respectable levels, the early years (1991–96) of 'benign neglect' of India by Russia left a deep mark on Indian policy-makers.

The situation changed when the new Russian Prime Minister Yevgeny Primakov (1998–99) started shifting from the previous pro-Western Russian foreign policy. To strengthen his country's relations with old allies, Primakov visited India in 1998 and pushed proposals for creating a Russia-India-China (RIC) strategic triangle, although RIC coherence remains questionable for some Indian commentators like Abanti Bhattacharya: 'the development of a strategic triangle would be unrealistic. The reasons can be easily found in the mutual suspicion between India and China'. The new Russian leadership under Vladimir Putin (president, 2000–08) reversed the Yeltsinera drift in India-Russia bilateral relations, signed the Declaration on Strategic Partnership with India in 2000 and established the institution of annual summit meetings. Moscow realized that as a Eurasian power, an active Russian role and influence in dynamic Asia would be limited without a solid partnership with old friends like India.

Indian commentators welcomed Putin's comment in his 2004 visit, that 'India is our strategic privileged partner [...] And speaking from the point of view of geographical representation [...] India is number one', as recognition of India's own rise:

The emphasis is to be interpreted both in the geopolitical context and also in the military context. In terms of geo-political interpretation one could say that Russia accords primacy to India in the Indian sub-continent and all that it implies. In the military context it stresses that Russia recognizes India not only as a strategic partner but also as a 'privileged strategic partner'. If this is Russia's emphasis truly, then the long range prospect of Russia-India strategic cooperation is pregnant with exciting prospects.

Despite its improving relations with the USA, China and Europe, India also did not want to abandon its time-tested relationship with Russia. In a world dominated by a single power (the USA), both the Indian and Russian vision of a multi-polar world coincided. The issue of terrorism has also brought the countries together. Within South Asia, Russia has consistently supported

India on the issue of Kashmir unconditionally over time or regime change and opposed its internationalization. These issues continue to be reiterated at their Summit Declarations. Another point which both the partners have been emphasizing after every important meeting is that their partnership is neither against any third country nor at the expense of their relations with other major powers, understandable given Russia's strategic links with China and India's with the USA.

State Linkages

Since 1992 about 15 summit meetings have taken place and about 135 agreements have been signed between the two countries. To improve their economic relationship, an Indo-Russian Inter-Governmental Commission on Trade, Economic, Scientific, Technological and Cultural Cooperation (IRIGC-TEC) has been working towards promoting bilateral co-operation. The Commission covers 11 joint working groups, namely: trade and economic co-operation; phar-maceuticals; petroleum; the coal industry; metallurgy; science and technology; cultural co-operation; information technology; power and energy; the environment and natural resources; and co-operation with the regions. In the 15th meeting of IRIGC-TEC, held in Moscow in October 2009, a new trade target of US $20,000m. by 2015 was agreed.

As already mentioned, a major turning point in their bilateral relationship was their formal Declaration on Strategic Partnership between Republic of India and the Russian Federation, signed during Putin's visit to India in October 2000.15 Broadly, this agreement meant enhanced co-operation in the political, economic, defence and cultural fields. It talked of 'deepening and diversifying cooperation in sectors such as metallurgy, fuel and energy, information technology, communications and transport, including merchant shipping and civil aviation', and of 'further development of cooperation in banking and finance, and improving credit and insurance facilities'. There was mention of simplifying rules and procedures for travel by entrepreneurs and businessmen of both countries. It was also agreed to jointly explore the possibilities of regional trading arrangements with third countries. Since then, summit meetings are taking place almost every year with many more agreements signed every year. The crux of all these summit meetings and accompanying declarations has been common positions on major global issues like international terrorism and desire for a multipolar world and close bilateral relations. These summits have been a very useful platform for formulating common positions and responses to emerging global political and economic issues.

However, what do these Summit declarations actually mean in real terms? There are many ways of looking at these developments. Every time the summit meeting takes place, the diehard proponents of old Indo-Soviet/Russian friendship emphasize the need to look at these agreements and declarations as a testimony of a time-tested, mutually beneficial friendship. They even go one step further and suggest that along with Russia, India should forge solid friendships with other like-minded countries including China to soft balance some of the negative trends of a unipolar world, dominated by a single economic and military power.

However, many people in the new generation of Indians, who have entered the business or academic professions in the post-Soviet period, have somewhat different impressions about these summit meetings and declarations. They argue that countless bilateral meetings have taken place since 1992, and a plethora of agreements have been signed between the two countries. Various inter-governmental commissions and committees are also working to improve bilateral relations. In addition, both the countries are in an avowedly 'Strategic Partnership'. Yet, despite all this rhetoric, India's exports to Russia have remained lower than countries like Bangladesh, Nigeria, Kenya, Thailand, Israel and Viet Nam. In today's Russia about 70% of the economy is in the private sector, yet India has not moved beyond public sector and government declarations. So it is argued that India needs to strengthen the commercial component of its relationship through the linkages between the dynamic sectors of Indian industry, commerce and services and the newly emerging Russian private sector. In the absence of this relationship, it is argued that 'strategic partnership' may soon start losing its charm.

There is truth in both arguments. Even 20 years after the Soviet collapse, India's relations with Russia were still in transition, particularly in the commercial field. After some disruption, both have been able to restore and improve their political linkages. In the economic and academic fields, however, most old India-Soviet linkages have broken and new India-Russia links have not developed to the same extent. Both governments have recognized this fact. Still, these summit meetings have been able to tackle the issue in a significant manner.

It could be argued that under new circumstances, business in both countries is no more the business of the governments. Therefore, it is up to the private sector to take advantage of conditions created by these agreements. Despite this, these high-level visits could have been used more effectively to promote Indian economic interests in Russia. Compared with India, Russians have done good business during these visits. Russia has a comparative advantage in the arms industry and India has purchased arms worth billions of dollars during these visits. Nine annual summit meetings over nine years were good opportunities for special bilateral economic relationships to have been created, even under entirely different circumstances. In 2005/06 trade still stood at a relatively modest $2,760m. In 2006 a Joint Study Group was set up to work out a programme for increasing bilateral trade to $10,000m. by 2010, and to explore the possibilities of a Comprehensive Economic Cooperation Agreement (CECA) between the two countries. The group submitted its lacklustre report in July 2007.17 Except for the recommendation of a CECA, there were few specific recommendations. Subsequently, a Joint Task Force between the Indian Ministry of Commerce and Industry and the Russian Ministry of Economic Development was set up in February 2008 to monitor progress on a CECA, but with few concrete results emerging from the exercise. Trade by 2008/09 had increased to $5,420m., but fell back to $4,550m. in 2009/10, some way off the earlier target set for $10,000m. by 2010.

DEFENCE LINKAGES

There are estimates that about 800 Russian defence production facilities are kept in operation by Indian defence contracts. Although China used to be the number one arms importer from Russia, India has emerged as number one since 2007. Some analysts have argued that in arms exports, geopolitical and economic factors will eventually force Russia to make a choice between China and India, a contest that India will probably win.

India's major purchases from Russia over the last 18 years have been varied and extensive, including aircraft (MIG 29, MIG 29 SMT, SU 30K, SU MK1), helicopters (Mi-17, Mi-18, etc.) and air-defence systems (AK 630 30mm, etc.). In June 2010 the Cabinet Committee on Security cleared another deal of more than $3,000m. to buy an additional 42 Sukhoi-30 MKI fighters from Russia. The deal came on top of the 230 aircrafts already contracted from Russia in three deals worth a total of $8,500m. The initial contract was for 50 fighters, at $1,460m. In 2000 the Government contracted the licensed production of 140 fighters by Hindustan Aeronautics Limited. Then another 40 were added to the contract. Some purchases have been of artillery and armoured vehicles (256M Tunguska), engines, sensors and a variety of missiles. Maritime purchases have been noticeable, including frigates (Talwar stealth class), submarines (Kilo/Sindhughosh), nuclear submarines (Akula-2 lease) and an aircraft carrier (the delayed Gorshkov purchase originally due for handover in 2008–09, now scheduled for handover at the end of 2012). Joint production has seen India also starting to producing significant portion of armaments at home, including Brahmos missiles, T72M1 tanks, radars, anti-ship and anti-tank missiles, etc. Most tanks and aircraft are also being assembled in India. In 2009 both countries agreed on a new military technical co-operation agreement for the period 2011–20. The new programme covers both ongoing projects, such as the Su-30 MKI fighter plane and the T-90 tank production in India, and 31 new projects, which include a fifth-generation fighter aircraft, the multi-role transport aircraft and a new multi-role helicopter. Under this programme India hopes to further shift from the buyer-seller relationship to joint design, development and production.

India also has a long tradition of collaboration in space with the USSR/ Russia. Thumba Equatorial Rocket Launching Station was set up with Soviet help and many Indian experimental and remote sensing satellites were launched with Soviet co-operation.

In 1990 India entered into a $350m. contract agreement with Russia to supply the cryogenic engines and technology for their manufacture within the country. Russia earlier agreed to provide India with the technology, but then reversed the decision after it signed the Missile Technology Control Regime agreement with the USA.

The USA objected to giving India the technology because of its potential use for nuclear missiles. Commercial and political factors later compelled Russia to sell the rocket engines while withholding the technology. Soon afterwards Indian scientists were able to develop Indian engines. Currently, both countries collaborate on many space projects, which include India's unmanned lunar space fight project (Chandrayaan-2), the human space flight project and the development of the Indo-Russian Student Satellite, Youthsat. Russia has also agreed to provide India with access to signals from its Global Navigation Satellite System (GLONASS).

Commercial linkages

One important point of the old Indo-Soviet friendship was a special bilateral trade and economic relationship. Although this arrangement had many of the usual weaknesses, like corruption and patronage transactions in low-quality products, it helped many small and medium-sized private Indian companies to become exporters. After the disintegration of the USSR, this relationship was badly damaged. Economic transformation in Russia from a centrally planned economy to a market economy in 1992 coincided with the policies of economic liberalization in India. These developments changed the nature and character of foreign economic relations in both countries. Therefore, despite having solid economic and trade relations in the past, most Russian and Indian companies are still struggling to adjust in each other's markets. Economic relations are still surviving mainly because of defence purchases and some public sector investments by India. Commercial initiatives are slow to take advantage of Russian economic transformation. Despite good intentions, both governments have been unable to facilitate any major economic initiative which could have given a new direction to bilateral commercial ties.

Background of trading linkages

Since 1953, when the first trade agreement took place, seven long-term agreements have been signed between the two countries up to the collapse of the USSR. This bilateral trade was conducted through a specific system of trade and payment called the Rupee Trade System, based on annual plans. The important point of the system was payments in non-convertible currency. The trade turnover between the two countries increased from less than 2 crores in 1953 to about 8,000 crores in 1990–91. In 1990–91 more than 16% of Indian exports went to the USSR and about 6% of imports came from there.

One of the most striking characteristics of the Soviet centrally planned economy was that it had created a system of exchange in non-convertible currencies with many of its trading partners. This trade behaviour existed not only with the Council for Mutual Economic Assistance (CMEA) countries, but also with some other friendly countries like India. The value of exchange between the Russian rouble and Indian rupee currencies was arrived at through periodic bureaucratic negotiations.

Most of the ideologically-motivated scholars in India regarded this arrangement as a Soviet version of bilateral aid. The mainstream academia in India also declared that India had 'derived substantial benefits from its trade with the socialist world'. In the late 1970s and early 1980s a few scholars in India had already warned that despite short-term gains, this type of arrangement would harm long-term requirements of efficiency and growth. After initial industrialization, India had problems of importing further machinery either for joint production for third countries or for the exclusive production for the socialist bloc. India did not want Soviet participation in those areas where it could get markets of its own. It also did not want 'captive units', the production of which could not be exported anywhere else but to the Soviet bloc and could give the Soviets the possibility of dictating terms. Except for a few works, academia in India by and large did not bother to critically examine this pattern. The whole arrangement reflected political imperatives rather than economic rationality. After the Soviet break-up, the new policy elite in Russia also found these 'irrational' arrangements with developing countries unaffordable.

The haste with which bilateral payment arrangements were scrapped in favour of payments in convertible currencies indicated that Russian and Indian policy-makers considered such bilateral arrangements undesirable under the new economic policy regimes in both countries.

After the collapse of the USSR, the Indian and Russian Governments renegotiated the entire trade regime. The 1993 agreement terminated the traditional rupee trade arrangement and mandated all bilateral trade transactions to be conducted on a hard currency basis. However, with this agreement the issue of repayment of civilian and military loans taken by India from the former USSR also came up. Finally, after prolonged negotiations, the rouble credit was denominated in rupees and a repayment schedule was drawn up. The agreement provided for an annual repayment of about the equivalent of $1,000m. in rupees to Russia over a period of 12 years starting from 1994, with smaller amounts for a further period of 33 years. The rupee debt funds were to be used by the Russian side for import of goods and trade-related services from India. The rupee debt funds are maintained in a central account with the Reserve Bank of India. Under a three-year perspective plan, which came to an end in 1997, a part of the rupee debt funds was allocated for the import of tea, tobacco, soya meal and pharmaceuticals to designated Russian agencies. The balance was either auctioned or allocated to various states or importing organizations in Russia. In January 1998 this mechanism was replaced with a weekly auction of rupee debt funds conducted by the Vnesheconombank (Bank for Foreign Economic Affairs). During 1999 allocations made for the import of pharmaceuticals and medical equipment from India were utilized by several ministries in Russia. Between 2000 and 2006 the utilization of rupee funds continued through the auctions. In 2007 it was agreed that India's restructured rupee debt would be invested in Russian projects in India. According to Indian finance ministry sources, in December 2007 India still owed $1,970m. in debt to Russia under this category.

Contemporary trading ties

As a result of these changes, contemporary trade between India and Russia is based on payments in freely convertible currencies. All Russian exports to India follow the new system. However, in the 1990s about two-thirds of Indian exports were financed through the renegotiated rupee debt-repayment mechanism. As a result of all these economic policy changes, traditional actors in Indo-Russian trade and other economic relations like the public sector units and state trading corporations are no longer as relevant as they used to be in the Soviet era. Sections of the Indian private sector, which used to get away with selling many products of questionable quality under the bilateral system, also found it difficult to adjust to the radically changed economic and commercial environment in Russia, driven by market forces.

Although Indo-Russian trade has improved in the last few years, it has hovered around a 1% share during the first decade of the century. In quantity terms, although its volume has gone up from $905m. in 1995/96 to $4,547m. in 2009/10, it is still a very small sliver of India's trade; indeed, a 1.98% share in

1995/96 down to a 0.97% share in 2009/10. Of course, statistics may not reveal the full story. Some imports from Russia, particularly metal, metal scrap, fertilizers, paper and paper products, may be sourced through international suppliers and are not reflected in these official figures. Similarly, many Indian goods enter Russia via 'shuttle trade' or through third countries. Still, this will not significantly change the broader picture. Russian trade figures have also included some of the arms exports in commercial trade figures in the last few years.

Main items of traditional exports from India are pharmaceuticals, tea, coffee, ready-made garments, cotton, tobacco, edible preparations, iron and steel, etc. Recently, some non-traditional items like machinery have also shown some growth. Imports from Russia include iron and steel, fertilizer, wheat, minerals, chemicals, paper, rubber, copper, nickel, nuclear machinery, project goods, etc. Apart from goods, services trade may also become more significant in coming years.

According to the Russian Central Bank, India and Russia had about $680m. in services trade in 2008. Russian services exports are mainly associated with construction and maintenance of equipment. In the last two years, services trade has moved in favour of India, with Indian exports in this category increasing from $90m. in 2003 to about $500m. in 2008.

Investment linkages

In the energy sector India's state public sector Oil and Natural Gas Corporation (ONGC) is active in Russia. In 2001 ONGC Videsh Limited (OVL) acquired a combined 20% interest in the Sakhalin-1 project. From 2006 this project started to generate positive cash flow. During 2008/09 ONGC's share of production was 1.853m. metric tons of oil and 0.372 billion cubic metres of gas. In 2009, at a total cost of $2,100m., OVL also completed the acquisition of seven blocks in the Tomsk region of western Siberia, previously held by a United Kingdom-listed company, Imperial Energy. At present, this Tomsk acquisition produces oil mainly from two fields and has its own infrastructure including pipeline network, field processing facilities and connections to the Transneft pipeline system.

The Indian ICICI Bank has opened its subsidiary ICICI Bank Eurasia in Russia, with branches in Moscow and St. Petersburg. TATA Motors launched a project to assemble its light-duty trucks at Russia's Urals Automobile and Motors plant and assembling plant for buses at Volz-hanin and Samotlor. The SUN group has also invested in Russia's food and real estate industries. Similarly, pharmaceutical companies like Dr. Reddy's Laboratories Ltd. and Lupin Ltd. have investments in Russia. Berger Paints has also started operations in Russia. Carborundum Universal has purchased an 84% share in Russia's Volzhsky Abrasive Plant in the Volgograd region. The GMR Infrastructure has participated in a tender for the reconstruction and maintenance of St. Petersburg's Pulkovo Airport. Other companies that are exploring possibilities for investment in Russia include GAIL, Indian Oil, Coal India, Reliance and Tata Tea.

Similarly, a few Russian companies are active in the Indian market. Silovyie Mashiny and Tekhnopromeksport are providing equipment and technical assistance for the construction of the Sipat thermal power plant in Chhattisgarh, Bihar and Uttar Pradesh. Two 1,000-megawatt nuclear power plants in Kudankulam, Tamil Nadu, are being constructed with the help of Russian Atomstroiekspor. In March 2010 both agreed on the construction of two more reactors (units five and six) at Kudankulam and two reactors at Haripur in West Bengal during India's 12th Five-Year Plan period, 2012–17. Their agreement also outlined the timeline for the steps to be taken for the construction of Kudankulam units three and four, and called for progressive indigenization of supplies for units five and six at Kudankulam. For all six reactors at Kudankulam, Russia will provide the equipment and components, while Nuclear Power Corporation of India will build them.

The Russian AFK Sistema owns a 73% share in the Indian telecom operator Shyam Telelink. It is constructing a pan-Indian transmitting network, Shyam. The Russian VTB bank has also started operations in India. Sberbank also intends to enter the Indian market. The numerous other infrastructure companies that are already operating in India include Transstroi and Tsentrdorstroi (road construction), Elektrostal and Tyazhpromeksport (metallurgical industry) and Stroitransgaz (gas pipeline). A joint venture between Russian truck-maker Kamaz and India's Tatra Vectra Motors is nearing completion. The unit will produce Kamaz-6540 dump trucks of over 25 metric tons and Kamaz-5460 prime movers. Zarubezhneftegaz is doing exploration work along with GAIL in the Bay of Bengal. Russia's Gidro OGK and India's SUN Group launched a joint venture called RusSUNHydro in 2009, with the newly formed company planning to participate in hydro-electric projects in India. At the India-Russia Summit in 2007 a decision was made to establish a joint India-Russia titanium product facility. In February 2008 Russia's State Property Committee, the St. Petersburg-based engineering company Tekhnokhim Holding and India's Saraf Group agreed to set up a plant in Orissa. The Russian share in the project is 55%, which is expected to be financed through Indian outstanding debts to Russia. Overall, however, Russian investment in India remains minuscule. According to the Indian Ministry of Commerce and Industry, total foreign direct investment (FDI) from Russia during the period between April 2000 and March 2010 was about $373m., which was 0.34% of total FDI inflows to India during that period.

Conclusions

Except for a very brief period in the early 1990s, India's relations with Russia have been based on mutual trust and confidence. In the mid-1990s relations were restored to respectable levels which have been further strengthened since the signing of their 'strategic partnership' in 2000. Currently, the main pillars of this relationship are strategic congruence, defence ties, nuclear power and hydrocarbons. The trouble for Indian policy-makers is that these areas still remain skewed in favour of Russia.

The major challenge for both India and Russia is how to sustain this relationship in the absence of dynamic commercial ties. Future bilateral economic relations will depend on Russia's importance to India's developmental needs and vice versa. In the past, the USSR played an important role in India's industrialization process. It had a comparative advantage in sectors like steel, which was central to its needs. India now has to assess where Russia has a comparative advantage. So far, India has been able to develop linkages in defence production, the oil and gas sector and in nuclear energy. Indian industry has already identified areas of mutual interest, namely information technology, pharmaceuticals, telecommunications, financial services, hydrocarbons, energy and power, oil and gas, food processing, financial consultancy, management services, textiles and diamond processing. The problems are well known, however, including lack of information, visa problems and logistical issues. Still, very little attempt has been made to address these issues. There was a lot of hope that a Eurasian north–south trade corridor would be able to tackle some of the transportation problems. Owing to low trade volumes, however, the trading community has not yet developed this route. The strong political will in both countries to improve bilateral economic relations could have been converted into real economic gains if some imaginative initiatives had been taken, particularly when the Russian economy was booming between 2000 and 2007. With the global economic slowdown impacting in 2008/09, things have become more complicated for increasing India-Russia economic links, with trade declining from $5,420m. in 2008/09 to $4,550m. in 2009/10.

Current Indo-Russian commercial relations are certainly not commensurate with existing potential. In the last few years India has signed bilateral trade deals with many partners and many are under negotiation. However, until Russia joins the World Trade Organization (WTO), it is highly unlikely that India and Russia will be able to sign any significant bilateral trade and economic co-operation agreements. In the last two decades the Indian and Russian economies have moved far from each other. With no major breakthrough, Indian and Russian economic ties will continue to depend on the arms trade, and nuclear and energy industry linkages. Russian exports to India are likely to be from the extraction industries and limited Indian exports will continue to be from low-volume, high-value and high-profit sectors.

It is clear now that defence ties constitute the core of bilateral relations. Russia has provided the most advanced aircrafts, tanks, rocket launchers, missiles, frigates and submarines to India. Through licensed production of arms, missiles and aircraft, India is slowly developing its own defence industry. There have been problems in defence supplies concerning product support, cost escalations, delays in delivery and incomplete transfers of technology. Still, substantial arms imports continue to come from Russia. With a changing foreign policy orientation in India, the importance of arms imports from Russia may see a declining trend in coming years. There was some uneasiness in Russia when India signed a Strategic Partnership with the USA in 2006, and there was talk of Russia being elbowed out as India's main arms supplier, particularly in the midst of troubled negotiations during 2008–10 over the sale of the Admiral Gorshkov aircraft carrier. Nevertheless, overall Russia remains an important factor in Indian foreign policy debates. Moreover, at the broadest level, the Indian elite believes that a strong Russia is important for maintaining a desired international equilibrium, both supporting the idea of multi-polarity and a rule-based international system, within which India can continue its rise. This remains India's basic 'strategic synergy'.

6

Cross-Cutting and Mitigating Factors in Triangular Relations

On nuclear security, the triangular dynamics between Russia, China, and India become far more complicated. Both Russia and China denounced India's nuclear tests in 1998, although Russia's criticism was milder, and both have urged India to sign the Comprehensive Test Ban Treaty and the Non-Proliferation Treaty. If the nuclear rivalry between China and India intensifies, Russia's nonpartisan stance as strategic partner to both may become less sustainable.

Possible U.S. deployment of national and/or theatre missile defence systems also elicits different kinds of concerns from Moscow, Beijing, and New Delhi. Russians are concerned about the deployment of a national missile defence system that could eventually compromise the Russian strategic deterrent. Although it is difficult to imagine that happening in the next ten to fifteen years, even if Russia reduced the size of its arsenal to one thousand deployed warheads, Moscow would incur some unwanted additional costs in developing countermeasures to defenses. The Chinese strongly oppose U.S. deployment of theatre systems in Asia and especially the potential sharing of such systems with Taiwan. But Beijing is also concerned about so-called "thin" national defenses designed to address small attacks and accidental launches, because those defenses would compromise existing Chinese deterrent capabilities. India is opposed to U.S. deployment of a national missile defence because it will likely hasten Chinese efforts to modernize and expand their nuclear forces, thus compelling India to deploy a more robust nuclear deterrent than it might otherwise do. All three states, however, share a dim view of the prospect that U.S. deployment of national and theatre defence systems to defend the homeland and U.S. troops will possibly allow it to deploy U.S. troops more liberally with less fear of reprisal.

The missile defence issue presents Moscow with tremendous challenges and difficult choices that affect the management of its relationship with China. If Russia were to reach agreement with the United States about modification of the Anti-Ballistic Missile (ABM) Treaty to allow for the deployment of a limited national missile defence system, the Sino-Russian relationship would suffer. The U.S.-Russian agreement at the June 2000 Clinton-Putin summit to explore cooperation on missile defence and to jointly monitor missile launches, followed by Putin's proposal to the Europeans in Rome the same month to cooperate on the development of a joint European theatre missile defence system, elicited serious concern from China. Presumably Putin had some explaining to do when he met with Chinese leader Jiang Zemin twice the next month, once in Dushanbe for the Shanghai Forum summit and once in Beijing. He was at least somewhat successful, as the two sides concluded with a more unified stance, once again denouncing U.S. plans for missile defence and upholding the ABM Treaty as a bedrock of strategic stability in the world. In the past, the Chinese and the Russians have discussed cooperation in taking joint measures to oppose U.S. missile defence, although apart from joint denunciations of U.S. activities and plans it is not clear what form such cooperation would take.

Moscow must beware of damage to the Sino-Russian relationship resultimg from a potential U.S.-Russian agreement on ABM Treaty modification, but Russian strategic thinkers are also concerned about catalyzing a more rapid Chinese nuclear build-up. With deployed Russian nuclear forces on a downward trajectory, the emergence of a more robust Chinese nuclear deterrent in the future is unsettling. Russia's choices will not be made easier by the new Bush administration in Washington, which has made very explicit its desire to deploy a national missile defence system more robust than that planned by the Clinton administration. As of February 2001, the Russian security establishment still appeared undecided about whether it would agree to accept modification of the ABM Treaty should the Bush administration seek to pursue one. President Clinton's decision to postpone a decision on national missile defence deployment, followed by a review by the Bush administration of economic and technical feasibility, provides a welcome breathing space for diplomatic efforts on a number of fronts. Nevertheless, Moscow will eventually face a fundamental decision on missile defence that will lay down a very significant marker in the consolidation of its post-cold war strategic approach. Should it jump on the bandwagon with the dominant global power or align with its rising power neighbor to balance against the hegemon?

Although far less likely than national missile defence deployment-but hardly unimaginable-Sino-American conflict over Taiwan could also potentially put Moscow in an awkward position. Moscow has consistently upheld a one-China policy, and at the July summit in Beijing Putin stated that Russia firmly supports China's efforts to reunify with Taiwan. But what would Moscow do if actual fighting broke out over Taiwan? Rumours circulated in Asia that before his trip to Beijing last summer Putin offered the Chinese direct military assistance in the event of a crisis in the Taiwan Strait. Supposedly the Russians would send their Pacific Fleet to cut off U.S. naval access to the strait. The rumour seems hard to believe since Russia stands to benefit little by actual involvement in a Taiwan crisis involving the United States-which speaks to the larger phenomenon that China seems to benefit more from the Sino-Russian relationship than does Russia. It would seem that Russia's interests are best served by continuing U.S.-Chinese tension over Taiwan because it increases Moscow's leverage with Washington and Beijing. It also seems slightly fantastic that the Chinese would take such an offer as credible given the decrepit condition of Russia's Pacific Fleet. Still, the story was not denied by Russian or Chinese officials, and there was no comment on the rumour either by top U.S. officials or by major media.

Currently the Russians and Chinese are negotiating a new treaty that would define and further elevate the status of the bilateral relationship. Although it series very unlikely that the new treaty would include security guarantees, it has been reported that it would broaden and deepen Russo-Chinese security cooperation in the fields of arms sales and weapons research and development. Reportedly, Moscow and Beijing are envisioning a fifteen-year cooperation plan that would include two stages. In the first stage (2000-05), China would be able to purchase up to $15 billion in weapons from Russia while expanding joint exercises and military training. In the second stage (2005-15) China and Russia would engage in joint research and development of new generations of military technology.

Although the Russian military-industrial complex could certainly benefit from the infusion of Chinese capital, it is not clear what technological benefit for Russia there would be in such extensive cooperation. In addition, it seems unlikely that Russian industry could quickly ramp up by a factor of three its current arms deliveries to Beijing.

Economic cooperation and trade between China and Russia continue to be sluggish. The announced goal of reaching $20 billion in bilateral trade by the year 2000 not surprisingly proved to be wildly unrealistic, as the overall figure failed to reach $8 billion last year. There is long-term growth potential in the energy sector, but it will require years to develop any major multilateral investment Like much in the Sino-Russian relationship, the rhetoric of partnership outstrips the reality. The overall relationship is better than at any time since the 1950s, but the foundation remains rather shaky. A measured and balanced look at the relationship would suggest that the two countries continue and even increase strategic cooperation, to meet the security interests of both without compromising their primary focus on economic development, which also requires cooperative relations with the West for both Beijing and Moscow.

Although Moscow has emphasized the long-term nature of its shared interests with China and India, the Sino-Russian relationship is controversial among Russian policymaking elites in a way that the Indo-Russian relationship is not. Russia shares a long border with China and a long history of often bitter and complex relations. There is an implicit Russian hedge position on China that is amplified by a growing sense of the economic and demographic vulnerability of the Russian Far East and, to a lesser extent, of Moscow's "sphere of influence" in Central Asia. Perhaps for the near future China will focus on its interests in Taiwan and the South China Sea, but there exists a barely veiled Russian fear that continued Russian weakness will invite Chinese infiltration and eventual control of some Russian territory. Russia shares no border with India, and despite the wild designs of nationalist politician Vladimir Zhirinovsky and the like for Moscow's "drive to the South," it is nearly impossible to foresee circumstances that could lead to conflict between Russia and India. This is not to say that conflict with China is at all likely, but rather that Russia's sensibilities toward China and India are different.

Initially giving longtime friendly partner India the cold shoulder after the collapse of the USSR, Russian diplomats fairly steadily sought to strengthen ties with New Delhi through the 1990s. This process culminated with Vladimir Putin's trip to India last October, when the "strategic partnership" between India and Russia was formally established. Despite this achievement and the signing of a number of arms sales agreements that amounted to more than $3 billion in new deals, however, reports in both the Indian and Russian press indicated some difficult discussions that suggest underlying tensions in this relationship. It was reported in the Russian press that India played hardball in the arms sales negotiations by demanding further price reductions, and that Russian defence officials were not fully satisfied with the deals, which consisted of agreements of intent rather than contracts. But even with arms transfers to India amounting to about $1 billion annually, the over-all Russo-Indian trade relationship over the past decade has fallen from $5.5 billion a year to about $1.5 billion. One Russian commentator, on the eve of the October summit in New Delhi, concluded that unless Russia and India can revitalize their trade relationship, the agreement about their strategic partnership "will be nothing but words on paper."

It was also clear from the summit and events around it that Indian and Russian interests do not precisely coincide regarding Pakistan or the Taliban. Just a week before Putin travelled to India, Sergei Yastrzhembsky went to Pakistan as a presidential envoy. His letter from President Putin addressed Russian concerns in Central Asia, Afghanistan, and Chechnya, including the role of camps on the Pakistani-Afghan border that are training soldiers to fight in Chechnya, Tajikistan, Uzbekistan, and Kyrgyzstan. Acknowledging that Pakistan and Russia do not agree on everything, Yastrzhembsky explained that Moscow hoped that Pakistan could play more of a stabilizing role in the region. Although Yastrzhembsky denied that the trip to Islamabad was designed to reach out directly to the Taliban, at a minimum Russia hoped that Pakistan could influence the Taliban to curb some of their activities. The trip also sent a message to the Indians that Russia intended to exercise all of its options, and it may help explain some of the chilliness of the meetings in New Delhi. The Russian press also reported that Putin made a significant political concession to the Indians to seal the arms agreements by condemning terrorism and noting in his speech before the Indian parliament that the same people were instigating terrorist acts "from the Philippines to Kosovo, and from Kashmir to the Caucasus." Putin also supported India's position that the Kashmir conflict should be resolved only by Pakistan and India and should not involve international mediators. Just after Putin made these very public statements effectively supporting India in its conflict with Pakistan, the arms agreements were: finally signed. Much of the Russian press concluded that India got the best of Russia in their summit deliberations, and that this reflected a shift in the balance of power of the Russo-Indian relationship in favour of New Delhi.

The Russo-Indian summit provoked some discussion in the Russian press about the prospects of a Sino-Russian-Indian alliance and especially its role in addressing religious "extremism" and terrorism, a popular theme of the Putin administration. Vladimir Lukin, deputy speaker of the Russian Duma and a veteran Asia hand who accompanied President Putin on his trip to India, described the trip as promoting the "emergence of a new centre of influence in Asia with the participation of Moscow, New Delhi, and Beijing." But he also noted the significance that "this tripartite interest is not negative in any way, i.e., it is not directed against anyone and is not anti-European or anti-American." In fact, Lukin went on to say that "the threat of international terrorism could help establish a kind of regional alliance of Moscow, Delhi, and Washington, crucial for maintaining stability in Asia." In his interview with Indian journalists, President Putin made some interesting remarks that emphasized the importance of maintaining transparency:

But everybody will understand us if we are going to say that India, China, and Russia have some common interests as countries located in that region, interests that we want to pursue jointly. I do not see anything special in this, nothing dangerous. But what is necessary is that all our proposals in the sphere of cooperation, both bilateral and multilateral, should be open for all our partners, understandable and transparent. I think this is something we can achieve.

Russian support for multilateral security institutions in Asia has a long history, going back at least as far as Brezhnev's proposal more than thirty years ago for a collective security pact in Asia. During the Gorbachev years these calls acquired more of a genuine positive-sum rather than zero-sum character when the Soviet Union improved relations with both China and the United States. Since the collapse of the Soviet Union, Russia has continued to support multilateral frameworks for addressing key Asian security issues. In that regard the Shanghai Forum, which grew out of the border and demilitarization agreement talks between China, Kazakhstan, Kyrgyzstan, Russia, and Tajikistan, is emerging as an interesting Asian multilateral institution with some potential to address regional interests in dealing with terrorism, drug-trafficking, and other common problems.

Implications for U.S. Policy

Conclusions that the Sino-Russian and Indo-Russian strategic partnerships have taken the place of the U.S.-Russian strategic partnership for Moscow, or that the leaderships in New Delhi and Beijing give relations with Russia a higher priority than ties with the United States, do not hold up to careful scrutiny. Particularly with Russia and China, but also with India, the United States holds a great deal of leverage-primarily by virtue of its position as global economic leader, but also as a global military leader and senior partner in the most powerful European and Asian alliances. When U.S. trade with China is more than ten times the level of Sino-Russian trade, for example, it is wrong to claim, as some do, that the United States is somehow "the odd man out."

It was very telling, for example, that last year President Clinton received a far warmer reception in India than did President Putin. And that should not be surprising since the United States can bring far more to the table that can influence India both positively and negatively than can Russia. If Sino-Russian and Indo-Russian relations became more threatening to the United States, this would represent failures of U.S. policy toward India and China at least as serious, if not more so, than those toward Russia. Currently Russia does not have alliance relationships with either China or India, and I contend that such relationships are not in the cards, absent some very ill-advised moves on the part of the United States.

That is not to say, however, that Sino-Russian and Indo-Russian arms sales and technological cooperation do not present U.S. policymakers with real challenges in several respects. Clearly they do. Increased conventional capacity could embolden China to take more risks over Taiwan. The sales encourage Sino-Indian arms racing, which will have spillover effects in South, Southeast, and Northeast Asia. U.S. policymakers would view most dimly transfers of ballistic missile technologies and cooperation that could possibly contribute to the development of Chinese and Indian nuclear forces. So far, however, despite the near-desperate straits of its military-industrial complex, Russian arms sales to China and India have not fundamentally changed the balance of power in South Asia or East Asia.

There is one near-term measure the United States could undertake that has the potential both to accelerate and deepen Sino-Russian and Indo-Russian strategic cooperation, as well as unleash a chain of potentially destabilizing events. If the Bush administration moves swiftly to unilaterally abrogate the Anti-Ballistic Missile Treaty in order to begin deploying a robust national missile defence system, the relative harmony in great power relations that has so far marked the post—cold war period will come under considerable pressure.

Simultaneously, the nuclear nonproliferation regime, weakened as it is, likely will not survive. For an administration in Washington that promises to bring more hard-boiled "realism" to U.S. security policy, the Bush team will need to conduct a very careful cost-benefit analysis of the potential impact of national missile defence both on our allies and on major powers in the international system, including, notably, Russia, China, and India.

On the campaign trail, usually in reference to domestic issues like crime and gun control, George W. Bush often mentioned that actions "have consequences." Realism, still the dominant paradigm of international relations theory, also would predict that unpopular unilateral measures taken by the dominant power in the system, the United States in this case, will have consequences. For the last thirty years, a central tenet of realism in the context of U.S.-Russian-Chinese relations calls for the United States to maintain stronger ties with China and Russia than they have with each other. National missile defence deployment will pose additional challenges to Washington policymakers trying to maintain the relatively favourable position of the United States in that triangular context. In other words, we may not be able to have our cake and eat it too.

Other consequences are not entirely predictable, but we can imagine some possible repercussions. The Russians have promised to abrogate the Strategic Arms Reduction Treaty (START) II agreement in response. Chances for deep cuts in nuclear arsenals will diminish and we risk scuttling a whole series of measures designed to bring greater safety and security to the Russian nuclear weapons and materials complex. It may still be unlikely that Russia, China, and India would respond by stepping up their strategic partnerships to the level of alliances directed against the United States, but their strategic cooperation to develop and share technologies to counter missile defenses would probably grow. National missile defence deployment will drive China to expand and modernize its nuclear forces more rapidly, and India will respond in kind, followed by predictable responses from Pakistan. If Sino-Indian relations were to sour and result in a greatly accelerated nuclear arms race, including more overt Chinese support for Pakistan's nuclear program—certainly one imaginable consequence-Russia's capacity to maintain strategic partnerships with China and India will come under much stress, as will peace in South and East Asia. Another possible chain of consequences developing from U.S. abrogation of the ABM Treaty to deploy national missile defence is a more rapid Chinese nuclear build-up that could lead Japan increasingly to question the credibility of U.S. nuclear guarantees.

There is still much uncertainty as to how the United States will handle the missile defence issue and its subsequent impact on other nuclear and non-nuclear states. But most fundamentally, the move would unleash a dynamic whose final consequences are unclear. One thing does seem fairly certain: U.S. deployment of a national missile defence that is not accompanied by the most adroit diplomatic and political handling of the concerns of allies, friends, and rivals alike may upset the relative stability that exists among major powers in the international system today.

CHINA-RUSSIA RELATIONS

The end of the long-held animosity between Moscow and Beijing was marked by the visit to China by Soviet President Mikhail Gorbachev in 1989. After the 1991 demise of the Soviet Union, China's relations with the Russian Federati on and the former states of the Soviet Union became more amicable. A new round of bilateral agreements was signed during reciprocal head of state visits. As in the early 1950s with the Soviet Union, Russia has again become an important source of military matériel for China, as well as for raw materials and trade. Friendly relations with Russia have been an important advantage for China, offsetting its often uneasy relations with the United States.

Russia's foreign policy toward China generally has had two goals: to preserve a counterweight against United States influence in the Pacific and to prevent Chinese regional hegemony and a Sino-Japanese alliance that could exclude Russia. This balancing act appeared in Russia's 1993 foreign policy concept in its call for weighing the benefits of increased Russian arms sales to China against the danger of re-creating a Cold War arms race in which the respective proxies would be Taiwan and China. Accordingly, the concept endorsed neighborly and substantive relations with China while ensuring that "third countries," such as the United States or Japan, would not be able to use China as an ally against Russia.

In the early 1990s, relations got a boost from China's interest in renewed weapons imports from Russia and other forms of military cooperation. In 1992 an exchange of visits by high defense officials established defense ties and included the signing of a major arms technology agreement with a reported value of US$1.8 billion. In 1993 another series of defense exchange visits yielded a five-year defense cooperation agreement. A strategic partnership, signed in early 1996, significantly strengthened ties.

In December 1992, Yeltsin went to China and signed a nonaggression declaration that theoretically ended what each called the other's search for regional hegemony in Asia. Another treaty included Russian aid in building a nuclear power plant, the first such provision since Sino-Soviet relations cooled in the late 1950s.

Chinese party chairman Jiang Zemin visited Moscow in September 1994 and concluded a protocol that resolved some borderdisputes and generally strengthened bilateral ties. During Yeltsin's visit to China in April 1996, both sides described their relationship as evolving into a "strategic partnership," which included substantially increased arms sales. At the April meeting, new agreements made progress toward delineating and demilitarizing the two countries' 3,645 kilometers of common border. Although border security and illegal Chinese immigration into the Russian Far East were controversial issues for Russian regional officials, Yeltsin demanded regional compliance with the agreements. Russia respected China's claim that Taiwan is part of its territory, although Russia's trade with Taiwan increased to nearly US$3 billion in 1995 and Russia planned to open trade offices on the island in 1996.

In 1994-96 China emerged as a major market for Russian arms, having bought several dozen Su-27 fighter aircraft and several Kilo-class attack submarines. Russia also had a positive trade balance in the sale of raw materials, metals, and machinery to China. A series of high-level state visits occurred in 1994 and 1995. Both countries pursued closer ties, in each case partly to counterbalance their cooling relations with the United States. In

March 1996, Russia announced that it would grant China a loan of US$2 billion to supply Russian nuclear reactors for power generation in northeast China, and further cooperation was proposed in uranium mining and processing, fusion research, and nuclear arms dismantlement.

China and Russia's joint perception of shared external threats drove warming relations. These threats include concerns that the they overtly sought to counter: terrorism, separatism and extremism. Russia actually perceives an expanding NATO as its primary external threat, and sought to use closer ties with China as a counterweight. China in turn sought to use this to counter U.S. military cooperation with Japan and South Korea in Northeast Asia. Sino-Russian cooperation in slowing down the push for additional sanctions against Iran was an example of a joint Chinese-Russian desire to counter the United States.

It is no coincidence that Dmitri Medvedev chose China [and Kazakhstan] for his first trip abroad as Russian president in May 2008. During the past eight years, Russia-China trade increased seven-fold, reaching $48-billion last year. The balance of trade is very much in China's favor. Russia basically exports oil and timber and precious metals to China. Russia supplies natural resources for Chinese industry, while China exports consumer goods and also increasingly industrial equipment, manufacturing goods. It's a very, very unequal relationship. And the Russians are not very happy with the fact that they seem to be almost, what they fear to be a raw materials appendage to the growing Chinese economy. The relationship in trade terms is almost acquiring a neo-colonial tinge to it.

By 2008, with the two countries' "strategic partnership" a decade old, China and Russia regularly emphasized the positive in relations between the two countries. Premier Wen Jiabao during his 05 November 2008 visit to Moscow declared that Sino-Russian ties are at their "best in history." Wen was celebrating the closing of the "Year of China" in Russia, which followed 2006's "Year of Russia" in China.

From the early 1990s until 2006, Moscow was Beijing's leading weapons supplier, averaging one-to-two billion dollars a year in sales. Top items included the Sukhoi SU-27 jet fighter, "Kilo" class submarines, missiles and destroyers. But analysts say that after 2006, arms sales had dropped. In 1992, China bought Russia's Su-27 fighter jets. Fifteen years later, Beijing unveiled J-11B aircraft which Moscow labeled as a copycat version of Su-27. Russia also accused China of producing cloned versions of Su-33 fighter jet, S-300 air defense system, the Smerch multiple rocket launcher and the Msta self-propelled howitzer in violation of intellectual property agreements.

What the Chinese had been essentially doing was reverse-engineering the Russian aircraft and destroyers, and they've stopped buying them now. And Russia is concerned that basically China has stolen the copies and now are going to put them in production and not buy Russian equipment. So after 2005, arms sales were stagnant. Russia was worried that that they had essentially sold out all of their know-how and technological expertise to China, and China had essentially committed copyright infringement and was building their own.

PRC military buyers have largely replaced Russian-made goods with domestically produced equipment due to rapid increases in quality in the Chinesearms. By 2008 the PLA was so impressed with the quality of Chinese-made arms that they no longer viewed Russian arms as important to their military procurement. In fact, the PLA was increasingly complaining about the quality of Russian-made arms China had previously purchased.

China and Russia shared common goals of limiting U.S. influence in Central Asia, maintaining political stability in the region and avoiding another color revolution like in Ukraine or Georgia. While China and Russia enjoyed political and security cooperation in Central Asia, the two countries competed economically in the region, particularly on energy issues. China was very interested in multilateral economic cooperation on cross-border infrastructure and transportation projects, while Russia was concerned that multilateral economic cooperation in Central Asia would primarily benefit China.

Despite China and Russia's public statements about the importance of their strategic partnership, neither country viewed its bilateral relationship as its top foreign policy priority. The main barriers to better relations between China and Russia were the lack of trust on both sides and the difficulty both countries faced translating the principles of their strategic partnership into concrete measures. Building good relations with Russia was China's second most important foreign policy priority after improving relations with the United States. Russia viewed relations with China as less important than its relationship with the United States, the European Union and the Commonwealth of Independent States (CIS).

China's close official ties with Russia were not reflective of Chinese officials' true views of Russia. In spite of PRC public support for the Sino-Russian "strategic partnership," many Chinese officials privately view Russia as "irrational, aggressive and untrustworthy". Chinese concerns about Russian aggression, as well as China's proximity to Russia, necessitated a careful, low-key approach to dealing with Russia. China's relationship with Russia was the best embodiment of China's foreign policy dictum of "hiding one's capacities and biding one's time".

China-Russia relations could experience big changes after 2012, as power passed from President Hu Jintao and Premier Wen Jiabao to a younger generation of leaders led by Vice President Xi Jinping and Executive Vice Premier Li Keqiang. Hu and Wen had come of age during the honeymoon period of China-Soviet relations in the 1950s and still felt affinity for Russia, whereas Xi and Li's generation had had relatively little exposure to Russian culture and had few good feelings about Russia. These younger leaders' personal attitudes about Russia could affect bilateral relations, particularly if tensions were to arise over energy or other issues.

In March 2013 Beijing and Moscow signed two arms-sale contracts in which China will buy Russian fighter jets and submarines. The deals, for 24 Su-35 fighters and four Lada-class submarines, raised concern among some regional players and media. Chinese observers said the reaction was "unnecessary" because the purchase is not directed at any third party. The purchase deals were signed before President Xi Jinping's visit to Russia. The purchases represented "the first time in nearly 10 years" that China had bought large military technological equipment from Russia.

Li Hong, secretary-general of the China Arms Control and Disarmament Association, said the recent purchases and joint building plan serve as an indicator of the evolution of the overall Sino-Russian strategic partnership. "It is the natural, well-deserved fruit of bilateral defense cooperation, and both sides have made it clear that the bilateral strategic partnership is not targeting anyone," Li said.

The enhanced agenda of bilateral defense cooperation also saw Xi, who is also chairman of the Central Military Commission, visit Russia's Defense Ministry. Xi is the first Chinese head of state to have made the tour, and he said the idea of visiting the ministry was proposed by Russian President Vladimir Putin. The world is still unequal, unbalanced and tumultuous, with challenges of both "traditional and nontraditional" threats, as well as the further spreading of turmoil in some areas, Xi said. China and Russia, in the face of complicated international situation, should strengthen their coordination, and work with the international community to deal with all kinds of challenges and threats, he said.

Chang Wanquan, Chinese State councilor and defense minister, said during a meeting with Russian Defense Minister Sergei Shoigu that wide-ranging and multilayer defense cooperation has become a cornerstone of the China-Russia comprehensive strategic partnership. "Given the complex international scenario today, China-Russia strategic cooperation and coordination will not only benefit the two peoples, but also help promote world peace and stability," he said.

In Russia, a sharp intensification of propaganda, "turning to the East" in 2014 led to the formation in a large part of society of ridiculous hopes on the progress of bilateral relations. As expected, they were replaced by an equally absurd "disappointment" in 2015 with the spread of absurd rumors about the "actual accession of China to the sanctions," and the absence of any progress in Russian-Chinese cooperation. One problem is especially disastrous in Russia against the background of well-known features of the Russian state propaganda, which ballyhoo d political plans as soon as they begin to acquire at least a vague outline. The formations are exaggerated, deliberately creating unrealistic expectations in order to gain short-term political payoff, which will inevitably lead to disappointment in the project and to discredit it. This in Russia in recent years has ruined the reputation of countless important reforms, economic and technological programs, which, strictly speaking, the actual point of view, could be regarded as a complete or partial success.

The June 2016 Sino-Russian joint statement on strengthening global strategic stability starts with a reference to "dangerous trend", associated with the desire to "certain states and military-political alliances to achieve determines the military and political superiority" in order to use force and the threat of force to advance their interests. Further declaration accusing "some countries and alliances" in the care of the dialogue on cuts the weapons that "are considered by them as a means to ensure military superiority." Russia and China refuse to consider strategic stability as a purely military category from the scope of nuclear arms. Russia and China clearly indicated that concerned the deployment of elements of US missile defense system in Eastern Europe and Northeast Asia "under false pretenses". Next, the two countries set out their own new understanding of the strategic stability, which, apparently, will serve as a basis for further negotiations with the United States on strategic issues. Russia and China refuse to consider strategic stability as a purely military category from the scope of nuclear arms. Both countries apparently consider nuclear weapons as one of the foundations of its security and intend to fend off any US anti-nuclear initiatives counterclaims to discuss the nuclear issue in the complex, taking into account conventional weapons and non-military aspects of security.

CHALLENGES TO US INTERNATIONAL STRATEGY

Some US officials admit that closer ties between Moscow and Beijing are cause for concern. They say, at the very least, debates are more complicated now on the UN Security Council, where Russia and China frequently make common cause against interventionist initiatives favoured by the United States and Britain. Deadlock on the UN Security Council reminiscent of the Cold

War era is becoming a regular occurrence. For instance, knowing that both Russia and China would probably veto military intervention in Kosovo, the Clinton Administration decided to work through NATO. Both Moscow and Beijing were concerned about external intervention on humanitarian grounds, which would be relevant to conflicts within Russia such as Chechnya, and within China such as its claims over Taiwan. Further, NATO was again conspiring to force the US value system on a Third World state.

Russia, China, and India watched the United States in conflicts throughout the 1990s and each learned the same lessons. Indian military and political sources were among the first to react to the Kosovo operation and to speculate on preliminary lessons to be learned. "We are studying what's going on there [in Kosovo] and drawing our lessons from it." A common theme in Indian, Russian, and Chinese thinking since Operation Desert Storm has been the importance of "force multipliers" provided by information technology, AWACs, mid-air refuelling, unmanned aerial vehicles, and electronic warfare capabilities. Analysts in all three countries believe their armed forces can succeed against a high-technology foe if they use these force multipliers in combination with clever low-technology tactics, urban guerilla warfare, financial terrorism, computer hacking, media warfare, diplomatic actions, and psychological warfare.

In light of the new "interventionist-oriented NATO doctrine" and the new capabilities of long-range precision conventional weapons, Indian military thinkers recommend upgrading its nuclear arms to deter Western intimidation and attack. This is a prime example of the drive toward nuclear weapons and its cascading effects predicted by

General Makmut Gareyev, President of the Russian Academy of Military Science. He believes that countries, including Russia, that are unable to match an opponent in high-technology conventional weapons will resort to nuclear weapons in order to deter conventional strikes. Until 1998, India held the principled position that nuclear deterrence was abhorrent to human sentiment, since it implies that if required to defend its own existence, a state will act with pitiless disregard for the consequences of its own and its adversary's people. But in remarks made on 15 March 1999, Prime Minister A. B. Vajpayee asserted: "The nuclear weapon is not an offensive weapon. It is a weapon of self-defence. It is the kind of weapon that helps in preserving peace. If in the days of the Cold War there was no use of force, it was because of the balance of terror." It is also true that India has begun revamping its conventional forces to push the nuclear threshold upward, creating more options with those conventional forces before resorting to nuclear weapon use.

In his article titled, "Nuclear Shadows on High Tech Warfare," Major General Wu Jianguo, former associate professor and dean of the Antichemical Warfare Academy, sums up the Chinese view of its nuclear capability: "When countries possessing nuclear weapons and high-tech conventional weapons are involved in a war in which the conflict is intensifying, the possible use of nuclear weapons cannot be ruled out. Nuclear weapons, therefore, are still a trump card in the hands of nuclear nations."

Many scenarios that would present a challenge to the United States could arise from the triangular strategic partnership. One possible conflict scenario is that of China and Taiwan. This is a possible conflict for several reasons. First, China is going through an economic modernization. This is good over the long run for encouraging political liberty. In the short run, however, as large state-owned enterprises are disestablished, the Chinese may have unemployment of millions to tens of millions and social and political disruption of one kind or another.

For thousands of years dictators have responded to domestic problems by playing the nationalism card and focusing attention on a foreign enemy or foreign problem. Taiwan will be front and centre because now it is a thriving, prosperous, free-enterprise democracy. Taiwan inescapably disproves those people in Southeast Asia and in the PRC who have said for years that Asians do not have an aptitude for democracy and need to be ruled with a firm hand. Taiwan is an affront to the leaders in Beijing the same way Poland's Solidarity movement in the summer of 1989 was an affront to the leaders in the Kremlin and the dictators in Eastern Europe. The Taiwan Strait is one of the most likely places over the next five to ten years where the United States might end up in a clear confrontation with another nuclear power.

How would such a conflict evolve? Top echelons of the PLA officer corps do not necessarily share a common point of view with regard to Taiwan, and the advice they give is not necessarily militaristic. However, a Western intelligence source surmises that high-ranking naval and air force officers support a militant stance in Taiwan. They, rather than the ground forces, have received the benefits of increases in the defence budget and are eager to test their new capabilities.

Beijing is not likely to haphazardly lob a few missiles over to Taiwan and see what happens. Beijing would have a plan and expect to win. The more probable scenario would be for the Chinese to effect simultaneous crises to distract the United States, forcing the Americans to choose between Taiwan and another ally. This quote from Chinese ultra-nationalist author He Xing lends credence to the "simultaneous crises" theory:

China must pay close attention to those countries that are opposed to American interests, or are potential strategic enemies. It must be borne in mind that the enemies of enemies are one's own allies.... Know this: the more the United States encounters trouble in other places in the world, the more difficult it is for it to concentrate its power on dealing with China and the greater the opportunities for China's existence and development.

Hypothetically, Beijing might cooperate with Moscow on the timing of an attack on Taiwan. Moscow could simultaneously start a conflict with emerging democracies in the Baltics or the Caucasus. Or Beijing and New Delhi could cooperate on timing, with India engaging Pakistan, perhaps with the support of Moscow. Both Russia and China are arming other enemies of the United States such as Iran and Iraq. Iraq could be persuaded by Beijing or Moscow to simultaneously start a conflict with Kuwait, Saudi Arabia, or Israel. China could concurrently attack Taiwan and stop the food flow to North Korea, forcing millions of refugees into South Korea, and causing the United States to choose between helping Taiwan and assisting South Korea.

The possibility of a nuclear dimension to a conflict between China and Taiwan is all too real. On 2 December 1998, the Defence Intelligence Agency (DIA) reported that the PLA had conducted exercises that included simulated nuclear missile attacks on Taiwan and on US military forces in the region. DIA analysts determined that the missile units were conducting mock nuclear attacks on Taiwan and against US Army troops based in South Korea. US marines on the Japanese island of Okinawa and mainland Japan also were targeted.

The missile exercise directly threatened the 37,000 troops based in South Korea and the 47,000 troops in Japan, including about 25,000 marines on Okinawa. All of these China-Taiwan scenario options are conjecture, but they are not beyond the realm of possibility and are worth considering. That may be particularly so in the aftermath of the terrorist strikes on the United States on 11 September 2001 and the US response. The volatility of the current situation calls into question many of our previous assumptions about stability and the likely course of international and regional relations.

The study of triangles in International Relations

The metaphor of a triangle has become increasingly popular in the historical-analytical studies of the big-power relations (Zha, 2001: 117). A triangle views the evolution of relations among three nation-states as an inseparable whole. It implies that one of the three actors adopts a particular foreign policy decision toward a second actor either as a result of or as an effect of managing its relations with the third actor. During the Cold War, relations among the United States, the Soviet Union, and China were considered to form a "Great Triangle". None of the three actors could act independently toward either of the other two without taking into consideration the third party.

The study of triangles has its origins in sociology and social psychology with a particular focus on the individual level of analysis (Woo, 2003: 33-63). The Levels of Analysis approach was first used by Kenneth Waltz and later elaborated by David J. Singer, which offered three different sources of explanations. If the individual level is the focus, then the personality, perceptions, choices, and activities of individual decision makers and individual participants provide the explanation. If the state level, or domestic factors, is the focus, then the explanation is derived from characteristics of the state: the type of government (democracy or authoritarianism), the type of economic system (capitalist or socialist), interest groups within the country, or even the national interest. If the international system level is the focus, then the explanation rests with the anarchic characteristics of that system or with international and regional organizations and their strengths and weaknesses (Waltz, 1961: 20-29). The purpose of theory is to guide foreign policy makers toward an understanding of which of these various explanations are necessary and sufficient to explain the behaviour of the states. Sociological coalition theory and the theory of structural balance have especially influenced the study of triangles in international relations. Coalition theorists maintain that the distribution of power among the players decides who is to align with whom (Caplow, 1956: 489-493). Structural balance theorists argue that the fate of the remaining side is determined by the nature of the other two relationships because players pursue cognitive consistency (McDonald and Roscrance, 1985: 57-82).

However, those above cannot be identified as sufficient explanations of interstate behaviour in a triangular setting. Lowell Dittmer has attempted to explain the strategic triangle from a rational choice perspective. He has viewed the triangle as some "sort of a transactional game among three players" (Dittmer, 1981: 485-515). Dittmer has developed the following typology, according to which there are three ideal patterns of interaction in a triangle: "the ménage-a-trois" consisting of symmetrical relations of amity among all the three players; "the romantic triangle" consisting of amity between one 'pivot' player and the two 'wing' players but enmity between the latter two; and "the stable marriage" consisting of amity between two of the players and enmity between each and the third.

The India-China-United States strategic triangle cannot be absolutely identified with any of these patterns. Each of these pattern dynamics has specific rules of rational play. Dittmer argues that the shift from one pattern to another is a function of the attempts of the players to freeze a given configuration through commitment to a treaty or a common ideology, interacting with periodic crises that test their commitments (Dittmer, 1981: 489).

The triangular pattern may assume various shades based on the mutual engagements amongst the players. It may be cooperative, or hierarchical, or competitive. Washington-based Indian correspondent, Seema Sirohi argues that the tendency of the relationship among the US, India and China can be characterised as a romantic triangle, implying that one country tries to benefit from the tensions between the other two; if ever the relationship between India and China deteriorates, the US will benefit from that deterioration and enjoy curry and Peking duck in the same meal (Sirohi, 2004). Will the US be able to maintain its advantageous 'pivot' position and benefit from the tensions between China and India? Such an assertion is perhaps too simplistic, because their relationships are much more complicated than that. The questions remain, "How does improving Indo-US relations affect India's relations with China?" or "What would be the American reaction to increasing co-operation between India and China?" or "Will India be marginalised as the United States and China dominate regional politics in the Asian sub-continent?" The end of the Cold War certainly did not mark the end of triangular politics.

India-U.S. relations: "Estranged democracies" to "engaging partners" During the first fifty years of India's independence, despite a common history of shared democratic values, India-U.S. relations drifted into a state of "estrangement" (Rajamony, 2002: 1-47). India, pursuing a policy of non-alignment, decided not to join the West in its crusade against Communism which offended the U.S. deeply. The 1960s and 1970s saw the United States veering towards Pakistan while the former Soviet Union offered political, military and economic support to India.

India – U.S. relations hit rock bottom in 1971 during the war with Pakistan over the liberation of Bangladesh. A virtual entente emerged between the United States, China and Pakistan against India. The United States sent its Seventh Fleet into the Bay of Bengal in what was seen by India as a blatant act of nuclear blackmail, and encouraged China to open a second front against India.

The end of the Cold War, the collapse of the Soviet Union and the launching of an economic liberalization program in India in the early nineties ushered in a new era in the estranged relationship. Although, there was greater interaction at the political, economic and the military levels, this cooperation was counterbalanced by tensions related to questions of non-proliferation. The conduct of nuclear tests and the announcement of a program of weaponization by India in May 1998 led to yet another low point in the relationship. The United States joined hands with China in leading international opinion against India and to call for a roll-back of its nuclear program. The United States further went on to impose military, economic, scientific and technological sanctions against India. After the Indian nuclear tests in 1998, the non-proliferation aspect of the Indo-U.S. bilateral relationship became more prominent, given the fact that India has always been a vociferous critic of the Non-Proliferation Treaty (NPT) regime which divided the world into nuclear-haves and have-nots.

The Kargil conflict of 1999 between India and Pakistan further provided the United States with an opportunity to play a positive role in the subcontinent by calling for a withdrawal of Pakistani infiltrators from across the Line of Control in Kashmir. Later, the visit of the American President Bill Clinton to India in March 2000 marked a major change in American foreign policy. By undertaking a five day visit to India and only a transit halt of a few hours in Pakistan, the Clinton administration made it clear that its priority within South Asia would be to engage India and strengthen its relations with India. The United States accepted that India, the largest democracy in the world and a potentially important economic partner could not be equated with Pakistan, a country, one seventh the size of India and facing serious economic problems as well as chronic political instability.

The U.S. developed a comprehensive and institutionalized relationship with India, covering broad fields such as economic ties, political dialogue and military exchanges. The U.S. also adopted a policy on the Kashmir issue-namely, calling for respect of the Line of Control (LoC), advocating direct dialogue between India and Pakistan, and opposing the use of force to resolve the dispute that was more favourable to India. India became the largest recipient of U.S. development and food aid in South Asia: U.S. assistance to India in 2000 reached a total of $170 million-second only to Indonesia among Asian states and more than 45 times that of Pakistan's ($3.78 million) (Guihong, 2003).

When George W. Bush ascended the White House in January 2001, his Republican Administration continued the Clinton policy of engagement in South Asia, with a special emphasis on U.S.-India relations. The realm of security was the first beneficiary of transforming U.S.-India relations.

The Bush Administration de-emphasized non-proliferation as the sole determinant of US policy towards India and moved away from its demands for India's signing of the CTBT (Comprehensive Test Ban Treaty). The second element of the transformation was in the area of defence cooperation followed by exchanges of high-level defence officials between the two countries and joint military exercises.

An indication of this new development was India's response to President Bush's 1 May 2001 speech on missile defence (Tomar, 2001). India is being slowly driven towards the idea of de-emphasizing the traditional agenda of reduced reliance on the use of nuclear weapons and is aligning itself with the new ideas such as missile defences and counter proliferation that have been highlighted by the radicals in the Bush Administration. There is a rising, complex view within New Delhi that it is in India's interest to adapt quickly to the changing international rules of the nuclear game, and within that framework the past emphasis on disarmament and no-first-use might no longer be the top priorities of Indian foreign policy.

Having recognised the proliferation of WMD as a serious threat to its own national security, India is deeply concerned about the spread of nuclear weapons into the hands of states or groups of terrorists who do not abide by the traditional rules of nuclear deterrence. India's own experience with Pakistan's nuclear blackmail and Islamabad's strategy of using the nuclear balance to foment terrorism across the border co-relates with the arguments put forward by Washington that there are forces out there who cannot be deterred by traditional means. Added to it is the concern that Pakistan might become a failed state or that nuclear weapons might fall into the hands of extremist forces in that country. This kind of approach paves the way for India to continue the security and strategic dialogue with the United States that had begun under the Clinton administration (Sidhu, 2001: 59-66).

From 2001 to 2003, the agenda for bilateral cooperation between the United States and India extended to diplomatic collaboration, military-to-military relations, counterterrorism cooperation, and public diplomacy. This paved the way for one of the Bush administration's major first-term diplomatic achievements, Next Steps in Strategic Partnership (NSSP). This agreement, which was announced in January 2004 after months of negotiation, drew its inspiration from the Bush-Vajpayee Joint Statement of November 2001.

The strategic dialogue initiated from this statement emphasized on global security issues, including India's quest for permanent United Nations Security Council membership, future defence cooperation, high-technology trade, and space-related collaboration, as well as regional issues pertaining to security in and around South Asia. The energy dialogue has the focus on energy security matters including the proposed Indian-Iranian-Pakistani gas pipeline, cooperation on nuclear safety, and, most important of all, ways of integrating India into the global nuclear regime so as to address New Delhi's desire for renewed access to safeguarded nuclear fuel and advanced nuclear reactors. The economic dialogue, which exists in a limited form, particularly compared with U.S.-China economic interaction, requires high-level political and private-sector participation in order to increase U.S.-Indian economic engagement (Tellis, 2005).

The September 11, 2001 attack and the war on terrorism that followed the tragic event provided a chance for the US and India to forge an even closer strategic cooperation. It has become a turning point in the Indo-US security relationship.

The two countries together implemented a co-operative framework of relationships based on three dimensions: democracy, economy, and security. As Stephen Cohen, the U.S. specialist on South Asia security issues has commented, the United States and India's relationship was "structurally changing" (Cohen, 2000: 1-37). He has continued to argue that India and the United States are each groping for a strategy to cope with the emergence of China as a major world power. There are significant numbers of people, both within the United States and India, which believe that China is a 'threat' to the interests of the two countries (Rajamony, 2002).

The Indo-U.S. defence agreement signed in Washington on June 28, 2005 between the Defence Ministers of the two countries has significant ramifications for the strategic framework involving China, India and the United States.

India has an obvious interest in enhancing cooperation with the world's sole superpower, as India strives to become a major regional power and eventually a powerful global entity. To achieve this goal, India seeks American support to join the Security Council as a permanent member, and also to acquire high technology from the United States and its G-8 partners, including military technology and civilian nuclear energy. The operationalization of the 123 Agreement between India and US on October 10, 2008 marked a watershed achievement in the history of their bilateral relations. The American interest in enhancing Indo-U.S. ties is two-fold. It seeks that India join the coalition forces in their counter-terrorism efforts as India is one of the very few nations in the world that has the trained manpower and logistics to contribute effectively to the cause of uprooting the seeds of violence. U.S. interest also lies in encouraging India to counter China to establish a new balance of power in Asia that would better serve American interests. However, the U.S. Ambassador in India Robert Blackwill had stated that "U.S.-India friendship will not be directed against any third party" (Blackwill, 2001).

Although both the United States and India share certain common interests, it is not imperative that they codify their commitments toward each other.

In today's era of open boundaries and economies, states have diffuse interests and threats and need to maintain fluid foreign relations.

The Indian Prime Minister, Mr Manmohan Singh concluded his momentous visit to the United States in July 2005 by assuring both Pakistan and China that what had been achieved in Washington was not directed against any other country (Dua, 2005). He spoke to the Indian press ensuring that India would continue with its "constructive engagement" with China. The assurance to both Pakistan and China had become necessary in view of the reports that both the countries were feeling concerned about the emerging relationship between India and the United States.

The Indian Prime Minister was confident that closer Indo-U.S. ties would not jeopardize improving Sino-Indian relationship which has completed 60 years of diplomatic relations this year. Obama's recent visit in November 2010 was marked by a pledge to support India's full membership in the Nuclear Suppliers Group (NSG), the Missile Technology Control Regime (MTCR), the Australian Group and the Wassenaar Agreement without insisting on India signing the Nuclear Non Proliferation Treaty (NPT) as a non-weapons state, which was a clear impossibility earlier.

India's membership in these regulatory bodies would give it an equivalent status to the five recognised nuclear weapons states and make it a genuine partner rather than a target of international non-proliferation efforts. In short, the Obama Administration was moving further along the road of US-India cooperation charted during the Bush Administration.

It is to be argued that as a regional power, India needs to consider its geo-strategic limitations and one of its major interests is to ensure that the changing contours of Indo-U.S. relationship do not disrupt the balance of power between India and China and consequently the peace and tranquillity in the neighbourhood.

Sino-U.S. relations: "Strategic partners" to "strategic competitors"

Since the founding of the Peoples' Republic of China (PRC), till the end of the Cold War, China's relations with the United States were overshadowed by ideological rivalry in the context of the East-West balance of power (Hook, 2005: 34).

Sino-American tensions lessened in the 1970s following the Sino-Soviet rift of late 1960s and the opening up of China by the efforts of Nixon-Kissinger duo. Despite the beginning of the economic modernization programme under Deng Xiaoping after 1976, Sino-U.S. bilateral relations continued to be plagued by U.S. complaints about Beijing's human rights policy, neglect of environmental problems, weapons transfers and arms sales to Iran, Pakistan and others and maintenance of protectionist trade policies. The Chinese leaders on the other hand continued to criticise the United States on international platforms as being hegemonic. The Tiananmen Square incident of June 1989 remained a pivotal event in the chronicle of Sino-U.S. relations. It fundamentally changed the way in which bilateral relationship between the two countries has been managed since President Nixon's historic 1972 visit to China (Lampton, 2001). With the collapse of Soviet Communism, the Chinese role in countering Soviet expansionism lost its rationale and the fundamental incompatibilities between the two systems became more pronounced.

However, with the end of the Cold War, the strategic importance of the Sino-U.S. relationship was further strengthened and the policy to 'engage' China for the greater purpose of global peace and stability was undertaken by the Clinton administration (Christopher, 1998: 516).

His regime specifically sought to revitalize relations with China through closer economic cooperation by encouraging China's entry into the World Trade Organization (WTO) and other global conventions. The President's policy was based on the neo-liberal presumption that China's inclusion in global economic and political regimes would encourage Beijing to moderate its internal political behaviour and conform to international standards.

The Bush administration's China policy has taken a significant departure from that of his predecessor (Sidhu and Yuan, 2003: 87). During the 2000 presidential campaign, the Bush campaign on several occasions characterized China as a 'strategic competitor' and a future challenger to critical U.S. interests in the Asia-Pacific region. Thus, the maxim that there are no permanent friends or enemies, only interests (Morgenthau, 1985) can be invoked to describe Sino-US relations. A certain group of academicians in America believe that neither idealism or imperialism, nor engagement or containment can be appropriately applied to the U.S. Policy towards China. The US administration cautioned that: "We don't have a strategic partnership or alliance with China. But we need to have constructive relations, there needs to be a continuing dialogue" (Grier and Thurman, 1999).

As the U.S Department of State Press Release on July 10, 2005 of the speech of the U.S. Secretary of State, Condoleezza Rice emphasized that the relationship between the United States and China is "complex" (U.S Department of State, 2005) with areas of divergent opinions like human rights and religious freedom particularly related to Tibet, Taiwanese independence, military build-up and arms transfers to Iran and Pakistan and favourable balance of trade towards China in the economic sector. However, both the countries have pursued cooperative strategies on issues like nuclear non-proliferation in the

Korean peninsula, counter-terrorism measures and an active economic engagement despite its complications.

Between 2001 and 2003, China's overall trade grew by two-thirds, from $510 billion to $851 billion and among the key factors in this surge in China's global trade were the exports from China to the United States, which grew by more than 40%, from $100 billion in 2000 to $156 billion in 2003 (U.S-China Business Council, 2005). The huge Sino-American trade imbalance has heightened the element of competitiveness in Sino-American relations which has had a positive impact on Indo-U.S relations. In recent years the sale of Patriot PAC-3 missiles worth about US$1 billion to Taiwan, Obama's meeting with Dalai Lama in February 2010 and the constant irritant, the human rights issue, have seriously undermined the US-China relations.

Rosemary Foot in "Chinese strategies in a US-hegemonic global order: accommodating and hedging" argues that the rise of China, especially marked in the 1990s, has prompted a realist argument that the unipolar order is leading to the establishment of a Chinese-led anti-hegemonic coalition, and to China's building up its internal economic and military capabilities in order to become a 'peer competitor' of the United States (Foot, 2006: 77-94). John J. Mearsheimer in "China's Unpeaceful Rise" has raised questions about possible American reaction to China's growing economic and military might. Historical records show that America does not tolerate peer competitors and it is determined to maintain its status as the world's only regional hegemon, if not the sole global hegemon (Mearsheimer, 2006: 160-162).

Despite its reassurances to the rest of the world that the new China would like to build amicable relationships based on mutual trust and long term bonds, the international community is not entirely convinced of China's new role as a harbinger of peace in Asia and the world. China however needs to create a greater sense of openness within its own walls in order for the international community to fully accept China's strategy of peaceful rise. The likelihood of outbreak of a Cold War between the two powers can be avoided if both subordinate national aspirations to a vision of a global order. Kissinger in a recent article in the Washington Post commented that "neither the United States nor China has experience in such a task. Each assumes its national values to be both unique and of a kind to which other peoples naturally aspire. Reconciling the two versions of exceptionalism is the deepest challenge of the Sino-American relationship" (Kissinger, 2011). In the American-Chinese relationship, the over-riding reality is that both countries will not likely be able to dominate the other and that conflict between them would exhaust the potential of their societies. Can they find a conceptual framework to express this reality?

For this, they need a consultative mechanism that permits the elaboration of common long-term objectives and coordinates the positions of the two countries at international conferences. Chinese scholars characterize the current state of affairs as a 'hot peace', not a new 'cold war'. To prevent turning this 'hot peace' into a 'hot war', the China-US relationship must be de-militarized and de-sensationalized. Neither power would gain anything from a head-on military confrontation.

PROSPECTS FOR THE RUSSIA-INDIA-CHINA STRATEGIC TRIANGLE

The Russia-India-China (RIC) strategic triangle is perhaps an under-emphasised theme in the discourse on multi-polarism and emerging groups in that direction. Last year the foreign ministers of these countries met within a fortnight of the meeting of the BRICS at New Delhi, and this year the meeting has yet to take place.

The three countries are rising pillars in a multi-polar globe and their contribution to international economic growth and peace and stability is beyond doubt. The countries' participation in, and being part of, various crucial groupings such as BRICS and G-20 and their economic growth despite global economic slowdown, and their contribution to the reshaping of global decision making process is acknowledged by the nations of the world. The point is: whether this grouping should continue its ad hoc like nature and end up in annual foreign ministerial meetings, or the members need to synergize their activities to match their potential?

The RIC strategic triangle concept, though older than the BRICS concept, is a post-cold war phenomenon. It was originally conceived by the former Russian Foreign Minister, later to become Prime Minister, Yevgeny Primakov. Succeeding an Atlanticist, Primakov was considered to be a Eurasianist. The initial years of complexity in terms of economic crisis had geared Russian foreign policy mechanism Westward. Post-Soviet Russia's first Foreign Minister, Andrei Kozyrev vigorously pursued a pro-Western policy with the belief that Western cooperation would salvage Russia from economic crisis.

In those formative years, there were various strands in Russia's foreign policy making process, including one dominant group advocating a pro-West policy, while another dominant group insisting on continuing the old policy, though in a modified way, of continuing and strengthening old friendships. Primakov belonged to this second group. After becoming Foreign Minister of Russia in 1996, even before that, he argued that Russia is a Eurasian power and must pursue a policy of 'near-abroad,' in which the relations with former Soviet republics and also other countries of Eurasia must be cultivated.

Primakov became Prime Minister in 1998. And the same year during his visit to New Delhi he pitched for a strategic triangle between Russia, India and China. His underlying arguments were the following. After the end of the Cold War, the world is no more divided into blocs. Rather, it is a world of multi-blocs or multi-poles. The rise of regional powers as well as rise of regional organizations complemented such a characterisation of the world order. He argued that in the evolving global order, the three powers must come together to reshape the global order. Russia and India, despite post-cold war changing equations and despite their adaptation to market economy and globalization, shared these viewpoints. Both the powers during this New Delhi visit of Primakov advocated for a multi-polar global order, and argued in favour of a peaceful resolution of the crises around the globe including the Palestinian crisis, crisis in Iraq, and other contentious issues. The triangle as envisioned by Primakov took a concrete shape in 2001.

The global situation has not fundamentally changed since then. The crises still persist or rather galore. The conflicts in the Middle East or in Korea, or the rising menace of extremism and terrorism, or the financial problems have contributed to uncertainty factor and raised questions about the sustainability of the prevalent global order. The last meeting of the foreign ministers in Moscow in April 2012 voices some of these concerns. For instance, the leaders criticised North Korea for rocket lunch but at the same time opposed any sanctions against the peninsular country, and advocated for a peaceful solution through six-party talks. The RIC in that sense can play the role of a balancer in global political and economic processes. Two of the members are permanent members of the United Nations Security Council, the most powerful body with wider acceptance among the nations. All the three countries' global visions converge on many accounts. All of them are in favour of coordinated mechanisms to counter terrorism and extremism, all of them favour a peaceful resolution of crisis in Syria, in case of Iran all of them argue for a peaceful resolution of the crisis, and in case of Afghanistan, the three countries share a common vision of a peaceful and stable polity in the war-torn country after the International Security Assistance Force departs.

There are no doubt differences among the three members, but a closer scrutiny reveals similarities of aspirations trump over dissimilarities of perceptions. India and China have differences over their border demarcations, the three countries have differing interests in Asia-Pacific, but that should not slight the prospects of gains from cooperation. The potentials of cooperation between these three countries are really vast. While Russia is energy rich country, both India and China are energy hungry countries. There can be vast networks of transport and communication between the three countries by exploring the Silk Road through Afghanistan and Central Asia with links with these three countries. In arms sector there are ample scope of cooperation as well. It is the economic diplomacy which needs to be prioritized in relations, while contentious political issues can be dealt with a spirit of moderation and negotiation. In this political sphere too, there has been tremendous progress. There has been no case of border skirmishes between these countries for decades together, and particularly in the context of India and China the high level meetings between national security advisors between the two countries is a regular phenomenon, which has helped in moderating tensions at borders.

The RIC has already many trilateral forums like RIC Trilateral Experts Meeting on Disaster Management, Trilateral Business Forum, and Trilateral Academic Scholars Dialogue. Perhaps this is time to further synergise the trilateral acts by institutionalising the meetings in terms of a permanent secretariat and permanent representatives. Besides foreign ministers, the triangle can also involve highest officials, President in case of Russia and China and Prime Minister in case of India. Perhaps that is an emerging imperative of the post-cold war global order.

STRATEGIC PARTNERSHIPS

But this is not an alliance in the making. Alliances are passé and only a few continue gingerly from the Cold War era. We live in a world today driven by "strategic partnerships". States find themselves in an interdependent system where the traditional power politics of yesteryear doesn't quite fit. After all, every major relationship characterised by strategic tension such as U.S.-China, Japan-China, India-China is simultaneously one of economic gain. The U.S. and China are each other's chief trading partners, while China ranks at the top for Japan and India. Besides, India might confront China at Doklam but it also wants Chinese investment.

Strategic partnerships carry certain characteristic features falling short of alliances. First, unlike alliances, they do not demand commitments to a partner's disputes with other countries. New Delhi does not take a strong position on Japan's territorial disputes with China and Russia. Likewise, Tokyo does not openly side with India in its quarrels with China and Pakistan. For instance, Japan's reaction to the Doklam stand-off, though critical of China implicitly, did not go beyond saying that "all parties involved should not resort to unilateral attempts to change the status quo by force." India's reaction to the verdict of the arbitral tribunal on the South China Sea last year, urging "all parties to show utmost respect for the UNCLOS", reflected a similar dispensation despite Japan's push for a stronger statement. There was also no explicit mention of the South China Sea in the latest joint statement.

Strategic partnership means, first, that both retain the flexibility to continue political engagement and economic cooperation with their common adversary. Second, they avoid "entrapment", or being dragged into a partner's disputes and potentially into conflict, which happened in the First World War. Third, regular high-level political and military interactions facilitate a collaborative approach to strategic policies over a range of economic and military activities. India and Japan, for instance, are not only moving forward on economic and defence cooperation but are also cooperating on other important issues such as civil nuclear energy and Security Council reform.

Given that resort to war is undesirable owing to economic interdependence as well as the presence of nuclear weapons, the aim of major strategic partnerships is to strengthen defences against marginal conflict, convey a determination to stand up to a strategic adversary and, overall, generate a persuasive environment that discourages potential intimidation. Occasionally, as between India and China, a "strategic partnership" is a way of opening a channel of communication and minimal cooperation intended to stabilise and develop the potential for a détente and conceivably something warmer. In this particular case, not much has been accomplished thus far, but it remains a low-cost option for expanding cooperation in the event the political fundamentals of the relationship show an upward swing.

Looking ahead

India's two main strategic partnerships, with the U.S. and Japan, are dovetailing nicely. For New Delhi, the U.S. will remain its chief backer both to enhance India's conventional defence capabilities and to draw political support in global political institutions, for example in components of the nuclear non-proliferation regime. Japan, in the meantime, is becoming its primary collaborator in developing its economic sinews and for building a geostrategic network that offers Indian Ocean states an alternative to dependence on China. Together, the emerging structure of triangular cooperation should give Beijing pause to think.

7

A New World Order: A View from Russia

Since around 2017–2018, the world has been living through a period of progressive erosion, or collapse, of international orders inherited from the past. With the election of Donald Trump and the rapid increase of US containment of Russia and China—which is both a consequence of this gradual erosion and also represents deep internal and international contradictions—this process entered its apogee. A period of collapse opens up possibilities for the creation of a new world order; hopefully, a fairer, stable, and peaceful order than has been previously experienced. Russia has a good chance of influencing the formation a new order.

However, the establishment of a new world order will take time, and in the meantime serious conflicts and crises could occur. The current state of US-Russia relations is just a beginning in this regard. In the medium term, the priority for major powers is to prevent a new large-scale war, which is becoming highly likely. In this regard, Russia, again, intends to act as a key security provider through its foreign and defence policies. Russian achievements in defence, declared by President Putin in his 2018 address to the Federal Assembly (Putin 2018), strengthen deterrence, and show that achieving military ascendency and changing the overall military balance is impossible, thus deterring an arms race, and creating the preconditions for dialogue with Washington. Russia's pivot to Asia will continue and the Greater Eurasia comprehensive partnership concept will gradually be substantiated and thus will become a zone of stability and a powerful unit within the global order.

No major improvement in relations with the United States is in sight, mainly because of the situation within both Western societies and the Western international community itself. At the same time, Russia will continue to deepen partnerships with China and India and to enhance cooperative relations with US allies and partners like Japan, South Korea, and, when possible, Western European countries. Neither major European allies nor Asian allies of the US support further escalation of the Russia-West and US-Russia confrontation. Maintaining these relationships seems the best way to forward the confrontation's conclusion on terms compatible with the current state of the world.

Russia's policy, therefore, is to remain tactically flexible, prepared for every eventuality, but also to be more strategic than ever in building a world order that is stable, peaceful, and comfortable for Russia. As the US and Europe are not ready to engage in order-building with Russia and other major non-Western actors, instead adopting an oppositional posture, and—primarily due to internal political reasons— because they are highly unlikely to so engage in the next decade, a new international order's emergence is more likely to occur in the 2030s or 2040s than in the 2020s, after the inevitable rotation of elites in the US and the EU.

Collapse of orders

The main reason for the general confusion among Western elites and the tension in world politics and the international economy is the simultaneous decay of most global and regional international political and economic orders, by which here we refer to systems of rules, norms, and patterns of behaviour accepted by a majority of actors at a particular time. This decay had been brewing for a long time but has only become visible in the last decade. Figuratively speaking, several tectonic plates on which international order and its underlying concepts have stood have begun to move.

The most dramatic shift is the end of the 500-year-long dominance of the West—firstly Europe, then the US and its allies—in politics, the economy, and ideology. This is chiefly due to loss of the military superiority the West had possessed since the sixteenth and seventeenth centuries.

Up until around the sixteenth century, Europe did not have primacy over most other civilisations. Many of the greatest scientific and industrial discoveries of the time were made in China, Persia, or the Arab world. A combination of factors then led to Western leadership in military technologies and organisation. Spanish and Portuguese navies, then latterly the British navy, led Europe to predominance in the building and use of warships. This capacity to project power abroad enabled Europe to conquer the Americas, Africa, and South Asia, as well as to subordinate China. Interestingly, China had possessed a far more powerful navy two centuries before the Europeans had built theirs, with substantially larger and more capable ships. However, perhaps due to assumptions of Chinese civilisational self-sufficiency or a fear of foreign influence, China destroyed its own navy in the fifteenth century.

In addition to naval and military supremacy, Europe's thirst for world domination was fuelled by its relative poverty, in comparison with other civilisations of the time, and the overcrowded limitations on European elites. Similar factors influenced the Crusades several centuries before the Age of Discovery. Despite the ideological and religious slogans, the major European imperative had been a desire to rob the Middle East of its riches.

The taking possession of colonies and semi-colonies resulted in a pro.found redistribution of global gross national product in Europe and the West's favour. It stimulated a flourishing of European science and culture, further development of military power, and it strengthened European and Western global dominance for several centuries. At this point, Russia was also part of the West. Russia's remarkably quick conquest of Siberia, which took less than a century, was possible not just because of Cossack bravery and desire to escape the lack of freedom in core Russia, but also because of their military superiority: They used canons and guns against the locals' bows and arrows. Unquestioned military superiority also enabled the Russian empire to easily conquer Central Asia in the nineteenth century.

World history as we know it was written by the victors: predominantly European victors. Ferdinand von Richthofen of Germany referred to the religion of economic and cultural interaction between China and the West as the Silk Road. Nowadays, China, reasserting itself ideologically, has branded its new initiative for the region One Belt, One Road. The terms Middle East and Far East were invented by the British and conveyed how far away these regions were from them. Yet the eastern regions of Siberia are still referred to as the Far East.

In the coming decades, the whole of humanity—not just scholars—will learn a new history of civilisation, not the one written by Europeans. Byzantium, which throughout the dark medieval era preserved and developed the best features of European culture in combination with the variety of cultures to Europe's east, will no longer be referred to disparagingly, but will be hailed as one of the triumphs of human civilisation. Whereas the Western Roman Empire collapsed under attack from so-called barbarians to the north, the Eastern Roman Empire, or Byzantium, was bled dry and eventually collapsed largely due to numerous—some might say barbaric—interventions from the west. The changing fortunes of Chinese, Indian, and Persian dynasties will be viewed as of equal importance to the alternating rules of the Stuarts, the Bourbons, the Habsburgs, and the Romanovs. The current generation's grandchildren will live in a world of different historical narratives. This will certainly challenge prevailing European—including Russian—cultural and historical identities.

The threshold moment in the centuries-old history of Western military supremacy and political and ideological ascendency occurred in the middle of the twentieth century, when the West's opponents—the USSR and then China—obtained nuclear weapons. The West lost supremacy over half the world. This was followed by the US failure to win the Korean War and its subsequent defeat in Vietnam. In both instances, nuclear escalation was considered but not employed.

The feeling of supremacy returned for a brief period in 1991–2007 when the Soviet Union fell apart and ceased to be a military-political balancer, while the West declared a "unipolar moment" (Krauthammer 1990/91) and proclaimed that the US-led and West-centric liberal world order should become universal and global. After political losses in Afghanistan, Iraq, Libya, and Syria, that sense of primacy is now falling apart, to the irritation of its architects. The Trump Administration was the first to officially recognise the loss of US military pre-eminence. The January 2018 National Defense Strategy claims that "For decades the United States has enjoyed uncontested or dominant superiority in every operating domain. We could generally deploy our forces when we wanted, assemble them where we wanted, and operate how we wanted. Today, every domain is contested—air, land, sea, space, and cyberspace" (Summary of the 2018 National Defense Strategy).

The crisis of 2008 showed, among other things, that the Western economic model was unable to deal with open competition when not backed up by military supremacy. The liberal trade and economic order mainly benefited those who had designed its rules, based on military and naval superiority, firstly the United Kingdom and then the United States. Their superior guns and warships, alongside efficient military organisation, made it possible to plunder colonies and dictate their own trading rules. The most vivid example is the series of wars in the nineteenth century that forced China to engage in the opium trade with British India, which was hugely profitable for the British, but intoxicated a considerable portion of Chinese society and accelerated its ruin.

The liberal economic order created by the West—primarily the US—at the Bretton Woods conference and expanded to the entire world since the 1990s is being undermined by a pile-up of contradictions and a reluctance of the rising new powers to play solely by the rules of the old powers. The new economic powers have certainly used the liberal order to progress economically. Western powers have encouraged this in the hope that the new powers would eventually transform themselves according to Western economic and political models and join the West as apprentice members. This is not happening. As the Trump Administration's 2017 National Security Strategy correctly put it, "the US post-Cold war policy was based on the assumption that engagement with rivals and their inclusion in international institutions and global commerce would turn them into benign actors and trustworthy partners. For the most part, this premise turned out to be false" (National Security Strategy 2017).

However, the main reason for the decay of this particular liberal economic order is the United States itself, and its protectionist and mercantilist turn upon realisation that when not backed up by military and political supremacy, the liberal order increasingly benefits new powers which refuse to yield to Western competitors. Trump's America first slogan is the hyperbolic epitome of the prevailing sentiments among the US elite and its broader population. The US and Europe still possess leading positions within the international economic system and continue to use them to redirect the benefits of the existing economic order in their favour. First and foremost, this occurs through sanctions, which target economic containment of adversaries rather than changes in their foreign policy. Thus, the US and Europe undermine both the liberal system and trust in themselves. It is no coincidence that the massive use of sanctions by Western countries is justified in order to apply pressure in the absence of the possibility of using military force.

Another fading system is the bipolar confrontation, even though both Americans and docile new Europeans are eager to renew divisions in Europe, and the US is trying to create new divisions in the Paci.c. Western Europe would like to avoid a confrontation with Russia, but it is holding on to Atlantic bonds which involve security being paid for by the US. The US is currently trying to distance itself from Europe, especially economically and strategically, while at the same time attempting to keep Europe dependent. The US is also taking steps to besiege China from the south and east through its Indo-Pacific strategy, an attempt to weaken Chinese positions by threatening trade and energy-supply routes in the Indian Ocean and South China Sea, by creating the Quad—the partnership of the US, Japan, India, and Australia—as a coalition to contain China, and by providing an alternative to the OBOR initiative (Swain 2018), while—in defiance of any reasonable foreign policy logic—pushing Russia and China into a de facto alliance.

It seems that faced with the apparent failure of attempts to include China and Russia within a US-led order as junior partners fully transformed in Western terms, as well as with the crumbling of this order, the US has decided to return to fully fledged containment (Suslov 2018). The US has intensified containment vis-à-vis both China and Russia in political, security, and economic fields, beginning with depictions of their roles across the world as profoundly negative and even predatory, and pushing other countries to pick sides: Either they are with the US as part of the liberal order, or against it, together with Moscow and Beijing. See, for example, Rex Tillerson's speeches on US policies in Latin America and Africa, given at the University of Texas in Austin on 1 February 2018, and at George Mason University on 6 March 2018. He describes China, and to some extent Russia too, as malevolent actors, and he cautions countries in those regions against deepening relations with them.

Finally, the US has adopted a new ideology of global polarisation and division, presenting Russia and China in the most recent National Security Strategy and other influential documents as a kind of united authoritarian bloc of revisionist powers committed to undermining the existing international order and opposing the free world. This aims to unite allies and partners under US leadership and to win a global confrontation for the second time.

However, attempts to restore a bygone bipolarity—let alone win a new global Cold War against Russia and China together—which are relatively beneficial for the US and the West more broadly, are actually doomed, the contemporary world being far more complex and far less dependent on the will of major powers than the world of the twentieth century. The overwhelming majority of US allies and partners in Asia, the Middle East, Latin America, and Africa are clearly resistant to the either–or choice between the US on one hand and China and Russia on the other, and would prefer to diversify their foreign economic and security relationships. The stronger US pressure is for countries to make such a choice, the weaker its influence and credibility will be. India, although a willing participant in the Indo-Pacific process and the Quad because of its growing concerns over Chinese economic and military advantage and what New Delhi sees as the policies of an encroaching Chinese hegemony in Southeast Asia and the Indian Ocean region, is nonetheless highly unlikely to dispense with its independent foreign policy, reject its Eurasian ambitions, withdraw from the Shanghai Co.operation Organization, and become just another US ally in the Indo-Pacific region.

Even if a new bipolarity were to ever become a reality, it would hardly bene.t the United States or the West. Given Beijing's pace of growth, its level of investment in science, education, and technology, and its ability to maintain an authoritarian political system—which is more effective in international competition when combined with a market economy—China is likely to become the world's number one power in fifteen years.

The Thucydides Trap, the danger of a war between a dominant power and a rising power, has been heavily discussed lately. Pressure from the east and the south and an increase in rivalry with the United States has forced

Beijing to progress westward and south-westward. This will have a dual effect. On one hand, this will spur the emergence of new clusters of development in central Eurasia and the formation of the comprehensive Eurasian partnership. But on the other hand, this will simultaneously intensify the opposite tendency, stoking concerns among China's neighbours about its growing power. To mitigate these concerns, China will need to allow greater multilateralism in its foreign policy and accept engagement in regional systems of rules and institutions, i. e., not rules imposed from the outside, but rules developed together with China. This is the kernel of the concept of Greater Eurasia.

The West's position

Could history have turned out less unfavourably for the West? The rise of the non-Western powers was inevitable, and Western military force lost potency not simply because of the Cold War years of strategic parity with the USSR/ Russia, but also due to other reasons. Still, these changes could have followed a softer trajectory.

In the early 1990s, Russia wanted to join the West and become a NATO member. Certainly, if it had joined the Western alliance, NATO would have taken a very different course. The US would have lost its hegemonic position. It would have been diffcult to impose the insanely incompetent deci.sions to initiate wars against Yugoslavia and Libya, and interventions in Afghanistan and Iraq. In any case, the West rejected this opportunity and failed to offer Russia a new Marshall Plan, as had been the case with Europe after World War Two, which strengthened Western military, economic, and ideological power for years to come. Without question, being a country with an almost sacred attitude to sovereignty, Russia could hardly have been fully integrated. Still, allied relations could have been established. This would have dramatically changed the world's military balance and history would have followed a different path.

Alas, the West decided that Russia was defeated, and that for the victory to be to complete, Russia needed to be pushed further back and deprived of any serious influence beyond its borders. Recall the Western mantra of the 1990s and 2000s that Russia must not have veto right over European security issues, including decisions on the use of force, and security and military architecture. Thus, instead of integration and a re-shaping of the Western order together with Russia, turning it into a broadly inclusive Northern Hemisphere order, the West launched a neo-Weimar policy vis-à-vis Russia with its primary manifestation being NATO expansion.

As a result, the West faced a geopolitically perked up, non-Western—or even anti-Western—Russia and doomed itself to a more rapid and sustained withering of its international standing. This chapter's senior author, who had initially pushed Russia to join NATO and later to establish an Alliance of Europe with the EU, was so shocked by the West's lack of reason when rejecting the Russian offer to build an alliance that he began to doubt the West's rationality. Western policy adventures that followed this episode have turned these doubts into a confidence in the West's historic incompetence.

Western countries, only recently regarded as examples of efficiency, are having a hard time. Western populations increasingly feel the negative impact of globalisation, with middle classes facing an unpromising future. The information revolution—primarily social networks—makes societies less subject to control by elites, parties, and traditional mass media. This is particularly evident in the United States, where swathes of the traditional middle class, in defiance of the regular channels of influence controlled by elites, voted for the non-standard presidential candidate who was able to express their views, fears, and concerns, if not their interests. It is this loss of control and the victory of a candidate who had campaigned against the establishment, rather than Donald Trump's unconventional personality or inexperience, which explains the fury, bordering on insanity, which has swept the majority of the American elite. Jimmy Carter, Ronald Reagan, and Barack Obama were also unconventional and relatively inexperienced, especially in foreign a.airs, but unlike Trump, they were part of the elite and were nominated by the elite in order to make necessary corrections after crises.

After its defeat in November 2016, the US establishment, and especially what is sometimes referred to as the deep state, has struggled to restore con.trol over the political system. This struggle is only partly directed towards Trump. Anti-Russian rhetoric also appears to be a cover for attempts to reform US domestic policy and make society more manageable, primarily by tightening control over social media, which made Trump's victory possible. Social media, which was originally seen as an open platform for the competition of ideas, and which helped the US to interfere in domestic a.airs in other countries like Egypt, Ukraine, and Russia, is now seen as the major channel of what is referred to as Russian meddling. As a result, the necessity of strengthening supervision and building defence against "Russian attacks against democracy" has already become a narrative in the US. In other words, traditionalist elites are trying to, as they present it, save democracy by strengthening authoritarian control over mass media.

The extraordinary avalanche of accusations that "Russian meddling" is undermining democracies all over the world seems to be cover for attempts to regain control. This certainly includes limiting opportunities for foreign actors to influence US policies.

As far as this chapter's authors are concerned, Russia would have been proud if at least 2 percent of these accusations were grounded in truth. The US elite must learn a lesson: People who live in glass houses shouldn't throw stones. This includes extensive long-term meddling in the internal a.airs of other countries, in most cases bringing chaos and bloodshed; Ukraine being a recent case. Fortunately, due to Russian involvement, a regime change in Syria that would have resulted in a profound strengthening of radical Islamist terrorism, was prevented. However, we doubt that even 2 percent of the accusations have any basis. In the meantime, US elites, divided and almost waging civil war against each other, are further undermining the moral and political standing of the West, and indeed of democracy itself.

Naturally, irritation with Russia has geopolitical causes, too. Russia is both symbolic of, and largely the reason for, the loss of US military supremacy. Russia intentionally opposed the US-led liberal world order, especially at.tempts to universalise it, whereby non-Western powers could take no part in order-building. Russia has opposed NATO enlargement since the 1990s, and has opposed illegal aggression in what was left of Yugoslavia in 1999, Iraq in 2003, and Libya in 2011. Russia has always demanded a role of co-designer, co-architect, and co-manager in the construction of a new international order, on parity with the West, and both Russian domestic and foreign policy, including nuclear weapons policy and policies with regard to the territory of the former USSR have clearly demonstrated Russia's refusal to be simply a junior participant in a US-led system.

The roots of anti-Russian policy run deep and a thaw in bilateral relations cannot be expected in the near future, especially if US elites fail to take control of the country's domestic situation. US-Europe estrangement is not too deep. However, the world to which Western elites had become accustomed, and the world which they desire, is crumbling, and Russia is both a symbol and a cause of this. The political positions of traditionalist elites are weakening across Europe, as shown by the rise of so-called right-wing populists and a stark fall in the popularity of mainstream political parties.

A return to the status quo of the 1990s and early 2000s is impossible. The US economy is dynamic and will likely be driven further by Trump's tax cuts and deregulation, which will maintain US strength for the next several years. The question is whether the US will opt for a partial isolationism and build a kind of fortress America, without totally abandoning global economic en.gagement, of course, as promoted by Trump's electoral campaign. Or, will the world once again face a policy of great-power revanchism, a bid to restore the US position as sole global leader? The latter outlook is favoured by the US military establishment, including those in the Trump Administration, and by hawkish internationalists among both Democrats and Republicans, and it could be more dangerous than in Reagan's time. Partial isolationism could prevail in the longer run because the traditionalist elite is losing ground and the world is becoming increasingly multipolar. This will create problems, both for Russia and for the world more broadly, but it will also o.er new opportunities.

Russia, foreseeing these tendencies in US policy, intends to keep the US at bay through a strategy of pre-emptive deterrence. The cutting-edge strategic systems which Vladimir Putin referred to in his presidential address to the Federal Assembly on 1 March 2018 aim to prevent US attempts to regain military superiority by showing that such attempts would be ine.ective and prohibitively expensive.

The situation in Europe is somewhat similar. Several European countries have accused Moscow of interference and claimed sight of a Russian trail in Brexit and the Catalonian separatist movement. So-called populists— who seem to represent a considerable portion of the electorate dissatisfied with current policies and deteriorating economic, social, and security conditions— are edging out elites, imposing their own agendas, and undermining traditional parties. However, no one knows who or what will replace the customary pro-Atlantic ruling class.

The European Union is facing four possible scenarios. The first would be to maintain an alliance with a less committed US, on deteriorating terms, possibly compensating and saving face by simultaneously making slight improvements to relations with Russia. The second scenario would be a pursuit of strategic independence through an effective security policy, but this would require enormous financial and political commitments and a revision of the basic principles of the European project itself. This could lead to either closer relations with the East, in order to respond to real challenges, or to a continued distancing from Russia. For the time being, the EU is trying to keep the faltering European project together with the help of anti-Russian sanctions, thus allowing the EU to speak with one voice. The third scenario would allow individual European countries and the European Union to join the Greater Eurasia project without breaking with the US. But this would be based on different values and political principles to those the EU is used to. Finally, the fourth scenario would involve the EU continuing to patch up holes without any strategic decisions having been made, while continuing to face the risk of the European project's erosion.

A majority among the current European elite dream of the second scenario and favour the first, but in reality, Europe is heading towards the fourth option. The third scenario could materialise in several years, after Europe has felt even greater consequences of the internal and external transformations in world affairs and understood the perils of alternative options, and especially given the likelihood of a more egotistical and detached US policy, and when the ongoing transformation of the European elite is far down the road. All of the above scenarios will require Russia to pursue a new and more active policy towards Europe.

Structurally, the situation in the West is so strained that it has become a serious challenge to international security. Whereas fifteen years ago the purpose of the international system was thought to be managing the rise of the new powers, it would now be more appropriate to speak about managing the decline of the old powers. Some prominent realist thinkers have already claimed—contrary to classic theories of power transition—that existing hegemons, in this case the US, are the real revisionist powers, whose policies violate the rules and practices of the existing order and thus constitute the major challenge to international stability (Schweller 2015).

The current state of international relations is often described as a new Cold War. In fact, the higher level of structural tensions, the number of unresolved problems, the proliferation of uncontrollable and irresponsible actors, and the lack of regulation mean that it is actually even more dangerous than that. To top it all, there is a new ideological confrontation, not between communism and capitalism, but within Western elites them.selves, who are trying to stop the slide of their ideological, political, and economic positions. This confrontation is no less severe than the Cold War. To be sure, the bellicose US ideological and military build-up are currently attempting to replay the Reagan strategy of the 1980s. This strategy is married to McCarthyism—a witch-hunt within the country. Just as in the 1950s, some leading US experts and think tanks are accused of pro-Russian sentiments (Young 2015). But neither Russia nor China, nor even the majority of US allies in Asia, the Middle East, or Latin America are willing to join in with a new game of old-style Cold War. Those in the West who want to play this game will have to do so alone, drifting towards new defeats and even isolation. Preliminary assessments of the new confrontation Washing.ton is trying to unleash—in particular, correlation of forces analyses—show that its chances of victory are slim. Russia, China, India, and the other so-called new powers are not engaged in ideological expansion and are generally content with the direction in which the international system is evolving. They are powers of an emerging new status quo being repulsed by old powers.

Security challenges

As international relations witness mounting structural tensions, there is an increasing danger of regional crises too. Old con.icts in the Middle East, previously suppressed by the old international system, are breaking out again. With a further awakening of the peoples and increasing incidence of nationalism across Africa, especially below the Sahara, further destabilisation is guaranteed. The rise of Asia is unfreezing old contradictions, previously suppressed by the bipolar world order and colonial powers, and creating new sources of tension.

Nuclear weapons are proliferating. It is unrealistic to expect North Korea to give up its nuclear goals after Israel, India, and Pakistan faced no penal.ties for moving forwards with their own nuclear programmes, and especial.ly after Iraq and Libya were devastatingly attacked after abandoning theirs. Crimea's incorporation within Russia was geopolitically necessary and historically fair. However, the action broke the pledge in the 1994 Budapest Memorandum—designed to reward Kiev for abandoning Soviet nuclear weapons (Memorandum on Security Assurances 1994)—to respect Ukraine's territorial integrity. As a result, the moral justification for the non-proliferation regime was undermined.

If the pressure on Iran and the threats to impose new sanctions and re.vise the Joint Comprehensive Plan of Action (JCPA) continue, Iran will obtain nuclear weapons sooner or later as well. Iran will be followed by Saudi Arabia and Egypt. South Korea and Japan may want to match North Korea and possess their own nuclear weapons as well, especially if the US makes a deal with Pyongyang which prohibits North Korea possessing intercontinental ballistic missiles capable of reaching the US mainland but does not result in its complete de-nuclearisation. However, even without such a gloomy scenario coming to pass, strategic stability is still in decline and the risk of a nuclear conflict is growing.

New kinds of weapons are emerging: nuclear, near-nuclear, and conventional. Cyber weapons are acquiring a strategic nature because they can cause comparable damage to weapons of mass destruction. If they are not con.trolled through joint e.orts, they could become ideal weapons for terrorists as they are relatively cheap, hard to trace, and can deliver stealth attacks on vital facilities, provoking international conflicts and producing a powerful multiplier effect. Biological weapons capable of causing significant damage may be in the making too. All this is happening at a time when the old system of nuclear arms control and its related structures of dialogue are crumbling, whereas new systems are not emerging. There has been practically no serious discussion of new threats. For the first time since the 1950s, the world could have no rules whatsoever governing strategic weapons, and this at a time when the strategic environment is far more complex and far less governable than it was in the early stages of the Cold War.

In part, the current situation is a result of free-riding in matters of security and what may be called strategic frivolity: the readiness for long-term risks including military conflicts with huge escalatory potential in order to achieve short-term tactical gains, because the materialisation of such risks is mistakenly perceived as unthinkable. States and societies have become used to a long period of relative peace and have preferred either to think it will last forever or to propose escapist plans to scrap all nuclear weapons, the fear of which is the main, if not the only, guarantee of relative peace. In this situation, current relations between Moscow and Washington are particularly alarming. On the surface, they are characterised by disdain on one side and near hatred on the other. This is a bad backdrop for strategic stability.

The growing number of actors and the lack of dialogue are compounded by intellectual confusion in elite circles. Meanwhile, the pace of change is increasing. The Fourth Industrial Revolution, just like the preceding Digital Revolution, will bring tremendous benefits but also heighten social and political tensions. Advances in medicine could save millions but could exacerbate demographic issues like ageing and overpopulation. Robotisation and localisation of production is reversing industrialisation in many developing countries, promoting re-industrialisation of the developed world, but most of the repercussions of this revolution are difficult to predict. In fact, just fifteen years ago the US counted on supremacy in the cyber sphere and rejected the very idea of it being internationally regulated. Russian concepts of information security and repeated proposals to develop rules of behaviour in the cyber sphere regarding both infrastructure and information were criticised as attempts to legalise censorship. Now the US has finally realised its own vulnerability. As we have argued above, social networks and other new media have been among the key factors contributing to the current political turmoil in the US. Therefore, the United States, which only recently advocated complete freedom of the internet—or rather, freedom for US media and ideas— is now seeking to limit it.

Fundamental geopolitical shifts, elite confusion, and new technologies not only increase the risk of war, but also thrust international relations back to basics. The skeletal foundation of military-power is increasingly visible beneath the economic, information, and political superstructure, which only recently was seen as dominant.

RUSSIA'S NEW GAME PLAN - ANALYSIS

On September 9, geopolitics unexpectedly hit the news headlines when Russian Deputy Foreign Minister Sergei Ryabkov made an important statement about the ongoing talks between Moscow and Islamabad on the delivery of Russian multirole Mi-35M attack helicopters and the latest Su-35 fighter jets. Ryabkov said Pakistan is Russia's "closest partner" and the ties between the two countries are evolving beyond the military sphere to include other sectors such as energy. At the same time, he also suggested that this will not have a negative impact on relations between Moscow and New Delhi.

Coming from a top Russian official, these statements cannot be considered as a mere kite flying stunt by the Russian media. Such a tectonic strategic shift may not have come as a pleasant news to Indian ears, but before we react to this startling change in the Russian position, it is important to first understand the deeper and nuanced aspects of Russia's motives.

Interestingly, within days of Ryabkov's statement, a prominent Russian political analyst *Andrew Korybko* provocatively detailed why Pakistan is gaining pivotal importance in the Russian geo-strategic calculus. The article, titled *"Pakistan is the "Zipper" of Pan-Eurasian Integration"*, appeared on 15 September on the website of the Russian government funded think-tank – Russian Institute for Strategic Studies (RISS) established by the President of the Russian Federation. The RISS puts up policy papers to the President's office, the Federation Council, the State Duma and the Security Council as well as to Government offices, ministries and departments. (*The RISS has closely interacted with IDSA in the past and the two institutions have signed a MoU for joint research. However, the Russian think-tank has not shown much interest for cooperation with IDSA in the past few years*).

As a keen watcher of Eurasian affairs, I thought it is important to share the significant points articulated by *Andrew Korybko in his rather* astounding article so that the Indian strategic community can understand the new thinking among informed Russian circles.

In Part I of his article, *Korybko* deals with the 'zipper' concept of how Pakistan can draw together four of Eurasia's most prominent economic entities, and examines the key imperatives for Russia to build a strong Strategic Partnership with Pakistan. In Part II, he does crystal gazing on the most probable ways in which the US can attempt to offset everything or derail Pakistan's future destiny of joining the Eurasian integration process.

Korbyko's article begins by saying that contrary to popular myth about Pakistan as a "backward land of terrorism and poverty" that carries little actual weight, the West purposefully neglects the country's rising geopolitical importance in Eurasia and its potential to connect the massive economies of the Eurasian Union, Iran, SAARC, and China to create an integrated pan-Eurasian economic zone.

The article then elaborates why Russia recognises Pakistan's prime geopolitical potential and how it is manoeuvring to speed up the development of full-spectrum relations with this "South Asian gatekeeper." It says that Russia's overarching goal is to provide a "non-provocative balancing component to bolster Pakistan's regional political position and assist with its peaceful integration into the multi-polar Eurasian framework being constructed by the Sino-Russian Strategic Partnership."

Interestingly, it draws attention to China's grand vision of building a trans-Pakistani trade corridor under the China-Pakistan Economic Corridor (CPEC), which could be a catalyst for connecting the four economic blocs together. This includes linking of the Russian-led Eurasian Economic Union (EEU) with SAARC intersecting at the Xinjiang-Pakistan junction to be developed under the CPEC.

From the Russian perspective, the article suggests, the CPEC not only represents a "geopolitical pivot for China, but also a geo-economic one", for "it'll position the country within easy access to the Mideast oil fields". This is the only way China will be able to quell the "externally orchestrated destabilization that it's lately found itself experiencing in Xinjiang."

It stresses the importance of the Iran-Pakistan-China pipeline project (a part of the CPEC) becoming a reality and suggests that "should Xinjiang succeed in becoming a significant Eurasian trading hub in connecting China, Eurasian Union, SAARC, and Iran, then it would catapult in geo-economic significance to become an ultra-strategic Heartland region."

On the prospect of India joining the Eurasian system, Korbyko's article says that the touchy issue of India's claim over "Pakistan-administered Kashmir" could come in the way. However, "if Indian companies employ this route, the economic allure might be too tempting to resist." Further, if Indo-Pak differences could be relaxed (perhaps within the SCO framework), then "the organization would finally be able to cash in on its economic capability and fully integrate with itself and the rest of Eurasia."

Importantly, the article discloses how Russia's strategic ties with Pakistan are moving towards very "exciting future possibilities" despite Russia being "India's closest friend". It notes that the emerging trend might appear somewhat "perplexing" but it isn't all that "unexpected." Because, the end of the Cold War and the subsequent emergence of South Asian "nuclear bipolarity" have reduced the intensity of Indo-Russian strategic ties as well as America's dealings with Pakistan. These shifts in focus (India's westward and Pakistan's eastward) do not, however, suggest that either India or Pakistan has completely deserted its erstwhile partner; only that they are seeking adjustments to protect their national interest in the changed context. But at the same time, these shifts in focus have not yet altered the Indo-Pak standoff. In this context, the article notes, both India and Pakistan seem to be willing to give multilateralism under Eurasia a chance, as evident from their entry into the SCO.

More interestingly, the author points to the Kremlin's calculation of its ability to intermediate between Beijing and New Delhi in the event of a major India-China crisis. But he also says that Russia does not enjoy the same leverage to do so in an India-Pakistan conflict situation. As a result, in the latter situation, Moscow would prefer to "push the US into the mix – giving it plenty of opportunity to divide and conquer according to the present geopolitical circumstances." Korybko then goes to point out that "if Russia were to compensate for its diplomatic 'blind spot' with Pakistan and reinvigorate the bilateral relationship with Islamabad, then it could mirror the role that it plays between India and China in also helping to balance the tension between India and Pakistan." This strategy, the article argues, would eventually "push the US out of the playing field, though India will still retain its current level of ties with the US but not for the purpose counterbalancing Pakistan." It suggests that both India and Pakistan would then rather rely on their same "trusted partner Russia", which for its part will be able to mediate between the two (like it does with India and China).

The article admits to the trust deficit between India and Pakistan as the weakest link in the 'zipper' vision, though the vision could still succeed without the SAARC component because the "EEU would gain by India's physical incorporation into the unified Eurasian infrastructural framework." Korybko also points to Russian diplomatic and strategic competence being capable of minimizing Indo-Pak discord and exploring the economic benefit of their peaceful collaboration.

The Russian analyst then explains how Russia made the first strategic move in this regard in June 2014 by offering to sell attack helicopters to Pakistan for the latter's drug-combating efforts.

Though the "paradigm shift" was attributed by many to Russia's concerns over post-2014 NATO withdrawal from Afghanistan, the main idea was to initiate the process of depolarisation in India-Pakistan tensions and to make the multi-polar concept more cohesive as a result. The article says that Russia's next move would be to help Pakistan with technical expertise for building a portion of the Iran-Pakistan-China gas pipeline in the near future.

According to the write up, Pakistan's own excitement has increased after sensing the enormous economic opportunities that will unfold after CPEC completion. Pakistanis could see the "writing on the wall" and even contemplate sealing a free trade agreement with the Eurasian Union. This signifies how seriously Russia takes its evolving partnership with Pakistan. The article underlines how the relationship is also gaining a soft power touch, with both sides preparing for their first-ever cultural exchange year. In a symbolic significance of what is likely to come, the article says that "Pakistan's national military band performed at the Moscow International Music Festival."

The article notes that "there should thus be no doubt at this point about the commitment of both sides for deepening the relationship as the ongoing interactions between the two are beyond passing convergence of business interests." It further says that "Both sides understand the larger significance of what they're doing", which is to work for the "shared vision of an integrated and multi-polar Eurasia."

However, on the down side and for the Eurasian enterprise to succeed, the author anticipates that CPEC and the 'zipper' plan could face a major blow either due to instability within Pakistan or India's possible refusal to participate in it.

Interestingly, the article notes that any possibility of all-round Russia-Pakistan engagement could speed up Indo-US proximity which, in turn, will lead to provocation by the "US and its information proxies". Things could also be exacerbated by an exaggerated "Indian threat assessment of Russia's activities." Any Indian paranoia over Russia's 'sliding away' to join the China-Pakistan 'axis' would consequently negate the main reasons behind the Russian-Pakistan strategic partnership, which is to "place Moscow in a position to intermediate between New Delhi and Islamabad and keep regional relations stable enough so as to jump start the envisioned multilateral economic partnership."

The author, however, argues that Russia's Pakistan gambit might fail most likely because of the United States playing dirty. In such a scenario, Russia would be worse off and risk losing a major strategic partner in India. Pakistan, on the other hand, will "never see its relation with Russia as equal level to one it has with China."

The article cautions that Russia needs to proceed delicately taking into consideration how the Indian establishment views Russia's evolving ties with Pakistan. It does not discount the ability of the US to split Russia and India through Pakistan, like it did with Russia and the European Union through Ukraine (although for different reasons).

The author fears the possibility of the US creating a rift through "information warfare" especially when Indo-US defence ties are deepening. He notes that this could have in a way "possibly played a part in influencing Moscow's decision to resume arms exports to Pakistan." The article draws attention to the saliency of "underreported military development" that makes the US more integral to India's national security, and this it says coincides with New Delhi's strategic overlap with the US in containing China. "The longer this progresses, the further the US will embed itself into India's deep state apparatus, with all of the unfortunate foreign policy consequences for the multi-polar world" the article notes.

The writer then dwells on the personal rapport shared between Modi and Obama and other aspects of the Indo-US friendship which, he thinks, could be an "exaggerated charade for political purposes, there's nothing tangible to indicate that this is the case" and by itself doesn't pose any worries for Russia." But what really worries Russia is the possibility of Obama leveraging his friendship with Modi to "enact certain policy shifts", such as "his encouragement to India's Act East policy for unstated reason that can aggravate relations with China." According to Korybko, Russian interests would be most endangered by the "US winning over India into viewing the Russian-Pakistan strategic partnership as a threat" and suggests that Putin should "continually reinforce his relationship with Modi so that the latter is insusceptible to being tricked by Obama into doubting the Russian President's intentions."(It is pertinent to note here that in his congratulatory message to Prime Minister Modi on his 65th birthday, issued by the Kremlin on September 17, President Putin praised how the Prime Minister rightly enjoys high international authority both in his homeland and abroad as a proficient politician and statesman. The message says "we highly appreciate your efforts to strengthen the special and privileged strategic partnership between our countries, develop Russian-Indian interaction in solving topical issues of the regional and global agenda.")

Further, the article points to the likelihood of American involvement in creating instability in Baluchistan. Baluch separatism driven by American interests is not just for destabilising Gwadar (the source of CPEC) or for the political fragmentation of Pakistan but to create a new geopolitical space to be carved out of the Iranian province of Sistan and Baluchistan as well. Such a Baluch proxy, it says, could provide the US with a greater degree of influence over both Iran and India in controlling trans-regional transport connectivity. Of course, the author cites the Pentagon's foremost author Lieutenant-Colonel Ralph Peters' infamous map *Blood Borders: How a Better Middle East Would Look,* which specifically earmarks a "Free Baluchistan" carved out of Iranian and Pakistani territory.

Korybko then moves beyond the Baluch separatist scenario to highlight the presence of militant Islamic radicalism in FATA – the most important destabilising factor in Pakistan. To add to that he draws attention to the rise of ISIL and its "expansive neo-Caliphate ideology" in Afghanistan's three provinces of Farah (west), Helmand (south), and Nangarhar (east). The ISIL, he says, could use Nangarhar province as a staging ground for pushing deeper into Pakistan by eliminating the Durand Line and "annex" the 'state of Hind' (Pakistan, India, Bangladesh, and Myanmar). Further, Korybko also says that if more "Taliban fighters defect to the up-and-coming group" a scenario of a birth of a "transnational 'mini-Caliphate' between Nangarhar and parts of FATA would evoke the shades of ISIL's prior successes along the Syrian-Iraqi border." Not just that, the article vividly points to how ISIL is also moving in the northern direction, citing the defection in May of Colonel Gulmurod Khalimov, the head of Tajikistan's Internal Special Forces, to ISIL. It hints at the possibility of ISIL gaining invaluable intelligence and employing Khalimov's knowledge in infiltrating into the most 'ideal' location in Gorno-Badakhstan region. If this occurs concurrently, the article suggests, the "US then would be keen, among other things, to take revenge for Kyrgyzstan denouncing its cooperation agreement with the US." Therefore, the article does not rule out the possibility of a quadrilateral South-Central Asian Caliphate emerging in "heavily fortified Pamir and Hindu Kush mountain ranges, with Pakistan being the southern peg of this vile construction."

The article paints another disruptive scenario of how the US could derail Pakistan's geo-economic destiny by engineering a possible "Colour Revolution against Prime Minister Sharif or any of his successors", although it also says that the violent protests last year did not pan out as a doom and gloom scenario for Pakistan. Korybko does not foretell the exact contours of the follow-up disruptive attempt, but says that with the "improved political technology available" it might likely embrace "anti-corruption" slogans led by an amorphous and superficially apolitical "civil society" in Pakistan. Such a structural innovation, the article suggests, would "allow the coup's leaders to readjust their social infrastructure (leadership, members, slogans, etc.) on the fly a lot more efficiently than if they followed the comparatively rigid practices of their predecessors in organizing the event around clearly defined political parties led by a few well-known (and easily compromised) individuals."

This scenario to be deployed in Pakistan would be "Colour Revolution 1.5". The article notes that this will be halfway between the comparatively 'docile' 2003 Colour Revolution 1.0 in Georgia and the "out-of-control Hybrid War mayhem of Colour Revolution 2.0 in EuroMaidan." Colour Revolution

1.5 in Pakistan could go either way, "towards 1.0 if it sputters out like in Armenia or towards 2.0 if it dangerously intensifies like it did in Syria." The article says that 1.5 could become a dangerous innovation to "regime change strategy" and that the US would be committed to apply it first with smaller targets before being "perfected and repackaged to Pakistan."

The article argues that Moscow has rightly taken the "bold step in reaching out to Islamabad and soliciting a strategic partnership" and the quick pace of the partnership taking a revolutionary shape is a "natural fit for both partners." But this trend, according to the article, has incited the US' "geopolitical jealousy", which is keen to call upon a "mixed bag of secessionist, terrorist, and Colour Revolution destabilizations to offset Pakistan's catalytic role in bringing Eurasia together." The author then calls upon Russia, China, and Iran to defeat the threat so that Pakistan can become Eurasia's economic 'zipper' and linking these (and perhaps even SAARC's) economies together in an emboldened multi-polar future.

The article concludes by saying that the EU is mistakenly staying out (due to US pressure) of this trans-Eurasian integration process, which is becoming the primary theme of the 21st century. But "the rest of the main continental economic powers – the Eurasian Union, Iran, SAARC, and China – stand poised for closer integration with one another owing to the infrastructural overlap that Pakistan's geostrategic location provides."

The central theme of Korbyko's article is to highlight the pivotal importance of Pakistan and the Russian eagerness to build a foundation of political trust with the Pakistani leadership so as to better assist in the management of Pakistani-Indian tensions.

To be sure, Pakistan can certainly help Russia shift its focus away from its current difficulties but Moscow should be doubly careful whether Pakistan will not become a staging ground to break up Russia further. The Americans have already tested the Pakistani betrayal, and China too sooner or later will become another victim of Pakistani treachery.

RUSSIA: VICTORIOUS, BUT WITH PROBLEMS

Russia's recent foreign policy has been extremely successful. It has harnessed a historical wave: renationalisation; a re-assertion of sovereignty; negative responses to globalisation in many societies; and a growing role of military-political factors. Sovereignty, the primacy of secu.rity issues, and traditional values have returned to the fore. Traditional val.ues almost universally include a prevalence of communal over individual interests, to be realised through public service and recognition. As explained by Rein

Mullerson, peace and prosperity in the second half of the twentieth century spurred the emergence of a new individualism in the West (Mullerson 2017), but globally, the inherently social nature of humanity has been more prominent.

Russia's resolutely swift takeover of Crimea and support of the rebellion in the Donbass have prevented the further expansion of the Western bloc. This expansion had been changing the balance of power to Russia's disadvantage and could have resulted in a large-scale war. Russia's remark.ably successful involvement in Syria has enabled it to regain the status of a top-level player. For the first time in 30 years, Russia has proved capable of not just preventing regime change by projecting power in a country outside of the former USSR, but also of creating a new geopolitical environment disregarding US preferences. Russian success in Syria has influenced the Middle East more broadly by encouraging regional powers to diversify their foreign policy and security relationships. The sense of victory and regain.ing of great-power con.dence, paired with the West's angry reaction, have so far rallied Russian society, nationalised elites, and marginalised comprador sentiments.

Russia has established a historically unique partnership: a near-allied relationship with China, which is destined to become the world's leading power in the near future. A majority among Russian elites have changed their geostrategic identity, turning from a marginal part of Europe, with an expensive and unguaranteed access to the centre, to central Eurasia. In other words, Russia is transforming itself in accordance with both the present and future state of world affairs. Having survived waves of hostile sanctions, it also senses a moral victory too.

The development and deployment of a series of high-tech strategic weapons, announced by President Putin in his 1 March 2018 address to the Federal Assembly, not only render most US investments in these fields obsolete, but guarantee for years, if not decades, the effectiveness of a Russian deterrent and its role as the main security provider globally and regionally. This role is crucial against a background of the incompetence and self-destructiveness of US policy and ongoing attempts to intensify simultaneous containment of Russia and China, re-creating a new bipolar global division. The world has seen what happened when the role of Russian deterrence weakened in the 1990s and 2000s due to its own internal crisis. The alliance of democratic countries ran amok, committing a series of interventions with horribly costly repercussions in Yugoslavia, Iraq, and Libya. The West began to aggressively export its political model, bringing chaos to countries and regions it influenced. The latest example is Ukraine, which has slid from a weak to an almost failed state. Still, despite apparent foreign policy successes, there are several strategic challenges Russia needs to deal with.

Apart from the objectively growing threat of war, the primary challenge is the lack of a coherent strategy for economic and social development. The fat Russia accumulated in the 2000s is running thin. Foreign policy successes are important in themselves, but poor compensation for social and economic troubles. No less risky would be a premature withdrawal from conflicts, as some in the Russian elite suggest. So far, Russia has acted intelligently and deftly, but failures are possible and likely to occur. Russia's relative economic weakness has limited its partners' desire for friendship and encouraged opponents to feud with it. If economic stagnation continues, geopolitical mishaps could ruin any aura of victory and expose economic weakness. A strategy of technocratic, conservative modernisation has been declared but is still to be implemented. So far the only area where Russia has undergone profoundly successful modernisation is its military.

Russia has lacked not only an attractive strategy for its own development but also a positive vision of a future world order. Just like China, Russia has been slow to fill the ideological vacuum created by the collapse of many of the previous international economic, political, and security orders and the Western recipes for international development. Contrary to conventional thinking, multipolarity throughout history is hardly a harmonious state of affairs, but is chaotic, characterised by almost endless conflicts, and wars among great powers like the two world wars of the twentieth century. Multipolarity has only been a useful concept as an antithesis to the bygone uni.polarity. But what could be next?

Besides strengthening its own capabilities for deterrence, Russia has not yet arrived at a coherent strategy to improve international security, which is currently under severe stress, if not under threat of total collapse.

Relations with the West are at their worst, although the majority of the blame for this does not lie with Russia. Nonetheless, Russia is also at fault because of its past weaknesses, foolishness, its giving of concessions in hope of gratitude, and its reluctance to foresee the inevitable problem in Ukraine for years on end. Russia has strengthened its economic and political positions by turning east, but further movement will be constantly impeded by the weakness of the western flank. Concessions to Western partners would not make sense and could even be dangerous. They wouldn't so much en.courage the kind of foolishly arrogant expansion attempted previously, but rather a desire to sort of finish Russia off, strengthening Western warmongers. Concessions would create the illusion that current US attempts to kind of replay the 1980s actually work and thereby stir even greater escalation. There should be no expectation of a lifting of sanctions in the foresee.able future, especially from the US. However, the present state of affairs is also counterproductive and harmful. Russia needs to make changes, look at the situation from a different angle, and give up its obsession with the West in both pro-Western and anti-Western forms.

FUTURE POLICY

The collapse of the previous international orders requires Russia's creative participation, on parity with other centres of global power, in the building of a new and balanced world order. The cornerstones of Russian strategy should be leadership in prevention of a new large-scale war and a transformation of itself into a leading provider of international security. This should be achieved by developing both capabilities and a doctrine of deterrence, and by offering, even insisting—as opposed to acting without permission—to jointly strengthen international strategic stability. This could be worked out not so much through traditional arms control channels, but by promoting a system of dialogue which would increase transparency and reduce the risk of accidental or escalating conflicts. If the United States were to balk at the task, Russia and China should start without it by inviting other states to join in. Another option would be a series of unofficial dialogues between US, Chinese, and specialists from other countries on how to strengthen international strategic stability.

Naturally, new creative approaches are needed to preserve peace, including joint efforts not to overcome nuclear deterrence, but to strengthen it, as the main instrument for preventing war in the foreseeable future. It is worth fighting against the proliferation of nuclear weapons. But there must be a forward-looking philosophy and a practice of dialogue that engage unofficial nuclear and threshold states in order to strengthen their security. This is the only way to mitigate or prevent the further spread of nu.clear weapons.

As a rule, international orders emerge after wars, but nowadays a major war would spell the real end of history. Russia should clearly declare a commitment to ensuring that history goes on. Russia is a major supplier of global security, as borne out by its policies in the Middle East and Central Asia, by its efforts to prevent the expansion of Western alliances in Europe which have created the risk of war, and also by its efforts to deter the United States and other major powers. It should formalise this status politically and intellectually.

Once the foundation of the future world order is built through mutual deterrence and dialogue between leading powers, a discussion of its principles can commence: cooperation; respect for sovereignty and territorial integrity; and the freedom of political, cultural, and value choices. The universalism of communism, liberalism, and other isms should be left behind.

Russia should revive the legalist tradition—a commitment to international law—which has been pushed to the side-lines by the so-called liberal.world-order era's law of the jungle. The necessary conditions for this, including a favourable balance of power, are re-emerging.

In geopolitical terms, the most promising option for Russia in the coming years would be a further pivot to the East to create a comprehensive partnership in Greater Eurasia. The US and its neighbours, alongside particular European and Asian states, will probably create their own centre.

Russia and China have reiterated their readiness to join forces with other countries in order to build a comprehensive partnership in Eurasia. Russia has supported China's One Belt, One Road initiative, which can, together with other projects, provide an economic foundation for future partnership. China has supported the Eurasian Economic Union and agreed to enlarge the Shanghai Cooperation Organization to include India and Pakistan: both necessary steps towards establishing the political, normative, and institution.al foundations for Eurasian partnership. But then Moscow suffered a loss of initiative, apparently due to the Russian character: we make a breakthrough and then relax. The idea of Eurasian partnership requires systemic interaction, primarily with China, India, Japan, South Korea, and the Eurasian Economic Union, SCO, and ASEAN member states.

The Greater Eurasian partnership is not only a conceptual framework for building a united Eurasia as a global economic and political unit and thus a key element of the future world order, but also a way of integrating China's growing power within a system of institutions, ties, dialogues, and balances. Beijing, which maintains a Middle Kingdom tradition of surrounding itself with dependent states, faces a difficult task of overcoming this tradition. In the contemporary world this will only lead to a Thucydides Trap, prompting other countries to pool their efforts against Chi.na. This can already be seen in the emergence of the Indo-Pacific strategy, designed precisely to contain China from the east and south. However, there is a good chance of China operating through a cooperative, multilateral, and less Beijing-centred order, once this order has been systematically built. Simplifying somewhat, we could say the Greater Eurasian partner.ship is supposed to achieve with Chinese power something similar to what European integration achieved with German power: after reunification, fuse together a system of multilateral rules and institutions, thus avoiding both unilateral hegemonic ambitions and fear among neighbours. The EU has successfully solved the German issue—Germany's predominant power and hegemonic ambitions having produced two world wars in the twentieth century. It is in everyone's interests to resolve the Chinese question before unilateral exercise of its power provokes a backlash.

Another important task is avoiding a bipolarisation of the Pacific into the Indo-Pacific with the US, the Quad, and US allies and partners on one hand, and Greater Eurasia with China, Russia, Iran, Pakistan, Central Asian states and perhaps others, on the other hand. This is being promoted by the US and, if successful, would constitute a new global divide, with the Pacific turning into the major front of the new global Cold War and Europe being a second front—a reversed reflection of the previous Cold War's geopolitical arrangement. Containing China with economic alternatives to OBOR and military components—the Quad and US-India partnership—of the Indo-Pacific strategy, combined with an intensification of Russian containment, the US is indeed pushing China towards the Eurasian landmass and push.ing Russia and China towards one another, thus accelerating the emergence of Greater Eurasia as a geopolitical and economic reality, albeit with Greater Eurasia and the Indo-Pacific region emerging as rival neighbours.

In order to avoid this, Russia, China, India, Japan, and other Asian and Eurasian actors should develop Greater Eurasia and Indo-Pacific partner.ships as cooperative, not adversarial, projects. This requires dialogue between Russia and India, Russia and Japan, and Russia and ASEAN, and perhaps the creation of a trilateral format between Russia, India, and Japan. Remarkably, none of these countries support a bipolarisation of the Paci.c, despite Japan and India's apparent desire to strengthen counter-balancing of China; meanwhile, smaller Asian states are resistant to having to make strategic choices between the US and China. Russia, India, and Japan should discuss alternative ways of managing Chinese power to containment, above all through a system of rules and institutions, which would diffuse Chinese power, and by combining the economic power of OBOR and the Indo-Pacific region, making connectivity and development projects in the region more inclusive. At a later stage, this system of dialogue could and should be complemented with a Russia–China–India–Japan format.

Three to four years down the line, when the Greater Eurasian partner.ship has already been consolidated and substantiated, and when the political problems in European states have settled down—either through traditional elites re-establishing control or through new elites taking their places—Russia should resume efforts to improve relations with leading European countries and the EU as a whole. This time, this improvement—including dialogue between the EU and Eurasian Economic Union—would not happen bilaterally. And unlike in the early 2000s, it would not imply Russia joining an EU-centric arrangement. On the contrary, it would happen within the wider context of Greater Eurasia and would constitute engagement of major European players and perhaps the EU within the ambitious Greater Eurasian partnership, comprising the creation of a China-Russia-Europe triangle of peace and development within which Russia would act as a link and as a balancing power. Promoting the compatibility of Greater Eurasia and the Indo-Pacific region will make the emergence of the China-Russia-Europe triangle much easier, as Europe would no longer perceive this as joining a Cold War.style adversarial bloc.

Russia must not repeat the mistake of the 1990s and 2000s by trying to strengthen relations with Europe through institutions of the Cold War era which keep reproducing the Cold War, like the OSCE or the Russia-NATO Council. These should be used instrumentally, wherever they can be useful—to regulate crises or prevent conflicts—but otherwise be pushed aside. Of course, it would also be good to improve relations with the United States, but this will depend on the internal politics of the US and will take time. It is unlikely that the US will be ready for a new partnership with Russia based on joint building and management of international order before the rotation of US elites, which began with the 2016 election, is complete. Still, the degree of tension should be eased wherever possible and Russia should seek to withdraw from current conflicts and avoid new conflicts. Russia has achieved everything it possibly could have through the strengthening of its strategic deterrent and its policies in Syria and Ukraine.

History, coupled with Russia's efforts in recent years, has made it possible for Russia to play a role in the building of a new world order. Russia paid for this right 75 years ago with millions of lives, but both international and domestic systems hampered further Russian success. Today, Russia should once again attempt to shape a new world order, but at lower cost and with great.er bene.ts. There is no way Russia can avoid this challenge. If it sits out the process, a new world order will be created without Russia, or even against it. Russia should continue to act deftly and maintain a systematic approach, being persistent, ready to cooperate, and to contribute to international balance, although these characteristics do not naturally fit Russian traditions.

8

Russia and India on The International Arena

Russia and India have similar positions on building a new architecture of global relations. Built around the principle of a polycentric world structure, these positions theoretically create new opportunities for interaction between the two countries in a variety of global and regional formats.

The two states' national interests coincide in the following areas:

- a unipolar world is wholly unacceptable;
- the absolute need to continue to combat political extremism and radicalism;
- aspects of economic globalization that have a negative impact on developing nations must be staunchly opposed.

The Russian Federation and India uphold similar views, with rare exceptions, during votes at the UN General Assembly sessions on problems related to global sustainable development, strategic stability and international security.

India's position, from the outset, has been directed at creating a world order based on the principle of "uniformity through diversity." This model incorporates consensusdriven world politics and international relations, while groups of "horizontally" organized states acting in accordance with the principle of coordination rather than subordination will inevitably become key players on the international arena.

Prospects for the development of Russia-India relations on a global scale largely depend on the nature of interaction displayed by India with regard to the key players on the international scene: relations with China and the United

States are of paramount importance for India just as they are for Russia. India has demonstrated a genuine interest in establishing an inclusive world order in which China could be one of the major, but not dominant, states. This does not run counter to Russia's interests.

Despite the positive trend in how U.S.-Indian relations are developing on a global scale, a latent growth in conflict potential between the United States and India can be observed as resulting from fundamental disagreements on geopolitical and geo-economic issues (especially during the sessions of UN bodies). As a result, Russia, in the absence of the expected results from its "reset" in relations with the United States, facing differences with the United States on a number of issues, alarmed – much like India – by neighbouring China's growing strength, could create an alliance with India, that proves to be strategically important to both parties, lending fresh impetus to political, trade/economic and cultural relations.

Renewed efforts in economic and political cooperation within the RIC group (Russia, India, China) have good prospects. Highly-efficient interaction is likely in areas involving Russian fundamental science and resources, India's engineering theory and Chinese production that boasts high-quality low-cost labour. Products generated by this linkup could enjoy a high capacity market: BRICS countries have the highest long-term growth rates in the world, and the purchasing power of their populations is invariably also on the rise.

Specific areas for cooperation may include agricultural production, joint development of mineral, fuel and energy and forest resources in Siberia and Russia's Far East, manufacturing industry, coordination of aviation projects, space exploration, power engineering, and machine building, in particular car manufacturing oriented towards markets in the countries under review. Establishing a special-purpose Energy Association (possibly with Japan and South Korea) could also prove useful.

India and Russia share the view that today's problems cannot be effectively resolved without broader involvement of developing nations in global trade, finance and investment. Developing countries can and must become the real drivers of global economic growth. Russia should reaffirm its position regarding support for India gaining the status of UN Security Council permanent member and call for comprehensive assistance to Delhi in its desire to become an APEC member.

India strongly opposes the involvement of external international forces in the solution of regional problems in South Asia, whether in Kashmir or in the Indian Ocean zone. India is watching the development of United States-Pakistan relations in the military and political spheres with great suspicion, given the

American forces' stated intention to withdraw from Afghanistan in 2014. Russia has invariably taken a low-profile stance on regional problems such as Kashmir and Tibet that are highly sensitive to India. Russian diplomacy has every reason to believe that the "internationalization" of these problems would be unlikely to facilitate their settlement and may damage India's political prestige.

Indian experts view the Indian Ocean as a key element in the country's policies and in its historical destiny. To the east of the Indian Ocean, India should enhance its efforts to strengthen ties with Myanmar, Indonesia, and Singapore as well as Vietnam, South Korea and Australia, potentially creating a kind of "diamond ring" of countries friendly towards India. It is highlighted that this initiative should not be a smokescreen for efforts to create an anti-Chinese alliance. At the same time China is acting as a major investor in the economies of these countries thus reducing the effect of the Indian foreign policy.

The development of Russia-India relations will also benefit from Russia's comprehensive support for India in interactions with other states in the region. It would seem reasonable to find a way of mentioning the fact that Russia is not rendering any military assistance to Pakistan (while highlighting arms supplies to Pakistan from the United States, France and other Western countries); it is also worth highlighting those foreign policy processes in South Asia that parallel Russia's post-Soviet realities, and the similar positions that India and Russia have respectively taken in these regions, in particular the remarkable similarity in the approaches that Russia has applied to solving problems faced by the CIS and those taken by India regarding issues in South Asia. India's policies on Afghanistan are determined by three key considerations: a) concerns over an Islamist victory, the spread of radical Islam across Central Asia and possible appearance of an Islamist bloc comprising Pakistan, Afghanistan and Central Asian republics characterized, among other things, by a radical anti-Indian thrust; b) undesirable strengthening of the great powers' influence in Afghanistan and their increasing involvement in regional affairs; c) the goal of transforming Afghanistan into a transit country between Central Asia and India.

It appears that the reason for India's activity in the Afghanistan-Pakistan (Af-Pak) conflict zone indicates Delhi's intention to increase the quality of its economic, political and possibly military positions in the regions, primarily at the expense of Pakistan and China.

There are no principal disagreements between Russia and India over the situation in Afghanistan, while the prospects of interaction between the two countries are quite explicit in the Af-Pak node of tension.

Specifically, a bilateral agreement on joint implementation of economic programs in Afghanistan is likely to be signed. It would also appear quite feasible to unite the two countries' efforts in the military-political sphere (for instance, in joint programs to train Afghan servicemen) while in the longer term it might be efficient to disseminate similar economic and military-political programs across Central Asia.

SOVIET UNION AND INDIA

A cordial relationship with India that began in the 1950s represented the most successful of the Soviet attempts to foster closer relations with Third World countries. The relationship began with a visit by Indian prime minister Jawaharlal Nehru to the Soviet Union in June 1955 and Khrushchev's return trip to India in the fall of 1955. While in India, Khrushchev announced that the Soviet Union supported Indian sovereignty over the disputed territory of the Kashmir region and over Portuguese coastal enclaves. The Soviet relationship with India rankled the Chinese and contributed to Sino-Soviet enmity during the Khrushchev period.

The Soviet Union declared its neutrality during the 1959 border dispute and the Indo-China war of 1962, although the Chinese strongly objected. The Soviet Union gave India substantial economic and military assistance during the Khrushchev period, and by 1960 India had received more Soviet assistance than China had. This disparity became another point of contention in Sino-Soviet relations. In 1962 the Soviet Union agreed to transfer technology to coproduce the MiG-21 jet fighter in India, which the Soviet Union had earlier denied to China.

In 1965 the Soviet Union served successfully as peace broker between India and Pakistan after an Indian-Pakistani border war. The Soviet chairman of the Council of Ministers, Aleksei N. Kosygin, met with representatives of India and Pakistan and helped them negotiate an end to the military conflict over Kashmir.

In 1971 the former East Pakistan region initiated an effort to secede from its political union with West Pakistan. India supported the secession and, as a guarantee against possible Chinese entrance into the conflict on the side of West Pakistan, signed a treaty of friendship and cooperation with the Soviet Union in August 1971. In December, India entered the conflict and ensured the victory of the secessionists and the establishment of the new state of Bangladesh.

Relations between the Soviet Union and India did not suffer much during the rightist Janata Party's coalition government in the late 1970s, although India did move to establish better economic and military relations with Western countries. To counter these efforts by India to diversify its relations, the Soviet Union proffered additional weaponry and economic assistance.

During the 1980s, despite the 1984 assassination by Sikh extremists of Prime Minister Indira Gandhi, the mainstay of cordial Indian-Soviet relations, India maintained a close relationship with the Soviet Union. Indicating the high priority of relations with the Soviet Union in Indian foreign policy, the new Indian prime minister, Rajiv Gandhi, visited the Soviet Union on his first state visit abroad in May 1985 and signed two long-term economic agreements with the Soviet Union. In turn, Gorbachev's first visit to a Third World state was his meeting with Prime Minister Rajiv Gandhi in New Delhi in late 1986. Gorbachev unsuccessfully urged Gandhi to help the Soviet Union set up an Asian collective security system.

Gorbachev's advocacy of this proposal, which had also been made by Brezhnev, was an indication of continuing Soviet interest in using close relations with India as a means of containing China. With the improvement of Sino-Soviet relations in the late 1980s, containing China had less of a priority, but close relations with India remained important as an example of Gorbachev's new Third World policy.

Russia and India

Relations with India have always been and I am sure will be one of the most important foreign policy priorities of our country. Our mutual ties of friendship are filled with sympathy, and trust, and openness. And we must say frankly that they were never overshadowed by disagreements or conflict. This understanding - this is indeed the common heritage of our peoples. It is valued and cherished in our country, in Russia, and in India. And we are rightfully proud of so close, so close relations between our countries.– *Dmitry Medvedev, about relations with India*

We are confident that India lives in the hearts of every Russian. In the same way, I can assure you that Russia also lives in our souls as a Homeland, as people who share our emotions, our feelings of mutual respect and constant friendship. Long live our friendship!– *Pratibha Patil, about relations with Russia*

Military Relations

Defence relations between India and the Russian Federation have a historical perspective. Russia has been an important supplier of defence goods for several decades. Today, the cooperation is not limited to a buyer-seller relationship but includes joint research and development, training, service to service contacts, including joint exercises. The last joint naval exercises took place in April 2007 in the Sea of Japan and joint airborne exercises were held in September 2007 in Russia.

There is an Inter-Governmental commission on military-technical cooperation co-chaired by the two Defence Ministers. The Seventh session of this Inter-Governmental Commission was held in October 2007 in Moscow. During the visit, an Agreement on joint development and production of prospective multi role fighters was signed between the two countries.

India–Russia original co-operation agreement was signed in December 1988. It has seen the trade of a multitude of defence equipment to India and also the emergence of that country as a development partner as opposed to purely a buyer. Two programmes that evidence this approach are the projects to form Indian-Russian joint ventures to develop and produce the Fifth Generation Fighter Aircraft (FGFA) and the Multirole Transport Aircraft (MTA).

Deba R Mohanty, a senior fellow in security studies at the New Delhi-based Observer Research Foundation, told Jane's on 13 October that the original co-operation agreement has laid a "very solid foundation" for India to develop further as a development partner. He added: "The mutual benefits are clear: India can acquire modern platforms and technologies while Russia gains access to India's growing defence market."

India and Russia have several major joint military programs such as those mentioned below:

- Brah Mos cruise missile program
- INS Vikramaditya aircraft carrier program
- 5th generation fighter jet program
- Sukhoi Su-30 MKI program (230+ to be built by Hindustan Aeronautics)
- Ilyushin/HAL Tactical Transport Aircraft.

Additionally, India has purchased/leased several military hardware from Russia:

- T-90S Bhishma program. (1000+ to be built in India)
- Akula-II nuclear submarine (2 to be leased with an option to buy them when the lease expires)
- Tu-22M3 bombers (4 ordered)
- US$900 million upgrade of MiG-29
- Mil Mi-17 (80 ordered)
- Ilyushin Il-76 Candid (6 ordered to fit Israeli Phalcon radar).

Russia's MiG-35 is competing in the Indian MRCA Competition and is considered to be the front-runner for the winning bid, given India's already, largely Russian-built air force. The Farkhor Air Base in Tajikistan is currently jointly operated by India and Russia.

Economic Relations

Bilateral trade turnover is modest and stood at US $ 3 bn in 2006-07, out of which Indian Exports to Russia were valued at US $ 908 mn. Main Indian exports to Russia are pharmaceuticals; tea, coffee & spices; apparel & clothing; edible preparations; and engineering goods. Main Indian imports from Russia are iron and steel; fertilizers; non-ferrous metals; paper products; coal, coke & briquettes; cereals; and rubber. Indo-Russian trade is expected to reach US$10 billion by 2010.

The India-Russia Inter-Governmental Commission on Trade, Economic, Scientific, Technological and Cultural Cooperation (IRIGC) has had 13 sessions so far and is co-chaired by the External Affairs Minister from the Indian side and a Deputy Prime Minister from the Russian side.

There are six Joint Working Groups [WG] under the IRIGC, namely, WG on Trade and Economy [trade and financial matters], WG on Energy [oil and gas, thermal and hydel power, non-conventional energy], WG on Metallurgy and Mining [steel, non-ferrous metal, coal], WG on Science & Technology; WG on Communication and Information Technology; and WG on Culture and Tourism. The 13th of the IRIGC was held in Moscow on 12 October 2007.

The two countries have setup India-Russia Forum on Trade and Investment at the level of the two Commerce Ministers to promote trade, investment and economic cooperation. The first Forum was held in New Delhi on 12–13 February 2007 which was attended by the Minister of Commerce and Industry and the Russian Minister of Economic Development and Trade, apart from a large number of business representatives from both sides. The Minister of Commerce & Industry, Shri Kamal Nath participated in the 11th Saint Petersburg International Economic Forum on 9–10 June 2007.

In February 2006, India and Russia also setup a Joint Study Group to examine ways to increase trade to US $ 10 bn by 2010 and to study feasibility of a Comprehensive Economic Cooperation Agreement (CECA). The Group finalized its report after its fourth meeting in Moscow in July 2007. It has been agreed that a Joint Task Force would monitor the implementation of the recommendation made in the Joint Stdy Group Report, including considering CECA.

Science and Technology

The ongoing cooperation in the field of science & technology, under the Integrated Long-Term Programme of cooperation (ILTP) is the largest cooperation programme in this sphere for both India and Russia. ILTP is coordinated by the Department of Science and Technology from the Indian side and by the Russian Academy of Sciences and Russian Ministry of Industry & Science and Technology from the Russian side.

Development of SARAS Duet aircraft, semiconductor products, super computers, poly-vaccines, laser science and technology, seismology, high-purity materials, software & IT and Ayurveda have been some of the priority areas of co-operation under the ILTP. Under this programme, eight joint Indo-Russian centres have been established to focus on joint research and development work. Two other Joint Centres on Non-ferrous Metals and Accelerators and Lasers are being set up in India. A Joint Technology Centre based in Moscow to bring cutting edge technologies to the market is also under processing. An ILTP Joint Council met in Moscow on 11–12 October 2007 to review cooperation and give it further direction. In August 2007, an MOU was signed between Department of Science and Technology and Russian Foundation of Basic Research, Moscow to pursue scientific cooperation.

North-South Transport Corridor

The North-South Transport Corridor is a term used to describe the ship, rail, and road route for moving freight from South Asia to Europe through Central Asia, the Caucasus, and Russia. The route primarily involves moving goods from India via ship to Iran. From Iran, the freight moves by ship across the Caspian Sea or by truck or rail to Southern Russia. From there, the goods are transported by truck or rail along the Volga River through Moscow to Northern Europe. In 2001, Russia, Iran, and India signed an agreement to further develop the route. The "North-South" Transport Corridor Agreement [INSTC] has been ratified by all the three original signatory states, viz. India, Iran and Russia, and has come into force since 16 May, 2002.

This route is expected to reduce the cost of movement of goods between India and Russia and beyond. The 3rd Coordination Council Meeting of the INSTC was held in October 2005 in New Delhi and the 4th meeting was held in Aktau, Kazakhstan in October 2007 to discuss further streamlining the operation of the corridor.

Cooperation in the Sphere of Culture

India–Russia relations in the field of culture are historical. Five Chairs relating to Indology have been established in Moscow, Saint Petersburg, Kazan and Vladivostok. Days of Russian Culture were held in India in November 2003, in Delhi, Kolkata and Mumbai. "Days of Indian Culture" in Russia were organized from September- October 2005 in Russia. 130th birth anniversary of Nikolai Roerich and 100th birth anniversary of Svyatoslav Roerich were celebrated in India in October 2004.

Chief Minister of National Capital Territory of Delhi led a delegation for participating in the event "Days of Delhi in Moscow" from 28 May-1 June 2006. The "Year of Russia in India" was held in 2008. It was followed by the "Year of India in Russia" in 2009. There is a Hindi Department, in the University of Moscow.

Terrorism

On international terrorism, India and Russia agree that there is no justification for terrorism, and this must be fought against, without compromise and wherever it exists. Russia has supported the Indian draft at the UN on Comprehensive Convention on International Terrorism [CCIT]. The two sides signed a MOU on cooperation in combating terrorism in December 2002. A Joint Working Group on Combating International Terrorism meets from time to time and its fourth meeting was held in Delhi on 24 October 2006.

Nuclear Deals

On 7 November 2009, India Signed a new nuclear deal with Russia apart from the deals that were agreed upon by the two countries earlier.

India and the EU: A Long Road Ahead

Indian-European Union relations date back to the 1960s, where India was one of the first countries to establish relations with what is now the European Union (EU). The two signed bilateral agreements in 1973, when the United Kingdom joined. The most recent cooperation agreement was signed in 1994 and an action plan was signed in 2005. As of April 2007 the Commission is pursuing a free trade agreement with India.

Trade

The EU is India's largest trading partner, accounting for 20% of Indian trade. However India accounts for only 1.8% of the EU's trade and attracts only 0.3% of European Foreign Direct Investment, although still provides India's largest source for India. During 2005 EU-India trade grew by 20.3%.

Trade between the two has more than doubled from 25.6 billion euros ($36.7 billion) in 2000 to 55.6 billion euros in 2007, with further expansion to be seen. "We have agreed to achieve an annual bilateral trade turnover of 100 billion euros within the next five years," Singh told reporters. A joint statement issued at the end of the summit said the EU and India would work to reach an agreement on climate change by the end of 2009. There was controversy in 2006 when the Indian Mittal Steel Company sought to take-over the Luxembourg based steel company, Arcelor. The approach met with opposition from France and Luxembourg but was passed by the Commission who stated that they were judging it on competition grounds only.

Agreements

The EU and India agreed on September 29, 2008 at the EU-India summit in Marseille, France's largest commercial port, to expand their cooperation in the fields of nuclear energy and environmental protection and deepen their strategic partnership. French President Nicolas Sarkozy, the EU's rotating president, said at a joint press conference at the summit that "EU welcomes India, as a large country, to engage in developing nuclear energy, adding that this clean energy will be helpful for the world to deal with the global climate change." Sarkozy also said the EU and Indian Prime Minister Manmohan pledged to accelerate talks on a free trade deal and expected to finish the deal by 2009.

The Indian prime minister was also cautiously optimistic about cooperation on nuclear energy. "Tomorrow we have a bilateral summit with France. This matter will come up and I hope some good results will emerge out of that meeting," Singh said when asked about the issue. Singh said that he was "very satisfied" with the results of the summit. He added that EU and India have "common values" and the two economies are complementary to each other.

European Commission President Jose Manuel Barroso, also speaking at Monday's press conference, expounded the joint action plan on adjustments of EU's strategic partnership with India, saying the two sides will strengthen cooperation on world peace and safety, sustainable development, cooperation in science and technology and cultural exchanges.

Reviewing the two sides' efforts in developing the bilateral strategic partnership, the joint action plan reckoned that in politics, dialogue and cooperation have enhanced through regular summits and exchanges of visits and that in economy, mutual investments have increased dramatically in recent years, dialogue in macro economic policies and financial services has established and cooperation in energy, science and technology and environment has been launched.

Under the joint action plan, EU and Indian would enhance consultation and dialogue on human rights within the UN framework, strengthen cooperation in world peacekeeping mission, fight against terror and non-proliferation of arms, promote cooperation and exchange in developing civil nuclear energy and strike a free trade deal as soon as possible. France, which relies heavily on nuclear power and is a major exporter of nuclear technology, is expected to sign a deal that would allow it to provide nuclear fuel to India.

India is an important trade partner for the EU and a growing global economic power. It combines a sizable and growing market of more than 1 billion people with a growth rate of between 8 and 10 % - one of the fastest growing economies in the world. Although it is far from the closed market that it was twenty years ago, India still also maintains substantial tariff and non-tariff barriers that hinder trade with the EU. The EU and India hope to increase their trade in both goods and services through the Free Trade Agreement (FTA) negotiations that they launched in 2007.

India is one of the growing economies that will reshape the global economy in the twenty-first century

Trade in goods:

- EU goods exports to India 2007: €26.2 billion
- EU goods imports from India 2007: €29.4 billion.

Trade in services:

- EU services exports to India 2007: €6.7 billion
- EU services imports from India 2007: €5.5 billion.

Foreign Direct Investment:

- EU outward investment to India 2006: €2.5 billion
- Indian inward investment to EU: €0.5billion.

SEARCHING FOR COMMON APPROACHES TO THE NUCLEAR NON-PROLIFERATION

According to the views of the Indian political class, India is a defacto nuclear state whether or not it is recognized as such by the Treaty of Non-Proliferation of Nuclear Weapons. Indian officials contend that there is no sense in joining a Treaty that has been criticized by Indian society for so many years. The fragility and contradictory nature of the nuclear non-proliferation regime is reflected in India's position: Delhi has invariably emphasized nuclear disarmament over nuclear non-proliferation. India has always viewed the proliferation of nuclear weapons as a threat to regional and global security, and as a consequence has viewed nuclear proliferation as illegitimate (hence non-proliferation, i.e. maintaining a privileged status of "nuclear club" members). India is scrupulous about compliance with this regime as it has categorically refused to transfer "sensitive" technologies and fissionable materials to other countries. The logic behind India's position on nuclear non-proliferation and nuclear security suggests that cooperation in this area between the two countries under review has no meaningful political prospects.

THREE STAGES OF INDO-RUSSIAN DEFENCE RELATIONS: A MILITARY PERSPECTIVE

Stage 1: The Soviet Era

The USSR was one country that sent its Ambassador, Kirill Novikov to establish diplomatic relations with India even prior to our former declaration of Independence -he reported on 15 Apr 1947. Even in military and defence domain, the relations between the USSR and India have always remained very warm and cordial, carrying a bit of the 'big brother flavour' on part of the former. Starting with early fifties, the signs of support and solidarity from the Soviet Union were clearly visible when it announced its support to the Indian sovereignty over the disputed territory in Kashmir and in Goa. In fact, by very judiciously declaring neutrality in the Sino-Indian war of 1962, it faced strong objections from China, but Premier Khrushchev remained firm. History has it that in the next war thrust upon our country in 1965, it was USSR that played a major role in brokering peace between two warring nations.

Most significantly, from fifties to late sixties, it was defence technology and equipment coming from the USSR that actually built the spine of the Indian military. In 1962, USSR agreed to transfer the technology to co-produce its frontline fighter jet MIG 21; something it had denied even to China earlier. What this supersonic fighter interceptor meant to India at that point in time, and how, is indicated by this absolutely marvellous design spanning all sense of time with a tenure extending from 1961 to 2017-18 when it is slated to retire, while its updated version Bison, is still to go on till 2022. By that time, it is slated to be replaced by Hindustan Aeronautics Limited 'Tejas'.

If the above time window is extended and is taken up to around eighties, about 60 to 70 percent of all military hardware for the Indian defence forces came from the USSR -MiG 27, MiG 29, IL 76, Mi 35, Mi26,Mi 17, Mi8 in the current inventory of the Indian Air Force (IAF), IL 38 and MiG 29 K in the current Naval Air Arm, AK series of assault rifles, general purpose and heavy machine guns for the Infantry, multiple types of bridge laying equipments of several makes for Engineers, T 72 Tanks for Armoured Corps, BMPs for Mechanised Infantry, howitzers (M46, D30),heavy guns (180 mm), BM 21 rocket launchers for Artillery and a whole series of Ground Based Air Defence Weapon Systems (GBADWS), complete with their command, control and support systems - ZU 23-2 Guns, Schilka Weapon System, Strela 2M Shoulder fired Missiles, Strela 10 and OSA AK Very Short Range Missile Systems and Kvadrat Area Air Defence System- all belong to this era. The above weapon system list is by no way comprehensive. It is merely indicative and only includes some of the weapons still continuing in the current arsenal of Indian defence Forces.

What was this type of defence relationship and the pattern of acquisition of Defence equipment? Well, most of these deals related to Government-to-Government (G2G) agreements that normally preceded or followed the visits of national leaders on either side to each other's country. Most of the above procurements were a kind of 'what came as a packet from USSR' - main weapon systems and spare line. There were no such encumbrances like Defence Procurement Procedure (DPP), Request For Information (RFI), water tight and non-negotiable Services Qualitative Requirements (SQRs) , long winded chains of series of approvals starting from Acceptance of Necessity (AoN), categorisation on the type of acquisitions by Services Capital Acquisition Committees and Higher Committees (SCAPCC and SCAPCHC) and finally the casting of dice at the Defence Acquisition Committee (DAC), the chain that is currently in vogue.

Seeing one such deal first hand (SAM 6 Kvadrat Weapon System), the ease associated with the series of receipts of sub-consignment was easy to be taken for granted. Equipment were simply taken over, duly cleared in a G2G agreement in sub-unit groups, complete with main equipment, live equipment based simulators, ZIP drives (spare support kits) and a host of training literature. This was preceded by a select lot of all ranks moving to USSR for a hands-on training package on the equipment which culminated into live firing.

It is no wonder therefore that from early sixties to late seventies or beginning eighties, the Indian armed force accumulated a huge percentage (nearly 60+%)of arsenal from the Soviet Union. Another important feature in those times was that since the equipment was comparatively new and all the production lines of the Original Equipment Manufacturers (OEM) were still open, the continuous supply of spares (which were in any case needed in lesser quantities) came directly as spare consignments while the ZIP spares largely remained intact!

That was the hey-day period for the Soviet arsenal. Receipt of complete consignment as packets with deliveries spaced over time and in smaller identifiable packages for specific fire units were being received in regular intervals. As said, since most of the equipment was in its first quarter life-cycle, requirement of deep spare support was very less while the running spares were smoothly coming with OEM production lines. Great times indeed!

Stage 2: Soviet Demise and Aftermath

And then the eclipse started to set in slowly. It all commenced in one way or the other with the demise of the Soviet Union on 25 Dec 1991. Besides a host of political and diplomatic upheavals arising out of what the newly independent States inherited from the erstwhile stature and the aura of Soviet Union, in the defence domain some earth-shaking events unfolded in the years that followed. These would leave some permanent scars on India's defence system for years to come.

The most significant of them all was the grim reality that the erstwhile comprehensive defence manufacturing base of a host of big and small industries, design bureaus, production units, et al, that was spread over the entire landmass of the Soviet Union. These had a capability to design, manufacture and sustain a whole hierarchy of weapon systems all on their own, but now lay scattered into 15 newly born independent States, each in its cradle (except Russia) and each governed by its own set of newly defined or undefined national priorities.

The effect of this 'scattering away' of 'one whole' under 'one control' into many an independent entities had a far reaching effect. First and foremost, the umbilical chain which ensured that multiple systems and sub-systems produced by different manufacturing units are seamlessly integrated into one end-product, simply gave way as independent countries now controlled various production bases each capable of a part but not the whole. The connection had now to be established through dialogues with each of the newly independent States, many of which were just about rising from the smouldering ruins of the collapsed giant called the Soviet Union. Also several newly independent states, barring a few (Russia, Ukraine, Uzbek, Belarus), were in fractured state of economy. Funds required to restart the wheels of the defence industry were simply not there. Besides there were hundred other priorities to attend to, internal unrest and civil wars not the least of them.

As years rolled, while Russia as the legally accepted inheritor of the Soviet legacy took the lead in picking up the threads of what was the precedents and traditions of the mighty defence industrial design and production base of the erstwhile USSR, in effect, it could never reach anywhere to 'what it was'. Over the years, many OEMs faced with a quagmire of political and economic compulsions started closing production lines. For several of them it was kind of a vicious circle of a *fait accompli*chain reaction since they produced sub-systems whose demand in the 'pull system' shrunk because the final assembler and integrator was either not operating in full gear, or was in a scale down mode.

For the Indian armed forces sitting over a huge Soviet inventory and used to the seamless ease of dealing with the USSR, the 'demise after-effects' were catastrophic to say the least, though their total de-stabilising effect was fully felt only over the years. In fact, the first couple of years after the break-up got spent in just trying to re-establish the severed links and trying to find a re-connect with a new and hereto unknown flag bearer called Russia, who while trying its best to pick up loose threads and get a move on, fell short on many counts.

The above state of things started to show their ugly faces to the user domain. The first unwelcome realisation started to come over the spares of main frame combat equipment. As the spare support, which first stared drying up to a minimal sporadic trickle, the ZIP packs started to get opened up. As the show had to go on complete with its rigour of regular training and live firing of equipment year-on-year, reserves of spares started to dip lower and lower while hardly anything fetched up from the OEMs. The scheduled overhauls (OHs) started to slip only to be replaced later by OH and Repair as Necessary (ORAN).While several Russian and its supporting conglomerate of companies represented by Rosoboron Exports (RBE) promised the moon in spare support, hardly anything actually fetched up on ground.

The user made desperate attempts for Last Time Buys (LTBs) but it fetched a near void. Several countries like Israel, Poland, Singapore etc. came forward with a promise of spare support but all of that proved to be 'too little and too late for joy'. Another thing that was noticed by the users at this time was that Russia, with the state of economy that it was in, actually started sky-rocketing the spares costs by wide margins - for some critical components the costs went up by more than a 1000%! A stage slowly emerged when the users were left with no choice but to carry out cannibalisation to keep a portion of the fleet operational at the cost of losing out on some numbers. Around this time (2000-03), efforts were put in to indigenise the spares. Directorate of Indigenisation (DOI) came up under the Corps of Electronic and Mechanical Engineers. The journey for DOI has been long and arduous with very less actual throughput till date - understandably so.

Besides the spares imbroglio, the delivery schedules started to slip, especially in case of ammunition and missiles. The catastrophic beating which their economy had taken showed up at many places. RBE started quoting unrealistic costs for mainframe equipment thus losing out in several big ticket procurements in multi-vendor scenarios - case in point, Tunguska Weapon system for Army Air Defence. Since the time was now approaching for the periodic OH of mainframe equipment, The OEMs started to make astronomical time and cost estimates for setting up facilities for the OH – a case in point being the overhaul of guns and missile systems of Air force and Army. Besides this, RBE stared to drag its feet on many offset negotiations or asking for unbelievable costs for Transfer of Technology (ToT).

Getting frustrated with the emerging realities, the armed forces stated looking elsewhere towards countries like USA, Israel, UK, Sweden, France, Singapore, Germany and Korea. The initial years were a NO-GO for USA due to a seemingly impassable disconnect between our DPP and their procedure of Foreign Military Sales (FMS). It is besides the point that today the No 1 arms supplier to India is not Russia but USA.

At that stage things were actually looking bad and difficult for the Soviet origin equipment.

Stage 3: Move to the Present and Future

As time passed, the debilitating effects of the break up started to loosen its suffocating bind and Russia primarily, along with Ukraine, Bulgaria, and a few others stared to rise from the mess, so to say.

In the meanwhile, a complete metamorphosis was underway in India as well. This was marked with the new found euphoria of 'Make-in-India', strengthening of Micro, Small and Medium Enterprises (MSMEs), shaking the Defence Public Sector Undertakings (DPSUs) from their deep slumber and the states of complacencies and despondencies. All this and more gradually started to usher a totally changed defence manufacturing eco system, made possible by the new found strength and techno-capability, as also a gradual coming of age of the defence private Industry.

Russia (as also the rest of the world) slowly came to realise that fuelled by DPP 2016, complete with its appendices and annexures, the defence eco system in India had 'new signatures and 'rules of survival' for the foreign OEMs. The new Code of Conduct now demanded a regime of *make in India, joint ventures, memorandum of understandings (MoU), co-development of niche equipment, joint production with buy back clause, compulsion of transfer of niche technology in the 'know why' domain, equal ownership in cutting edge development projects,* to name some. That code actually summed up the current and futuristic status of our defence procurement scenario. Thanks to the 'slow but sure' growth (though there are many a glitches yet) of the private industry and the opportunities for strengthening of the indigenous muscle of the defence procurement base by the DPP 2016, every foreign OEM came to know too well, the compulsions of following the spelt out mandate. Accordingly, it was not uncommon to see many OEMs aligning themselves to the tune of 'Make in India'. In fact one of them has adopted the punch line 'Made in India'.

The Russian block was no exception. They adopted themselves nicely to the changed rules of the game. To sample these developments; some old, some new:-

- The BrahMos success story is actually the crown jewel in the Indo-Russia defence co-operation on equal footing. The project prides itself of co-design, co-development and co-production with equal rights on niche technology areas. This was prominently visible recently in the open source literature relating to the ongoing development of the miniature version of BrahMos or while developing the hypersonic velocity technologies (6 Mac+).
- Contract to sell the S-400 Air defence and BMD system is another example of contemporary defence relationship. A weapon system of

such a capability (range 400 km, altitude coverage 20 km) is a totally way-up induction in what the capability is currently possessed by the existing weapon inventory of GBADWS across the three Services. This niche technology is poised to come to India aligned with the new DPP.

- Of the 200 Kamov KA 226 T helicopters, only the first 60 are coming in the fly away condition. The balance 140 are to be made in India with complete transfer of technology. Similarly in the co-development and co-production of the futuristic fifth Generation Fighter, T 50 PAK FA, issues like work share, Intellectual Propriety Rights (IPR) on ToT, access to codes and roots et al, are played between India and Russia on near-equal footing. In fact, an earlier one-sided imbalance in favour of Russia in the niche work share rights over technologies related to PAK FA actually delayed the project till a mutually acceptable balance was achieved.

Conclusion

And finally, a word on the age-old dictum, 'There are no permanent friends or permanent enemies of a State, what is permanent is national interests'. In difficult times post the break-up of USSR, as also in the recent past (2012-2015 period) when India started to look elsewhere for its big ticket items (futuristic multirole fighter jets, artillery mainstay guns/howitzers etc), in 2015, Russia lifted arms embargo against Pakistan and sold to them 4 MI-35 attack helicopters. Again in Dec 2016 India was excluded by Russia from its joint exercise with Afghanistan, Pakistan and China. In essence, our historical warmth and goodwill notwithstanding, the Russia-China-Pakistan axis is also a reality that cannot be wished away. Its dormancy/ resurgence is driven by the perception of Russian national interests at any point in time. It is also a kind of 'tool of reciprocal behaviour' driven by Indian moves 'as perceived' by our friend.

Such are the three shades of Indo-Russian defence relations which have unfolded in the last seven decades. As it stands today, the future of these relations is likely to be driven by the new and emerging contours of resurgent India and will be tweaked by what measure of success we can turn in on our new found dream of MAKE IN INDIA.

BILATERAL RELATIONS: INDIA-RUSSIA RELATIONS

Relations with Russia are a key pillar of India's foreign policy, and Russia has been a longstanding time-tested partner of India. Since the signing of "Declaration on the India-Russia Strategic Partnership" in October 2000 (during the visit of Russian President H.E. Mr. Vladimir Putin to India), India-Russia ties have acquired a qualitatively new character with enhanced levels of cooperation in almost all areas of the bilateral relationship including political, security, trade and economy, defense, science and technology and culture. Under the Strategic Partnership, several institutionalized dialogue mechanisms operate at both political and official levels to ensure regular interaction and follow up on cooperation activities. During the visit of the Russian President to India in December 2010, the Strategic Partnership was elevated to the level of a "Special and Privileged Strategic Partnership."

Political relations

Annual Summit meeting between the Prime Minister of India and the President of the Russian Federation is the highest institutionalized dialogue mechanism under the Strategic Partnership between India and the Russian Federation. So far 15 Annual Summit meetings have taken place alternatively in India and Russia with the 15th Annual Summit held in New Delhi during the visit of President Putin to India on 11 December 2014.

During the Summit, 20 documents were signed covering cooperation in nuclear energy, defence, hydrocarbons, science & technology, trade and investment etc. Prime Minister Shri Narendra Modi and President Putin also adopted a Joint Statement "'Druzhba-Dosti: A Vision for strengthening the Indian-Russian Partnership over the next decade."

Besides the Annual Summit meeting in December 2014, our PM met the Russian President on the sidelines of the BRICS Summit in Fortaleza in Brazil on 15 July 2014 and the Russian Prime Minister H.E. Mr. Dmitry Medvedev ahead of the 9th East Asia Summit in Nay Pyi Taw (Myanmar) on 13 November 2014. President Shri Pranab Mukherjee participated in the commemoration of the 70th anniversary of victory in the World War II on 9 May 2015 in Moscow, and on the sidelines held a bilateral meeting with President Putin.

There are regular high-level interactions between the two countries. Two Inter- Governmental Commissions - one on Trade, Economic, Scientific, Technological and Cultural Cooperation (IRIGC-TEC), co-chaired by the External Affairs Minister (EAM) and the Russian Deputy Prime Minister (DPM) and another on Military Technical Cooperation (IRIGC- MTC) co-chaired by Russian and Indian Defense Ministers, meet annually.

Russian DPM Dmitry Rogozin visited India thrice last year, including to co-chair with External Affairs Minister the 20th session of the IRIGC-TEC. The Foreign Ministers of India and Russia met on the sidelines of the Russia-India-China (RIC) Foreign Ministers meeting in Beijing on 2 February 2015. The last annual Foreign Office Consultations was held in Moscow from 15-17 April, 2014. Foreign Secretary met Deputy Foreign Minister Igor Morgulov in Moscow on 8 May 2015. Chairman of the State Duma (Lower House of the Russian Parliament) visited India in February 2015 to co-chair with Lok Sabha Speaker the 3rd session of the India-Russia Inter-Parliamentary Commission. He also called on the President and Vice-President of India. In March 2015, Russian Minister of Telecom and Mass Communication, Nikolay

Nikiforov visited Delhi, where he met his Indian counterparts the Minister of Communication and IT, and the Minister of State for Information and Broadcasting.

In April 2015, Indian Minister of State for Defence visited Moscow and attended the 4th Moscow Conference on International Security and also addressed the Assocham-Sberbank Conference on Defence Industry Cooperation.

The Chief Justice of India and the Minister of Law and Justice participated in the St Petersburg International Legal Forum in May 2015. In June 2015, Commerce and Industry Minister visited St Petersburg to participate in the 15th St. Petersburg International Economic Forum (SPEIF) and also met the Russian Minister of Trade and Industry, Mr. Denis Manturov.

Russia assumed the BRICS Presidency in April 2015, and since then, it has been organizing a number of events and meetings under the BRICS format. The Minister of State for Environment, Forest and Climate Change visited Moscow for the BRICS Environment Ministers' Meeting on 21 April; Secretary (East) attended the BRICS Consultations on Middle East and North Africa in Moscow on 22 May; National Security Adviser visited Moscow to participate in the 5th Meeting of BRICS High Representatives for Security Issues from 25 - 26 May; and Chairman of the Parliamentary Standing Committee on External Affairs participated in the BRICS Parliamentary Forum in Moscow on 8 June 2015.

Defence Cooperation

India has longstanding and wide-ranging cooperation with Russia in the field of defence. India-Russia military technical cooperation has evolved from a simple buyer - seller framework to one involving joint research, development and production of advanced defence technologies and systems. BrahMos Missile System, Joint development of the Fifth Generation Fighter Aircraft and the Multi Transport Aircraft, as well as the licensed production in India of SU-30 aircraft and T-90 tanks, are examples of such flagship cooperation. Last year in June, the Prime Minister dedicated to the nation the Russian-built aircraft carrier INS Vikramaditya at a special ceremony off the coast of Goa. The two countries also hold exchanges and training exercises between their armed forces annually. An Indian contingent participated in the military parade in Moscow on 9 May 2015 during the 70th anniversary of the victory in the World War II.

The Inter Governmental Commission on Military Technical Cooperation (IRIGC-MTC) co-chaired by the two Defence Ministers and its Working Groups and Sub-Groups review defence cooperation between the two countries. The Russian Defence Minister, Sergei Shoigu visited New Delhi for the last meeting (14th session) of the Commission on 21 January 2015 to review the ongoing cooperation and future opportunities for progressing bilateral defence cooperation. In December 2014, the two governments signed the Agreement for Training of Indian Armed Forces Personnel in the Military Educational Establishments of the Defence Ministry of the Russian Federation.

Economic Relations

Enhancing trade and economic cooperation between India and Russia is a key priority for the two governments. During 15th Annual Summit, the two leaders set a target of US$30 billion bilateral trade by 2025. Bilateral trade during in 2014 amounted to US$ 9.51 billion, with Indian export amounting to US$ 3.17 billion (an increase of 2.6 % over 2013) and imports from Russia amounting to US$ 6.34 billion (decline of 9.2 % over 2013).

Major items of export from India include pharmaceuticals, miscellaneous manufactures, iron & steel, apparels, tea, coffee and tobacco. Major items of import from Russia include defence and nuclear power equipment, fertilizers, electrical machinery, steels and diamonds.

Indian investment in Russia are estimated to be about US$ 7 billion which include Imperial Energy Tomsk; Sakhalin I; Volzhsky Abrasive Works Volgograd; and Commercial Indo bank. Russian investments in India total about US$ 3 billion, including Kamaz Vectra in Hosur; Shyam Sistema Telecom Ltd, Sberbank and VTB. Inter- Governmental Commission on Trade, Economic, Scientific, Technological and Cultural Cooperation (IRIGC-TEC) is the apex G2G forum to review economic cooperation. It reviews sectoral cooperation under working groups on trade and economic cooperation, priority investments, modernization and industrial cooperation (sub-groups on civil aviation, mining, fertilizer, and modernization), outstanding issues, energy & energy efficiency, science and technology, communications & IT, tourism and culture, and sub-groups on banking & financial matters and on conservation of tigers & leopards. The 20th session of the IRIGC-TEC was held in New Delhi on 5 November 2014.

India - Russia Forum on Trade and Investment co-chaired by the Commerce and Industry Minister of India and the Russian Minister for Economic Development, and India-Russia CEOs' Council are the two primary mechanisms to promote direct bilateral business-to- business contacts between India and Russia. Mechanisms such as India-Russia Business Council (partnership between FICCI of India and CCI of Russia), India-Russia Trade, Investment and Technology Promotion Council (partnership between CII of India and RUIE of Russia), India–Russia Business Dialogue (partnership between CII of India and Russia's Business Council for Cooperation with India) and India-Russia Chamber of Commerce (with focus on SMEs) supplement the efforts to build direct business - to - business ties.

The 8th India-Russia Forum on Trade & Investment was held in New Delhi on 5 November 2014. During the 15th St. Petersburg International Economic Forum (SPIEF) in June 2015, India and Eurasian Economic Union (EaEU) signed a joint statement to undertake joint feasibility study for the FTA between India and EaEU.

Hydrocarbons is an active area for exploring cooperation between the two countries. In May 2014, ONGC and Rosneft signed an MoU for bilateral cooperation in subsurface surveys, exploration, appraisal and hydrocarbons production in the offshore Arctic region of Russia. In June last year, a Russian company Gazprom International signed an MoU with Oil India Limited for cooperation in the oil and gas sector which include joint exploration, training, development of oil fields and sharing of information.

In December 2014, Rosneft signed an MoU regarding the possibility of a long-term contract with the Essar group for supply of crude oil.

Nuclear Energy

Russia is an important partner in peaceful uses of nuclear energy and it recognizes India as a country with advanced nuclear technology with an impeccable non-proliferation record.

In December 2014, Department of Atomic Energy (DAE) and Russia's Rosatom signed the Strategic Vision for strengthening cooperation in peaceful uses of atomic energy between India and Russia. Kudankulam Nuclear Power Plant (KKNPP) is being built in India with Russian cooperation. KKNPP Unit 1 became operational in July 2013, and attained full generation capacity on 7 June 2014, while its Unit 2 is in the process of commissioning in the later part of 2015. India and Russia have signed a General Framework Agreement on KKNPP Units 3 & 4 and subsequent contracts are under preparation. Secretary, DAE visited Moscow on 9 June to review the wider cooperation in the field of peaceful uses of nuclear energy.

Space Cooperation

India-Russia cooperation in the field of peaceful uses of outer space dates back to about four decades. This year marks the 40th anniversary of the launch of India's first satellite "Aryabhatt" on a Russian (then USSR) launch vehicle 'Soyuz.' In 2007, India and Russia signed a framework agreement on cooperation in the peaceful uses of outer space, including satellite launches, Glonass navigation, remote sensing and other societal applications of outer space. In June 2015, the space agencies have signed an MoU on expansion of cooperation in the field of the exploration and use of outer space for peaceful purposes.

Science & Technology

The Working Group on Science and Technology functioning under IRIGC-TEC, the Integrated Long Term Programme (ILTP) and the Basic Science Cooperation Programme are the three main institutional mechanisms for bilateral Science and Technology cooperation, while the Science Academies of the two countries promote inter-academy exchanges.

ILTP during its 25-year long implementation period, supported over 500 joint R&D projects and setting up of 9 thematic centers in India and Russia that resulted in generation of over 1500 joint publications and many new products, processes, facilities, and research centers besides developing over 10,000 scientific contacts.

India-Russia Science and Technology Centre with a branch each in Delhi-NCR and Moscow was set up in 2011-12 in order to promote two-way transfer of technologies and their commercialization.

Two new Programmes of Cooperation in the field of Science, Technology and Innovation and in Biotechnology concluded in October 2013 have become active mechanisms; these have already supported first batch of 11 joint R&D projects in 2014. In December 2014, Indian Council of Medical Research and Russian Foundation of Basic Research entered into an MoU for cooperation in health research. On 8 May 2015, Department of Science & Technology (DST) and Russian Science Foundation signed an agreement to support basic and exploratory research.

Cultural Cooperation

There is a strong tradition of Indian studies in Russia. Jawaharlal Nehru Cultural Centre at the Embassy of India, Moscow (JNCC) maintains close cooperation with leading Russian institutions, including the Institute of Philosophy (Moscow), Russian State University for Humanities(Moscow), Institute of Oriental Studies(Moscow), Institute of Asian and African Studies at the Moscow State University, School of International Relations at the St. Petersburg University, Kazan Federal University, Far Eastern Federal University (Vladivostok), and Russian Institute for Cultural Research (Krasnodar).

There is a Mahatma Gandhi Chair on Indian Philosophy at the Institute of Philosophy, Moscow. About 20 Russian Institutions, including leading universities and schools, regularly teach Hindi to 1500 Russian students. Apart from Hindi, languages such as Tamil, Marathi, Gujarati, Bengali, Urdu, Sanskrit and Pali are taught in Russian Institutions. There is general interest among Russian people in Indian dance, music, yoga and ayurveda. JNCC conducts classes in yoga, dance, music and Hindi for approximately 500 students every month. There are regular cultural initiatives to promote people-to-people contacts between India and Russia, including reciprocal Years of each others' culture. The President of India inaugurated the Year of Indian Culture 'Namaste Russia' in Moscow on 10 May 2015. About 15 performances in 8 cities are planned as part of 'Namaste Russia' across various parts of Russia over 2015. On 21 June 2015, the first International Day of Yoga (IDY) was organized across Russia covering more than 60 regions with over 250 events and involving about 45000 Yoga enthusiasts.

Indian Community

Indian Community in the Russian Federation is estimated at about 14,500. In addition, about 1,500 Afghan nationals of Indian origin live in Russia.

About 500 Indian businessmen reside in Russia out of which around 200 work in Moscow. An estimated 300 registered Indian companies operate in Russia. Majority of Indian businessmen/companies in Russia are involved in trading while some represent Indian banks, pharmaceuticals, hydrocarbon and engineering companies. Tea, coffee, tobacco, pharmaceuticals, rice, spices, leather footwear, granite, I.T. and garments are amongst the products being imported by these companies from India. There are approximately 4,500 Indian students enrolled in medical and technical institutions in the Russian Federation. About 90% of them pursue medical studies in about 20 universities/institutions across Russia. Hindustani Samaj is the oldest Indian organization in Russia functioning since 1957.

Other Indian organizations in Moscow include, Indian Business Alliance, Overseas Bihar Association, AMMA (All Moscow Malayalee Association), DISHA (Indian-Russian Friendship Society), Textile Business Alliance, Bhartiya Sanskritik Samaj, and Ramakrishna Society Vedanta Centre. Embassy of India School in Moscow is affiliated to Kendriya Vidyalaya Sangathan in New Delhi with teachers deputed from India. The School has classes from I to XII and has about 350 students.

MODI'S PERSONAL TOUCH TO INDIA-RUSSIA RELATIONS

The one-day visit of Prime Minister Narendra Modi to Sochi on May 21 heralded a new beginning as far as the question of India-Russia relations is concerned. It can be termed as a new initiative because the visit of Modi to Russia took place when the relation was slightly strained. This can be partly attributed to Russian policymakers' ambivalent policy on giving sophisticated weapons to Pakistan (known for sponsoring cross-border terrorism) and keeping mum on Chinese aggressive policy towards India. The third issue is Moscow's engagement with Taliban which certainly created jittery among the policymakers in New Delhi. The fourth concern is low level of bilateral economic relations between these two countries which certainly provide opportunity to introspect why after so many years the mutual economic relations are not on a higher pedestal.

Another interesting aspect that needs to be discerned here is that the PM visited China and held a similar informal interaction with Chinese President Xi Jinping last month at Wuhan. The two successive visits of Modi in a short span of one month are a reflection of "spirit of multipolarity", which India is espousing since long. The two visits silenced many critics who are quite vociferous in stating that India is following the footsteps of the United States.

Modi's intention to add a new substance to the gloomy bilateral relations between India and Russia can be evident from the fact that before leaving to Sochi, Modi on his personal twitter account (as quoted on the PMO website) stated "the talks with President Putin will further strengthen the Special and Privileged Strategic Partnership between India and Russia". One interesting inference can be concluded from the twitter message that Modi intended to give the informal relationship to a new "strategic level" between these two civilisational powers.

The issue of fight against terrorism and extremism figured prominently in the Sochi informal meeting between Modi and Putin. The Informal Summit Declaration stated "determination to combat terrorism in all its forms and manifestations." The Declaration relating to Afghanistan assumes significance against the backdrop of resurgence of radical activities by Taliban as well as ISIS. One may recall here that a few days back the radical Taliban forces took Indians working in Afghanistan hostage. It is an undeniable fact that since the breakup of the Soviet Union, radicals from Afghanistan played a direct or indirect role in inciting terrorist activities in the Northern Caucasus region. Despite greater bonhomie between India and Russia in fight against radicalism, in recent years, Moscow is showing sign soft-pedalling both the dreaded Taliban and its ideological mentor, i.e, Pakistan. The most intriguing aspect of Russian engagement with Taliban came to light when just after signing the Sochi Informal Summit declaration with India, Russia sent a feeler to Taliban leadership for negotiation as reported in newspapers. Similarly as reported in news reports, China after snubbing Pakistan (for harbouring terrorist activities) last month is providing backdoor support to Hafeez Saeed. This double-standard of both Russia and China is an impediment to a cohesive fight against radical and terrorist forces.

The second issue which cropped up during Modi's interaction with Putin is to maintain strategic equilibrium both at the regional as well as at the global levels. Both the leaders agreed to contribute to the ushering of a "new multipolar world". In this regard, a specific mention was made to underline the significance of "India-Pacific Region". One may add here that this part of the world is emerging as a major "strategic fulcrum" of global geopolitics because of its strategic location. It also acts as a major global "trade and energy corridor". All the major global powers the USA, China, Japan, South Korea, along with these two civilisational powers, are taking keen interest in dominating this region. It is in this context, the India-Russian cooperation can act as a hedge against expansionist policy of other external power which may have a spillover-effect on the security of both the countries directly or indirectly. One may add here that the "multipolarity" which the informal declaration touched upon can be inferred in the context of limiting the role of Washington and China (both having ambitious strategic goals) in the India-Pacific region.

The core issue which got affected following US sanctions on Russia is supply of Defense equipment. It should be underlined that since Soviet times, India used to get bulk of military supplies and heavily depended on Moscow. Because of additional sanctions the Trump Administration imposed on Russia for the Crimean crisis ("CAATSA Section 231(d) Defence and Intelligence sectors of the Government of the Russian Federation") in October 2017, India is facing the problem in getting Defence equipment. When Indian Defence Minister Nirmala Sitharaman visited Moscow last month, both the sides agreed to expedite the deal relating to "S-400 air defence missile systems". However, no concrete result has been achieved till now. Though Washington is mooting exemption to New Delhi from CAATSA for purchase of missile defence system, they have not done anything in this direction. Without mentioning this Defense deal, the Sochi Declaration stated "the significance of longstanding partnership in the military, security and nuclear energy fields and welcomed the ongoing cooperation in these areas."

Another critical area that got full attention in the Informal Declaration at Sochi was cooperation in the field of energy cooperation. Since the signing of the Sakhalin deal, India has signed deals in the Siberian, Far East and Arctic regions of Russia. As per the OVL website, India has three major stakes at "Imperial Energy, Vankor as well Sakhalin-1 projects". Rosneft is also thinking of entering into the oil market of India. The informal Declarations has also appreciated the "long-term agreement between Gazprom and GAIL", which can be a game changer as far as energy cooperation is concerned as the Declaration mentioned that through this deal it will bring substantial amount of "LNG" to India.

What is worrisome in India-Russia relations is that the economic cooperation has not reached its potentiality. One may add a footnote here that while India's economic cooperation with the EU, the US and China is growing, that with Russia is quite stagnant. In this regard, the operationalisation of the International North South Transport Corridor Project (INSTC) will facilitate greater economic cooperation between the two countries. Along with INSTC, Russia should take initiative for inclusion of India in the Eurasian Economic Union. It is a known fact that with India's support, Russia can balance Chinese penetration in the Russian economy. A good example in this regard can be cited (as reported in Bloomberg.com, March 14, 2016) from the fact that it is India which tamed the Chinese monopoly in the Russian energy sector.

The informal meeting between Modi and Putin can be remembered for one thing that both the leaders gave personal touch to strengthen the bilateral relationship between the two countries.

THE COMING INDIA-RUSSIA SPLIT

The Russian-Indian partnership has experienced an upward trend in the past years. Russian President Vladimir Putin and Indian Prime Minister Narendra Modi enjoy cordial relations, meet regularly, hold telephone conversations, and seek ways to boost further bilateral trade. Although the official presentation of mutual ties seems cloudless, fundamental shifts are happening behind the curtains.

The previous year was a breakthrough in bilateral relations for Moscow and New Delhi. Both nations experienced impressive 22 percent growth in trade and boosted cooperation in a number of spheres ranging from agriculture to energy to pharmaceuticals. Earlier, Russia's largest oil producer, Rosneft, closed a $12.9 billion purchase of India's second largest private oil refiner, Essar Oil, which marked one of the biggest foreign investment in India. New Delhi likewise was the major guest country of the St. Petersburg International Economic Forum (SPIEF) in 2017, Russia's top national event for international cooperation, and hosted the pavilion titled "Make in India" along with Modi's participation in a plenary session next to Putin.

The two countries likewise seek stronger ties in the military sector. The Kremlin keeps its competitive edge and remains the largest supplier of weapons to the Indian market. Both nations signed an inter-governmental agreement for the purchase of the S-400 Triumf advanced Air Defense Systems (NATO: SA-21 Growler) estimated at $4.5 billion. Moscow and New Delhi also agreed on the import of Kamov Ka 226T light utility helicopters and collaboration in manufacturing of four *Admiral Grigorovich*–class guided-missile stealth frigates. The previous calendar year was likewise marked by a rare feat: the Indian defense minister and national security advisor each visited Russia twice.

Growing trade and new defense contracts combined with the personal friendship between Putin and Modi facilitate an impression of strategic bilateral relations. But shifting geopolitical dynamics driven by the rise of China, international sanctions against the Kremlin, and its never-ending economic stagnation point to imminent changes for India-Russia relations in the coming years.

The Kremlin played a key role in facilitating New Delhi's membership in the Shanghai Cooperation Organization. Moscow pushed forward India's membership in order to dilute China's dominance in the group. Its efforts likewise played vital role in maintaining the Russia-India-China trilateral format, during which the nations reconcile on a mutually shared vision and responsibility for the future of the Eurasian continent. The Kremlin also perceives such meetings as vital steps for pushing forward its ideological agenda of a multipolar world and challenging Western dominance, but India maintains a far more pragmatic vision.

New Delhi has great capacity to effectively respond to structural and geopolitical shifts and is extremely skillful in learning to adjust to changing power dynamics. For instance, in 1971 India signed a treaty of friendship and cooperation with the Soviet Union to balance Sino-U.S. rapprochement. After the end of the Cold War, India was keen on joining the Moscow-led Eurasian movement and agreed to embrace institutional cooperation with Beijing. The impetus was to secure its geopolitical ambitions as well as resist Washington's threats to roll back New Delhi's nuclear goals and possible interventions in a regional dispute with Pakistan over Jammu and Kashmir.

Currently the geopolitical realities in the region are changing again. Growing Chinese power and Indian ambitions mean that sooner or later both nations will start confronting each other more. The new setting prescribes the need to revise previous formats of interactions and seek diversification in foreign policy. Given Moscow's weakness and growing dependence on Beijing, India will need to look for another strong player to maintain its geopolitical ambitions.

Beijing is currently posing the biggest geopolitical threat to India. Both nations have a disputed border, which was highlighted during the recent standoff on the Doklam plateau in territory claimed by both China and Bhutan. China and India likewise compete for influence in the Asia-Pacific region and the Indian Ocean. With China's current GDP four times larger and its defense spending almost three times bigger than that of India, the broken parity pushes New Delhi to seek for ways to counter its neighbor's power.

Sino-India relations have been deteriorating for the past decades, while U.S.-India relations have experienced improvement simultaneously. The White House supports New Delhi's claim for a permanent seat at the United Nations Security Council and its entry into the Nuclear Suppliers Group – moves that are opposed by Beijing.

The United States likewise is more keen on supporting India's pursuit for regional leadership in its opposition to China's ambitions in South Asia and the Indian Ocean and has lots to offer in terms of trade and defense technologies. The latter is particularly appealing in lights of India's quest to diversify its military suppliers.

Washington's previous support for Pakistan has posed a serious challenge to India's geopolitical ambitions and the two nations' relations. In effect, the Trump administration's latest unexpected move to freeze aid to Pakistan could deliver positive vibes to India-U.S. relations. New Delhi has a lengthy record of accusing Islamabad of supporting cross-border terrorism, claims that might find support in Washington considering its own criticism of Pakistan's poor efforts in combating terrorism.

The Kremlin could still help New Delhi with some of its cutting-edge technologies and international diplomatic support, but India will ultimately keep shifting to the pro-Western orbit. Despite augmenting trade volumes, Russia's exports to India are barely 2 percent of India's total imports and in an economic sense, Russia's struggling economy has little to offer to India in the long-term. The Kremlin's growing political and economic dependence on Beijing ultimately means that the current momentum of Russia-India relations will be imminently challenged in the upcoming years.

For New Delhi, the anticipated shift will necessitate rational support for its independent foreign policy, which aims to diversify political relations while nurturing the goal of keeping "India first." The latter is proven by India's participation in a November 2017 working-level meeting of the so-called "Quad" of countries along with Japan, the United States, and Australia to counter China's growing influence in the Asia-Pacific. As a growing power, India needs to find its ways to improve its weight in the world order and it's unlikely that its historically pro-independence foreign policy will make an exception for the Kremlin.

INDO-SOVIET TREATY OF FRIENDSHIP AND COOPERATION

The Indo–Soviet Treaty of Peace, Friendship and Cooperation was a treaty signed between India and the Soviet Union in August 1971 that specified mutual strategic cooperation. The treaty was a significant deviation from India's previous position of non-alignment in the Cold War and in the prelude to the Bangladesh war, it was a key development in a situation of increasing Sino-American ties and American pressure. The treaty was later adopted to the Indo-Bangladesh Treaty of Friendship and cooperation in 1972.

Indo-Soviet relations

Early relations

India's relation to Soviet Union initially after the former's independence was ambivalent, guided by Nehru's decision to remain non-aligned, and his government's active part in the Commonwealth of Nations. However, in February 1954, the U.S. administration of President Dwight D. Eisenhower announced the decision to provide arms to Pakistan, followed a month later by Pakistan joining the SEATO and subsequently the CENTO. These agreements assured Pakistan the supply of sophisticated military hardware and economic aid.

The developing situation alarmed India, which had uncomfortable relations with Pakistan. Since Pakistan also was near the Soviet Union, it also provided Moscow with the necessity as well as the opportunity to develop its relations with India.

India's status as a leader of the Non-aligned Movement would also allow the USSR to bolster Soviet policy in the Third World. India and the USSR therefore pursued similar policies based on common security threat born out of the US interests in Pakistan.

It was in this context that India and Soviet Union exchanged military Attaches. Although Indo-Soviet cooperation had begun, the investment of soviet-military aid to India only begun in the context of deteriorating Sino-Soviet and Sino-Indian relations. Following the 1962 Sino-Indian war, the Sino-Pakistani axis was also an impetus for growing cooperation between India and the Soviet Union.

1971

Following the general elections in Pakistan (March 1971), the Pakistani head of state, general Yahya Khan, was utterly dissatisfied with the large victory of the Awami League, the Bengali party which had its power base in East Pakistan (current day Bangladesh). To pacify East Pakistan, which voted overwhelmingly for the Awami League, he imposed martial law, a curfew, heavy censorship, and the persecution of the Awami League leadership.

The Pakistani military, under the orders of general Tikka Khan, used heavy gunfire for almost a week to gain control of East Pakistan's largest city Dacca. After having secured control of the cities, they then turned to the Bengal countryside, where Tikka Khan targeted almost exclusively the Hindu population. This led to a mass exodus of (mostly Hindu) Bengali citizens, who all fled to India.

The Indian government, under the leadership of Indira Gandhi, saw itself confronted to a major humanitarian catastrophe, as eight to ten million Bengali fled from East-Pakistan to overcrowded and underfunded refugee camps in India. Indira Gandhi decided in April that a war was needed to stop the exodus and make millions of Bengali refugees return to their homes. However, the Pakistani leadership was very well connected, as Yahya Khan had a close personal friendship with American president Richard Nixon, and harboured excellent diplomatic relations with Mao's China. Under these circumstances, Indira Gandhi was apprehensive about sending an army to East-Pakistan. She knew that India would easily defeat the Pakistani forces in East-Pakistan, but could not be sure about the reactions of Nixon or Mao. The latter had defeated India in a war in 1962.

To her relief, the Soviet leadership was open to negotiations. The ensuing Treaty of Friendship and cooperation, signed in August 1971, was very loose but sent a strong signal to Washington and Beijing. The treaty was a strong additional incentive for Nixon and Mao to pursue their planned meeting, which took place in February 1972. Eventually, since Nixon needed Brezhnev to end the Vietnam War, the frictions between the two superpowers were streamlined which paved the way for the immensely important summit that was convened in Moscow in May 1972.

The Treaty

The Indo-Soviet Treaty of Peace, Friendship and Co-operation, 9 August 1971. Desirous of expanding and consolidating the existing relations of sincere friendship between them, Believing that the further development of friendship and cooperation meets the basic national interests of lasting peace in Asia and the world,

Determined to promote the consolidation of universal peace and security and to make steadfast efforts for the relaxation of international tensions and the final eliminations of the remnants of colonialism

Upholding their firm faith in the principles of peaceful coexistence and co-operation between States with different political and social Systems,

Convinced that in the world today international problems can only be solved by co-operation and not by conflict,

Reaffirming their determination to abide by the purposes and principles of the United Nations Charter,

The Republic of India on the one side, and the Union of Soviet Socialist Republics on the other side,

Have decided to conclude the present treaty, for which purposes the following plenipotentiaries have been appointed:

On behalf of the Republic of India: Sardar Swaran Singh, Minister of External Affairs.

On behalf of the Union of Soviet Socialist Republics: Mr A. A. Gromyko, Minister of Foreign Affairs.

Who, having each presented their credentials, which are found to be in proper form and due order, have agreed as follows:

(ARTICLE I)

The High Contracting Parties solemnly declare that enduring peace and friendship shall prevail between the two countries and their peoples. Each party shall respect the independence, sovereignty and territorial integrity of the other party and refrain From interfering in the other's internal affairs. The High Contracting Parties shall continue to develop and consolidate the relations of sincere friendship, good neighbourliness and comprehensive cooperation existing between them on the basis of the aforesaid principles as well as those of equality and mutual benefit.

(ARTICLE II)

Guided by the desire to contribute in every possible way to ensure enduring peace and security of their people, the High Contracting Parties declare their determination to continue their efforts to preserve and to strengthen peace in Asia and throughout the world, to halt the arms race and to achieve general and complete disarmament, including both nuclear and conventional, under effective international control.

(ARTICLE III)

Guided by their loyalty to the lofty ideal of equality of all peoples and nations, irrespective of race or creed, the High Contracting Parties condemn colonialism and racialism in all forms and manifestations, and reaffirm their determination to strive for their final and complete elimination.

The High Contracting Parties shall cooperate with other States to achieve these aims and to support the just aspirations of the peoples in their struggle against colonialism and racial domination.

(ARTICLE IV)

The Republic of India respects the peace-loving policy of the Union of Soviet Socialist Republics aimed at strengthening friendship and co-operation with all nations.

The Union of Soviet Socialist Republics respects India's policy of non-alignment and reaffirms that this policy constitutes an important factor in the maintenance of universal peace and international security and in the lessening of tensions in the world.

(ARTICLE V)

Deeply interested in ensuring universal peace and security, attaching great importance to their mutual co-operation in the international field for achieving these aims, the High Contracting Parties will maintain regular contacts with each other on major international problems affecting the interests of both the States by means of meetings, and exchanges of views between their leading statesmen, visits by official delegations and special envoys of the two Governments, and through diplomatic channels.

(ARTICLE VI)

Attaching great importance to economic, scientific and technological co-operation between them, the High Contracting Parties will continue to consolidate and expand mutually advantageous and comprehensive co-operation in these fields as well as expand trade, transport and communications between them on the basis of the principles of equality, mutual benefit and most-favoured nation treatment, subject to the existing agreements and the special arrangements with contiguous countries as specified in the Indo - Soviet trade agreement of 26 December 1970.

(ARTICLE VII)

The High Contracting Parties shall promote further development of ties and contacts between them in the fields of science, art, literature, education, public health, press, radio, television, cinema, tourism and sports.

(ARTICLE VIII)

In accordance with the traditional friendship established between the two countries, each of the High Contracting Parties solemnly declares that it shall not enter into or participate in any military alliance directed against the other Party.

Each High Contracting Party undertakes to abstain from any aggression against the other Party and to prevent the use of its territory for the commission of any act which might inflict military damage on the other High Contracting Party.

(ARTICLE IX)

Each High Contracting Party undertakes to abstain from providing any assistance to any third country that engages in armed conflict with the other Party. In the event of either being subjected to an attack or a threat thereof, the High Contracting Parties shall immediately enter into mutual consultations in order to remove such threat and to take appropriate effective measures to ensure peace and the security of their countries.

(ARTICLE X)

Each High Contracting Party solemnly declares that it shall not enter into any obligation, secret or public, with one or more States, which is incompatible with this Treaty. Each High Contracting Party further declares that no obligation be entered into, between itself and any other State or States, which might cause military damage to the other Party.

(ARTICLE XI)

This Treaty is concluded for the duration of twenty years and will be automatically extended for each successive period of five years unless either High Contracting Party declares its desire to terminate it by giving notice to the other High Contracting Party twelve months prior to the expiration of the Treaty. The Treaty will be subject to ratification and will come into force on the date of the exchange of Instruments of Ratification which will take place in Moscow within one month of the signing of this Treaty.

(ARTICLE XII)

Any difference of interpretation of any Article or Articles of this Treaty which may arise between the High Contracting Parties will be settled bilaterally by peaceful means in a spirit of mutual respect and understanding.

The said Plenipotentiaries have signed the present Treaty in Hindi, Russian and English, all text being equally authentic and have affixed thereto their seals.

Done in New Delhi on the Ninth day of August in the year One Thousand Nine Hundred and Seventy One.

On behalf of the Union of Soviet Socialist Republics

(Sd.) A. A. Gromyko,

Minister of External Affairs,

On behalf of the Republic of India

(Sd.) Swaran Singh, Minister of External Affairs.

RUSSIA AND INDIA: AN 'ORPHANED' RELATIONSHIP?

On June 29, experts from Carnegie Moscow Center welcomed their colleagues from Observer Research Foundation (ORF), a leading think tank in India. Together they discussed the current state of Russia-India relations and proposed potential ways to boost ties between the two longstanding partners.

"This is, in my view, a relationship that is not given its due, in terms of the breadth and depth of its discussion. Most people feel complacent about the relationship, take it for granted," Dmitri Trenin, director of Carnegie Moscow Center and chair of its Foreign and Security Policy Program, said while opening the panel.

According to him, the general trend is that a lot of people, including those at a high level, find the relationship essentially non-controversial, learning to live with this excellent relationship without properly appreciating it. "This is a major issue, that unless we tackle it could lead us downward not upward," he said.

Transforming the nature of economic cooperation

Russia has been a reliable partner for India in a variety of areas, and high-ranking state officials in Delhi regard Russia as one of the allies that will help India, no matter what happens, said Manoj Joshi, head of the National Security Program at ORF.

Looking at Russia's potential competition on the Indian market from countries like the U.S, France or Israel, Petr Topychkanov, associate in the Carnegie Moscow Center's Nonproliferation Program, believes that there is nothing to worry about yet.

With numerous examples of cooperation in defense and nuclear energy, Russia enjoys a unique position and it is unlikely that the U.S. or any other country may offer more attractive opportunities.

For instance, in nuclear energy, Moscow not only participates in active plant construction and localization of nuclear technologies in India, but also offers India post-Fukushima technologies to ensure safety of the nuclear technologies that are already used at the Kudankulam nuclear power plant.

No one else, including the U.S., can offer this. What's more, only Moscow is ready to talk with Delhi about joint cooperation in construction and development of power plants in countries outside of Russia or India, the expert explained.

The countries' traditional cooperation in defense allowed India to benefit from technologies and military products developed in Russia. However, in order to move forward, it is necessary to transform the nature of economic cooperation between the two countries, moving to cooperation in other industries, argues Joshi. Here the key difficulty is logistical, the expert pointed out. Indian products become more expensive by the time they get to Russia and this is an urgent issue that businesses need to address.

Exploring the potential behind the big initiatives, such as the One Belt One Road project (the plan to connect the Asian, European, and African continents through transport and infrastructure development in Eurasia) and the International North-South Transport Corridor (linking the Indian Ocean and Persian Gulf to the Caspian Sea via Iran, then connecting to St. Petersburg and North Europe), Joshi argues that if successfully implemented, they might significantly increase trade flows within the region and benefit Russia-India cooperation.

"If this healthy potential is developed into a smoothly functioning rail and road corridor, there will be an access from India via Iran to Central Asia and Russia," he said.

Domestic problems lead to international collaboration

According to Nandan Unnikrishnan, vice president of the ORF, placing the Moscow-Delhi relationship in the context of wider economic and political changes is also quite important. The current shift towards multipolarity brings more instability, with different powers becoming more suspicious of each other. Addressing problems in the Russia-India relationship in this regard is very important, he said.

"India is going through tremendous internal challenges which, if India wants to be a major power, it has to resolve in a reasonably tight time frame," Unnikrishnan argued.

Touching upon these problems, most importantly, social and economic ones, the expert believes that even though the Indian economy can be best described as "functional anarchy" the growth will eventually occur as a result of reforms.

In order to successfully resolve domestic problems, the country needs good relations with everyone. "If India wants to develop it needs everyone else to ride along on its development story," the expert argued.

Such issues, like the lack of public access to healthcare, require India to cooperate with external assistance, whether in building infrastructure or providing technologies to deal with the effects of climate change, and the country is willing to pay for this help.

Russia's pivot to China worries Delhi

Another point is that the world is continually changing and it is not going to wait for India, so it has to make quick decisions without necessarily being ready to do that. In this context, Russia is important, said Unnikrishnan.

Moscow's shift in focus from the West towards more cooperation with China worries Delhi, which has a quite unique relationship with Beijing. The two countries have strong economic but poor political ties and it doesn't help that China is growing phenomenally, turning into the locomotive of world development.

At the same time, China occasionally flexes its military muscles, which makes India quite nervous. "In that context, Delhi is also very nervous about how close is Russia with China.

There is a doubt which naturally results in India seeking a more permanent and solid balancer and there is, therefore, a natural motivation for an improvement of relations with the U.S.," Unnikrishnan explained. He warned that this could potentially affect all aspects of Delhi-Moscow cooperation.

Focus on the future

India owes a lot to Russia dating back to the 1960s, but given the changing geopolitical situation, this longstanding partnership might be at risk. India owes a lot to Russia dating back to the 1960s, but given the changing geopolitical situation, this longstanding partnership might be at risk.

Therefore, it is vitally important to understand that it is not enough to bring just specialists on Indo-Russia relations to discuss the future of the relationship, but also to bring together a widest spectrum number of experts and specialists in a range of fields (science, technology, innovation and international affairs) and create a multitasking working group to give a some kind of a roadmap for the future of the strategic partnership, believes Unnikrishnan.

"Unless this is done very quickly, the relationship is going to stagnate, the difference between us is going to grow," the expert believes. Warning against focusing on the historical nostalgia of the relationship that distracts from resolving current problems, he called for more discussion of the present and the future that is at risk. Topychkanov agrees that the vision for the long-term is missing.

Even though there are two commissions – on trade and defense cooperation – there is no instrument to discuss the strategy for the relationship.

"For example, with Pakistan we have a working group on strategic stability and this group meets every year in Moscow and Islamabad, but we don't have the same working group with India," the expert said. Such a group could be useful to discuss a range of urgent questions, such as such as Delhi's concern regarding China, Moscow's tensions with the West, or the situation in Afghanistan.

G. Balasubramanian, deputy chief of mission at the Embassy of India in Russia, adds to this point, noting that the needs and opportunities for cooperation are vast, but the long-term vision is absent. According to him, more government supported programs and professional exchanges are needed.

Similarly, Topychkanov raises a concern over the humanitarian field in general.

In the period of important geopolitical and domestic changes – when greater humanitarian cooperation to understand each other's interests and goals is key – the area of soft power seems to be in a poor state, Topychkanov said.

For instance, in the field of media, one of the recent events was the closure of Russian state-owned media company Sputnik International's websites in Urdu and Hindi. In a situation when virtually no Indian mass media are working in Russia, this raises serious questions.

"My feeling, frankly, is that no one is in charge. No one is looking at the relationship as an integral relationship that has different aspects to it and that the relationship itself has a strategic significance to Russia," Trenin said, pointing out once again that focusing on historical nostalgia is bound to be unproductive.

The cooperation between Moscow and Delhi lacks the kind of high-level support that is present in the Sino-Russian relationship. What might be discussed as a potential way out is a possibility to form an Indo-Russian foundation to explore the potential and bring it to a strategic level. As he concluded, the question of the Delhi-Moscow relationship can no longer be taken for granted.

To avoid the risk that the partnership might turn into an "orphaned" one, leadership on both sides should take active action, for example, by creating a platform to discuss the strategy of Russia-India cooperation in the future, experts suggested.

RUSSIA AND INDIA: A 21ST CENTURY DECLINE

As strategic relations go, few countries can match the enduring partnership that India and Russia have shared since the 1960s. For close to half a century Russia has been New Delhi's foremost military supplier. In fact, defense trade became the *raison d'être* for strategic relations between the two nations – particularly in the post-Cold War era. Yet Russia's share of military sales to India is now in steady decline. In consonance with India's enhanced geopolitical status and strategic rapprochement with the U.S., New Delhi has found new partners in the West. And what was once the defining aspect of the bilateral relationship with Russia is threatening to become a heavy burden for both partners.

This shift has been a decade in the making and can be traced back to the 123 Agreement that India signed with the U.S. The pursuit of a "strategic partnership" with India is perhaps the most enduring foreign policy legacy of President George W. Bush.

On the back of rising religious extremism in South Asia, the Bush administration was convinced that India could be a driving force for political stability in the region. Taking confidence from what Washington perceived as convergent geo-political interests, the U.S. initiated proceedings to elevate India to the status of a strategic ally.

What followed was a reversal of a decades old non-proliferation policy that culminated in the signing of the Indo-U.S. civil nuclear agreement in 2005. America's strategic rapprochement with New Delhi marked a watershed moment in India's defense engagement with the world.

Sanctions against many Indian defense entities were lifted and high technology export controls were slowly eased. Foreign aerospace and defense majors were given expanded access to Indian markets and within the space of a decade Indo-Israel defense trade rose to $10 billion, while India's defense trade with the U.S. has since topped $9 billion.

All this has had an adverse impact on Indo-Russian defense trade. Despite robust numbers in absolute terms, Russia's share of India's defense pie will continue to fall, at least in the short term. In recent years, the Kremlin has lost out to other emerging export hubs for big-ticket Indian defense contracts. These include, amongst others, the 36 MMRCA contract worth $7 billion to France; 10 C-17 Globemaster-III strategic airlift aircraft worth $4.1 to the U.S.; and eight P-8I maritime patrol aircraft worth $2.1, again to the U.S.

At present, Russia's defense industry is sustaining its considerable ties with India on the strength of the execution of contracts already in place. Barring the upcoming $11 billion contract for the joint design and development of the Fifth Generation Fighter Aircraft (FGFA) program with Russia, there are no specific plans to purchase new Russian arms.

And although Russia is taking part in various Indian military tenders currently open to foreign firms, it is not a clear frontrunner in any. The EADS Airbus A330 MRTT has emerged as the preferred vendor over Russia's Ilyushin Il-78 to supply six aerial tankers for the Indian Air Force in a $1 billion contract; Russian platforms have also fared poorly in the rotary-wing aircraft category, where Boeing's AH-64 Apache and the Chinook CH-47F won the

Indian attack and heavy-lift helicopter tenders respectively. Thus, with the fulfillment of contracts signed in previous years, there is a considerable risk that Russia will lose its decades long stranglehold on the Indian arms industry.

Downgrade

Already there is trouble brewing on the horizon; all signs point to Russia downgrading its military-technical relationship with India from that of an exclusive partner to a preferred partner.

Such pragmatism should come as no surprise given that India has diversified its own military import portfolio and no longer considers Russia as its exclusive trading partner. Russian military export overtures towards Pakistan are now perceptible.

In a noteworthy development, Russia recently decided to supply Mi-35 *Hind* attack helicopters to Pakistan. Prior to this, Moscow had refrained from supplying lethal military equipment to Pakistan on account of New Delhi's strained relationship with Islamabad – the legacy of this Indo-Russian military exclusivity can be traced all the way back to the Indo-Soviet Treaty of Friendship, Cooperation and Peace of 1971. Consequently, the Pakistan deal caught many geo-political commentators by surprise; some, like Pavel Felgenhauer, have even gone so far as to call it an "important, key change in Russian policy in the region." Conscious of Indian sensitivities, Russian diplomats have been quick – perhaps too quick – to point out that the negotiations are part of an "ongoing cooperation with Pakistan in the field of defense and counter-terrorism." However, like a canary in a coal mine, Moscow's recent repositioning on the matter could herald a revised Russian arms policy for the region.

This shift is significant, and is driven by what IDSA scholar, Jyotsna Bakshi, calls Moscow's "compulsive" need to sell weapons. One of the most important issues following the dissolution of the Soviet Union was the distribution of its external state debt and assets among the fifteen successor states. Russia inherited a mammoth military-industrial complex (MIC) that comprised 1,600 defense enterprises staffing nearly two million people. Today, that number has grown to include between 2.5 and 3 million workers, representing 20 percent of all manufacturing jobs in Russia. However, Russia did not inherit an equally robust economy to support its expansive MIC. Average military expenditure as a percentage of GDP in the three years leading up to the break-up of the Soviet Union was 14.1 percent, compared with 3.8 percent for Russia between 1992 and 2013 was 3.8 percent. To make up for the deficit in military expenditure and maintain the economies of scale to sustain its resource hungry defense and R&D facilities Russia became increasingly reliant on military exports. As Bakshi points out, former Russian Deputy Prime Minister Ilya Klebanov once stated that arms exports were the "life buoy for our defense industries now that the defense budget is so small and military state orders are so few." Thus, in addition to fostering strategic cooperation with other countries, the sale of Russian weapons to foreign nations is driven by the financial imperative of bankrolling its own domestic defense industries. In all likelihood, Russia's decision to revive military exports to Pakistan and others is essentially motivated by the economic need to maintain a high level of military exports.

The recent upsurge in Sino-Russian military cooperation has also not gone unnoticed in India. By selling the advanced Su-35 fighter aircraft to China, Russia is potentially creating a conflict of interest for itself. With every sale of military equipment to China, Russian military hardware becomes less appealing in the Indian market; this is particularly true for the aerospace sector, where a major portion of the Indian Air Force fleet is made up of Russian imports. Some argue that the configuration of equipment supplied to India surpasses that which is supplied to China, but that claim is hard to conclusively verify given that the Chinese configuration does not go through technical evaluations or trials in India. The fact remains, New Delhi could be tempted to pursue military hardware from alternative sources, preferably from a manufacturer that could guarantee a competitive edge against Chinese imports. The Chinese arms industry is known for reverse engineering foreign-origin military hardware and has already burned Russia in the past when it acquired a small number of Russian Su-27 Flanker jets and then reverse-engineered the J-11B aircraft. In comparison, Indo-Russian military transfers do not have such a checkered past. If China's questionable reverse engineering practices and its already developed industrial base were factored into Russia's decision-making calculus, India would emerge as a far superior long-term partner for the Russian arms trade. Going forward, a period of dissonance is to be expected, before India and Russia can adjust to the *realpolitik* of the present.

INDIA-RUSSIA RELATIONS AS A METAPHOR FOR CHANGING GEOPOLITICAL EQUATIONS

First, the US displaced Great Britain as the global hegemon and underwrote world peace and prosperity, largely but not always as a benign hegemon. Second, the Soviet Union was established as the bastion of international communism, achieved superpower status and then imploded with accompanying geographic, demographic and economic shrinkage. Although Russia retains a massive nuclear arsenal that can destroy the world and has recovered some political and economic stability over the past decade, it is unlikely to emerge as a multidimensional major power anytime soon.

Third, the US's relative decline from its dominant position at the end of the Cold War continues apace. It retains an unchallengeable capacity to wreak military destruction, yet has suffered serial reverses in several conflict theatres in the capacity to impose an American order after military victory. Similarly, while the US remains the biggest, best balanced and most productive and innovative economy, its global economic dominance has declined on most measures, including share of global output, automotive manufacturing and international trade.

Fourth, China has acquired impressive power in both relative and absolute terms. How China develops economically, evolves politically and behaves domestically, regionally and globally, are among the most pressing questions for the world. The answers will help to shape the destiny of nations and the fate of billions of people. Moreover, while the most critical global geopolitical relationship is the one between China and the US, the most critical Asian geopolitical relationship is the one between China and India.

These trends hold acute lessons for Australia. They also offer insights into one of the less noticed bilateral relationships in recent years: that between Moscow and New Delhi, which shaped the previous geopolitical order in Asia. The relationship peaked in 1971 with a bilateral treaty that came close to constituting a defence pact. In the context of the looming India–Pakistan war that was midwife to the birth of Bangladesh, it provided political cover for India at the United Nations while buying it military insurance against the Nixon–Kissinger move on the geopolitical chessboard to detach China from the Soviet embrace.

The end of the Cold War upended India's world order completely. An acute balance of payments crisis in 1991, and the total discrediting of the command model of the Soviet economy that India had borrowed heavily from, added to the panic caused by the collapse of the Soviet superpower. India scrambled to readjust to the changed unipolar world and recalibrate relations with the US while still heavily dependent on Soviet military supplies. Since then, India has fared rather better than Russia in world affairs.

So where exactly do India–Russia relations stand now? The relationship is, in fact, quite a good metaphor for the polycentric world of offsetting ties of cooperation and competition as the sun sets in turn on US unipolar dominance. Russia has been engaged in its own Asian pivot, which it views as an attractive and feasible alternative to the current US-centric system of global financial, economic and political relations.

President Vladimir Putin paid a two-day visit to India on 5–6 October. Among the documents signed with India were agreements to develop six new nuclear power projects and a contract for Russia's S-400 Triumf air-defence system worth US$5 billion. The latter deal was especially significant because India ignored repeated warnings (including ahead of PM Narendra Modi's informal meeting with Putin in Sochi in May) about triggering the Countering America's Adversaries Through Sanctions Act (CAATSA, 2017), which mandates US sanctions on entities engaged in 'significant' defence transactions with Russia.

Resource-rich Russia and resource-hungry India are well matched economically. But there's even greater historical inertia to India's defence procurement from Russia. India and the US have been trying to promote increased Indian purchases of US defence systems, both to reduce dependence on Moscow by diversifying and to deepen India–US ties.

Every year in the 2012 to 2017 period, with one exception in 2015, and cumulatively for this six-year period, India has been the world's largest arms purchaser, buying 42% more than Saudi Arabia, the second-biggest arms purchaser. For the same period, the US has been the biggest arms seller; over the six years, it sold 48% more than Russia, the next big arms seller. The source of the bulk of India's purchases over the six-year period was Russia (67%), followed by the US (12.4%), Israel (9.9%) and France (3.8%). But if we compare 2012 with 2017, Russia falls from 86.5% to 60.1%, while the US increases from 3.1% to 7.5% and Israel from 3.7% to 21.3%.

It's hard to see how disrupting this trendline would be in the US's economic or security interest. That's especially so in light of America's stated intention to court India 'as a major defence partner' that has 'an indispensable role in maintaining stability in the Indian Ocean region'. In July, US defence secretary James Mattis urged the Senate to empower the secretary of state to waive CAATSA sanctions: 'Doing so allows nations to build a closer security relationship with the US as they continue to transition from reliance on Russian military equipment.'

Bibliography

Alam, Aftab : *US Policy Towards South Asia: Special Reference to Indo-Russia Relations*, Raj, Delhi, 1998.

Anil, K.C.: *Military and Democracy in South Asia : Challenges, Politics and Power*, Sumit Enterprises, Delhi, 2009.

Arbatov, Alexei: 'NATO and Russia', *Security Dialogue*, 1995.

Averre, Derek: *'Russia and the European Union: Convergence or Divergence?'* 2005.

Bhambhri, C.P. : *Indian Politics Since Independence*, 1999.

Bhat, T.P. : *India and China : Trade Complementarities and Competitiveness*, Bookwell, Delhi, 2008.

Budge I: *The New Challenge of Direct Democracy*, Oxford, Polity Press, 1996.

Buzan, Barry : *Security: A New Framework for Analysis*. Boulder: Lynne-Rienner Publishers, 1998.

Coakley, J.: *The Territorial Management of Ethnic Conflict*, London: Frank Cass, 2003.

Dan Nabudere: *The Political Economy of Imperialism*, London, 1977.

Dixit, A.K. : *Military Wars and Rescue Techniques*, Cyber Tech Pub, Delhi, 2010.

Ellis, F. *Rural Livelihoods and Diversity in Developing Countries*. New York: Oxford University Press, 2000.

Evelyn Goh, *Meeting the China Challenge: The Russia in Southeast Asian Regional Security Strategies*, DC: East-West Center, 2005.

Gaur, Mahendra : *Indian Political Parties Annual*, Delhi, Kalpaz Pub., 2006.

Goldstein, Joshua S.: *Three-way Street: Strategic Reciprocity in World Politics*. Chicago: University of Chicago Press, 1990.

Gottlieb, Thomas M.: *Chinese Foreign Policy Factionalism and the Origins of the Strategic Triangle.* Santa Monica, CA: RAND Corporation, 1977.

Habberton, William: *Anglo-Russian Relations Concerning Afghanistan 1837-1907*, Urbana, University of Illinois, 1937.

Haukkala, Hiski: *The EU-Russia Strategic Partnership: The limits of post-sovereignty in international relations*. Oxon: Routledge, 2010.

Hoffman, Bruce, *Inside Terrorism in Afghanistan*, New York: Columbia University Press, 1998.

Hurewitz, Jacob C.: *Diplomacy in the Near and Middle East: A Documentary Record 1535-1914*, Princeton, New Jersey, 1956.

Ikenberry, John G.: *After Victory: Institutions, Strategic Restraint, and the Rebuilding of Order after Major Wars*. Princeton, NJ: Princeton University Press, 2001.

Imtiaz, A.: *State and Foreign Policy: India's Role in South Asia*, New Delhi, Vikas, 1993.

Kanet Roger E., *Russian Foreign Policy in the 21st Century*, Palgrave Macmillan; 2011.

Kelly, John B.: *Indian Military and Pakistan War*, Oxford, Clarendon Press, 1968.

Keohane, Robert O.: *After Hegemony: Cooperation and Discord in the world Political Economy*. Princeton, NJ: Princeton University Press, 1984.

Kunju, N. : *Indo-Pak : Nuclear Cold War*, Reliance, Delhi, 2002.

Kutchins, Andrew C.: *The Future of China-Russia Relations*. Lexington: University Press of Kentucky, 2010.

Laquer, Walter, *The New Terrorism: Fanaticism and the Arms of Mass Destruction*, Oxford: Oxford University Press, 1999.

Lieven, Anatol. *The Baltic Revolution : Estonia, Latvia, Lithuania and the Path to Independence*. Yale University Press, 1994.

Martin, Terry. *The Affirmative Action Empire: Nations and Nationalism in the Soviet Union, 1923-1939*. Cornell University Press, 2001.

Mary, W.: *Asian Power and Politics: the Cultural Dimensions of Authority*, Cambridge, Belknap Press, 1985.

Moravcsik, Andrew: *The Choice for Europe: Social Purpose and State Power*. Ithaca, NY: Cornell University Press, 1998.

Nayyar, K K : *National Security : Military Aspects*, Rupa, Delhi, 2003.

Northrop, Douglas T. *Veiled Empire: Gender and Power in Stalinist Central Asia*. Cornell University Press, 2004.

Oksana Antonenko and Kathryn Pinnick: *Russia and the European Union*. Oxon: Routledge, 2004.

Olcott, M. B.: *The Great Powers in Central Asia*. 2005.

Phuskele, Preeti : *India and China : Emerging Superpowers*, ICFAI University, Delhi, 2009.

Pipes, Richard. *The Formation of the Soviet Union: Communism and Nationalism, 1917-1923*. Harvard University Press, 1997.

Popescu, Nicu: *EU Foreign Policy and Post-Soviet Conflicts: Stealth Intervention*. London: Routledge, 2011.

Posen, B.R.: *The Sources of Indian Military Doctrine*, Ithaca, 1984, Cornell Univ. Press.

Prabla, Dixit: *Communalism: A Struggle for Power*, New Delhi, Orient Longman, 1981.

Raeff, Marc. *Understanding Imperial Russia*. New York: Columbia University Press, 1984.

Rosen, P.: *Societies and Military Power: India and its Armies*, Ithaca, Cornell University Press, 1996.

Simon, D. : *Public Administration and Policy of Indian Military*, New York, Knopf, 1950.

Slezkine, Yuri. *Arctic Mirrors: Russia and the Small Peoples of the North*. Cornell University Press, 1996.

Smith, David J. et al. *The Baltic States. Estonia, Latvia and Lithuania*. London: Routledge, 2002.

Spector, Leonard S., *Going Nuclear*, Cambridge, MA: Ballinger Publishing Company, 1987.

Stein, Arthur A.: *Why Nations Cooperate: Circumstance and Choice in International Relations*. Ithaca, NY: Cornell University Press, 1990.

Stites, Richard. *Russian Popular Culture: Entertainment and Society since 1900*. Cambridge: Cambridge University Press, 1992.

Terras, Victor. *Handbook of Russian Literature*. New Haven: Yale University Press, 1985.

Thampi, Madhavi : *India and China in the Colonial World*, Social Science Press, Delhi, 2010.

Theodore, William : *The Buddhist Tradition in India, China and Japan*, New York: Vintage Books, 1972.

Weber, Katja: *Hierarchy amidst Anarchy: Transaction Costs and Institutional Choice*. Albany, NY: State University of New York Press, 2000.

Weitz, R.: *Averting a New Great Game in Central Asia*. 2006.

Wilborn, Thomas L.: *International Politics In Northeast Asia : The China-Japan-United States Strategic Triangle*. Carlisle Barracks, PA: Strategic Studies Institute, 1996.

Wishnick, Elizabeth: *Mending Fences: The Evolution of Moscow's China Policy from Brezhnev to Yeltsin*. Seattle: University of Washington Press, 2001.

Wooten, Sara. *Donald Trump: From Real Estate to Reality TV*. Enslow Publishers, 2009.

Zhu, Zhiqun: *US-China In The 21st Century: Power Transition And Peace*. London and New York: Routledge, 2006.

Zubok, Vladislav. *Inside the Kremlin's Cold War: from Stalin to Krushchev* (Harvard University Press, 1997)

Index

F

G

I

K

L

M

N

O

P

R

S

T

V

W

❑❑❑